Creases in Culture

Creases in Culture
Essays Toward a Poetics of Depth

Dennis Patrick Slattery, Ph.D.

fisher king press

Creases in Culture
Essays Toward a Poetics of Depth

Copyright © 2014 by Dennis Patrick Slattery
First Edition
ISBN 978-1-77169-006-5 Paperback

Published simultaneously in Canada and the United States of America by Fisher King Press. For information on obtaining permission for use of material from this work, submit a written request to:

permissions@fisherkingpress.com

Fisher King Press
5485 W 170th St N
Skiatook, OK 74070
www.fisherkingpress.com
fisherking@fisherkingpress.com
+1-831-238-7799

Many thanks to all who have directly or indirectly provided permission to reprint their work. Every effort has been made to trace all copyright holders; however, if any have been overlooked, we will be pleased to make the necessary arrangements at the first opportunity.

Front cover image © is from an original etching by Mel Mathews.

Dedication

To my teachers, who transform me
To my students, who challenge me
To my family, who sustains me
To my wife Sandy, who inspires me

Incipit

Here I am working toward a psychology of soul that is based in a psychology of image. Here I am suggesting both a poetic basis of mind and a psychology that starts neither in the physiology of the brain, the structure of language, the organization of society, nor the analysis of behavior, but in the processes of imagination.

—James Hillman[1]

I have suggested that myth is a moral, organizing force in a society and provides that society's members with security and purpose. It may be regarded, then, as a total outlook that affects the lives of individuals and of society as a whole.

—Louise Cowan[2]

---

1 Hillman, J., *Revisioning Psychology*, p. xvii.
2 Cowan, L., "Myth in the Modern World," in *Texas Myths*, edited by Robert F. O'Connor, p. 9.

Contents

Foreword

One of my lifelong secret desires – which I am now shamelessly exposing – has been to climb into the mind of a truly creative, original thinker and rummage around in there for glowing ideas and rich insights that will help me in my own life. Now I've done it – I've been inside the mind of Dennis Slattery in this extraordinary book, and I can tell you that I also found a treasure of heart and soul there too.

There is a certain subtle seductiveness in the work of a man who is both a scholar *par excellence* and a poet by nature. Example: I hadn't thought I'd be interested in motorcycles, which I had come to hate – one of my dearest friends was nearly killed riding one – but I was hooked into the essay, "Motorcycles as Myth and as Metaphor," and found myself transported (pun intended, it is the only word for this) to a world in which I too grew up, the late 1950s-early '60s. But far beyond and much deeper than the circumstance of time and place, a whole *new* world of vision and experience opened to me, a realization that, as in everything else, motorcycles are not *merely* motorcycles – the *thing* is not *merely* or *only* the thing – but conveyances and expressions of one's soul and one's deepest longing. A symbol of freedom and the means to get there. A sleek sculpture of surpassing beauty and a killing machine. And more.

Do you want to travel – or better still, *wander*? Dennis has wandered almost everywhere and is the perfect guide to anywhere, because he is a true pilgrim, he knows how to *see,* and see into, where he is. He notices. He notices everything. He lets everything in, is willing to be changed, and then, because he is a poet, he offers back to us all of it – a world of mystery and myth, poetry and problems, laughable failings and unbearable sorrow, that is the world each of us lives in.

Do you want to be free? In a real sense, all these essays are about freedom: of the spirit, of the mind, of the soul's deepest longing and fear.

Do you want to laugh? What can surpass the humor of an Irishman among friends – even when the talk is about loss and grief? Dennis has somehow found a way to coax a smile even out of the most curmudgeonly and solemn-minded people we know, and sometimes are.

The book is a *tour-de-force*, in the breadth and wealth and depth of its ideas, in the beauty of its language, of a sort that doesn't appear often in modern times. So this is my suggestion as you pick up this volume: find a comfortable chair, make sure your cell phone and computer and television are turned off, try to get everyone out of the house, a fireplace on a cool evening is recommended if possible, and let yourself go rummaging around in Dennis Slattery's mind. Motorcycle helmets are optional.

—Lyn Cowan, author of *Tracking the White Rabbit: A Subversive View of Modern Culture* and *Portrait of the Blue Lady: The Character of Melancholy.*
Groundhog Day, 2011.

Acknowledgements

Formal Essays

"Psychic Energy's Portal to Presence in Myth, Poetry and Culture." *Eranos Jahrbuch*, Ascona, Switzerland. Ed. Riccardo Bernardini, 2010. 435-474.

"The Wonder of Wandering: Archetype, Myth and Metaphor in William Faulkner's 'The Bear.'" Special issue on *Home and the Wanderer, Spring 85: A Journal of Archetype and Culture*, Spring 2011. 165-86.

"Mytho-Poiesis: The Shared Ground of Psyche's Dreaming and Poetic Impulse." *Quadrant: Journal of the C.G. Jung Foundation for Analytical Psychology*. XXXXI: 1 Winter 2011. 71-85.

"Thirteen Ways of Looking at a *Red Book*: C.G. Jung's *Divine Comedy*. *Jung Journal: Culture and Psyche*. Summer 2011, vol. 5, no.3. Edited by Dyane Sherwood and Murray Stein. 116-127.

"Mimesis, Neurology and the Aesthetics of Presence." *Psychological Perspectives: A Quarterly Journal of Jungian Thought*, 56.3.268-288.

Cultural Essays

"Motorcycles as Myth and as Metaphor" presented to the Bikes, Blues and Barbeques Conference and Rally, Fayetteville, Arkansas, 3-5 October 2002.

"The Power and Poetry of Love" to the Jung Society of Utah, Salt Lake City, 4 February 2010.

"The Soul's Claim: Choose It or Lose It." *Marked by Fire: Stories of the Jungian Way*, edited by Patricia Damery and Naomi Ruth Lowinsky. Carmel, California: Fisher King Press, 2012. 123-35.

"Introduction: Humanities Education: Necessities for Cultivating the Whole Person."
In *The Soul Does Not Specialize: Revaluing the Humanities and the Polyvalent Imagination*. Edited Dennis Patrick Slattery and Jennifer Leigh Selig. Carpinteria, California: Mandorla Books. Xvii-xix.

"Poetics of Soul: *Revisioning Psychology* as Mythical Method." Lecture to The Dallas Institute of Humanities and Culture, 3 December 2011. *Essays in Honor of Robert Romanyshyn*. Ed. Michael Sipiora. Trivium Publications, 2013.

"The Memorable Teacher: Father Zosima's Active Love and Learning in *The Brothers Karamazov*." A revised version of this essay appeared in a collection of essays on the subject, *What Is a Teacher?* Ed. Claudia Allums. Dallas: The Dallas Institute Publications, 2013, 147-69.

Introduction

Not long ago, the poet, farmer, short story writer, essayist and novelist, Wendell Berry delivered a talk at the National Endowment for the Humanities Jefferson Lecture series. It was slightly altered and appeared in *The Progressive* magazine with the title "It All Turns on Affection."[1] There he outlined the difference between what his mentor, Wallace Stegner, called "boomers" and "stickers." The former comprises that group of people who want to acquire enormous wealth in whatever they do, without regard for consequences or for injuries inflicted in their mad desire for money. The other group, the "stickers" by contrast, comprises the folks who settle, who settle *in* and "who love the life they have made and the place they have made it in."[2] Their motivation is love of place rather than love of acquisitions.

From there Berry goes on to speak about the loss of imagination in the first group and the fierce imagination that drives the second. Their purpose resides more in stewardship of the land and place, whereas the first group is propelled by a depersonalized efficiency to extract the most gold from whatever area they have identified to pillage. I offer the above distinction as a way to introduce what Berry believes the imagination is and then to a description of the essays in this volume.

He offers that the "sense of the verb 'to imagine' contains the full richness of the verb 'to see.' To imagine is to see most clearly, familiarly, and understandingly with the eyes, but also to see inwardly, with 'the mind's eye.'" To do so, Berry conjectures, is to see with not only a "force of vision" but with "a visionary force."[3] Why this is so indispensable a human faculty, he goes on to reveal, is that belonging to place, respecting place and dwelling fully and with respect in a place "without destroying it, we must imagine it." To imagine in this fully human way is to love the place that one lives in because one imagines it fully, "illuminated by its own unique character and by our love for it."[4] What develops and flourishes in such an imaginal rapport with place is a deep affection for it that grows directly from a sense of sympathy with it: "And in affection we find the possibility of a neighborly, kind, and conserving economy" out of the hands and the narrow grasping greed of the boomers. Today, however, the stick-

---

1 Berry, Wendell, *The Progressive*, pp. 16-21.
2 *The Progressive*, p. 17.
3 *The Progressive*, p. 18.
4 *The Progressive*, p. 18.

ers are struggling to sustain place even as boomers seem to gain in both power and force as they unleash their own desires on locales, with the quality of affection stuffed far down on their poverty scale.

So much more is contained in this clear-eyed vision of where the nation is today and under what throes it suffers both person and place. I bring forward Berry's understanding of the imagination as a way of revealing affection for what one has, is, and where one is in place. I understand this same sense of imagination in the essays that follow, each of which was written more out of affection than out of a need or desire to master its subject matter. To inhabit a particular subject matter is to dwell in its place, to converse with it, to gain access to it, not in a rapacious but more in a respectful way so that the ideas in place can be seen and understood from where they are, and accompanied by a complete sympathy for their well being. Such an attitude has been called poetic knowing, a knowing by connaturality, in the language of James Taylor when he reflects on the work of the philosopher and theorist Jacques Maritain. It is a "knowing in sympathy with."[5] I think ideas themselves, as well as the images that often grow from them, need and even invite our affection, our homing in on them with a considerate heart so they can illuminate our own space and we can, in this process, thrive in their flowering. To me, this is the essence of affectionate scholarship; writing is a rhetorical way to show love to what presents itself to us. When we reveal an authentic affection to our subject, then it is invited to appear affectively to us in their fullness. If we can entertain with not a little fondness what wants to be revealed by means of us, then we enrich the place of the ideas and the understanding of others in a nutritive way, not in a numbing avaricious impulse towards wrenching them of their treasures.

Each of the essays in this volume, then, serves some angle of affection from me towards the subject matter. I mean by this that I befriended every one of these ideas to request from them what they wished to make present to me in their own form, with my words serving as both midwife and catalyst to what wanted to be known. In this process, boundaries between disciplines were not only crossed, they were ignored or simply dismantled, so that ideas incarcerated in the realm of literature, say, or depth or archetypal psychology, or incidents in my own life, were allowed to speak across the table to one another in a café called Free Exchange of Ideas. What I think they all serve on various levels of intensity is the imagination implicit to humanities learning,

---

5 Taylor, James S., *Poetic Knowledge*, p. 82.

an interdisciplinary feast where casseroles can linger with lemon meringue pie and a glass of Pinot occupy the same place setting as an IPA brew.

My sustained hope in such an approach was to let ideas and angles of understanding from many disciplines socialize at the same outing in such a way that some new correspondence would awaken, some clearer insight roll forward, a new sympathy between ideas inspire and provoke a fresh guest in the room. Key works in poetry, depth and archetypal psychology, literary theory, neurology, aesthetics, dreamscapes, the nature of the humanities themselves, history, historical persons, politics, teaching, personal history—all have an abode on the roster and, taken as a whole, perhaps form some new patterns of awareness that I cannot see, so close am I to the guest list. Together they comprise a free range grazing where barbed wire fences separating subject matters have been booted flat so that inhabitants of one pasture can taste and be nourished by those of another. Living in Texas, it is very difficult to avoid cattle and grazing metaphors.

Gathered from writing done over a number of years, the essays reveal a loose-fitting unity of design: they balance along the beam that separates poetics from psyche to reveal each in its own way the mythopoeic structure of soul making. Personal experiences mingle with depth and archetypal awareness, often couched in works of poetry to reveal some third dimension that wishes to crop up between them. Executed less as a book length work written from start to finish, these essays are successive vignettes, forays into the same field over time and for varied publications that have now been herded together to create a unitary effect; such is my hope and intention. Much more needs to be done in this fertile interstice between depth psychology and poetics. Let these essays stand as inaugural attempts to flush out where the psyche may be poetic and where poetry gathers itself around mythos. The result is a way of understanding mythopoiesis in the making.

In Section I: "Formal Essays," the book begins with Chapter One," Psychic Energy's Portal to Presence in Myth, Poetry and Culture." It explores C.G. Jung's sense of psychic energy in the creation of metaphor and as the ground of mimesis in poetry. Several works of literature and poetry are used to illustrate the pull of presencing that these energy fields cultivate. Chapter Two, "The Wonder of Wandering: Archetype, Myth and Metaphor in William Faulkner's 'The Bear'" lists the wanderer in literary history and then illustrates poetically the force of the archetype of the Wanderer in the figure of the young Isaac McCaslin in a section of *Go Down, Moses*. Chapter Three,

"Mytho-poiesis: The Shared Ground of Psyche's Dreaming and Poetic Impulse" continues my exploration of poetic and oneiric expressions by focusing on a section of Goethe's *Faust*, Joseph Campbell's work on myth and my own personal dreams.

Chapter Four, "Thirteen Ways of Looking at a *Red Book*: C.G. Jung's *Divine Comedy*" proposes that the structure and the plot of Jung's magnificent work on his own psychic journey dramatically parallels the action of Dante's medieval poem of individuation by showing many parallels with the tripartite structure of the two works. In it we glimpse the power of Jung as visionary poet. Chapter Five, "Mimesis, Neurology and the Aesthetics of Presence," yokes some of the findings of neuroscience with the mimetic impulse in the soul and its consequent manifestation in poetic expression. It ends with a discussion of beauty and its impetus to create a just life in the individual.

In Section II: "Cultural Essays," chapter Six, "Motorcycles as Myth and Metaphor" offers a history of my own relation with motorcycles, which I have been riding for 45 years and traces the liberation they offered me at an early age. The essay pushes further into the motorcycle as cultural symbol and as mythic structure that has spawned several large industries globally. Chapter Seven, "The Power and Poetry of Love" remembers and commemorates the history of Valentine's Day as a classical-Christian amalgam of two historical events, after which it moves into a discussion of Love as Dante Alighieri understood it in *La Vita Nuova* and in the *Inferno* of his *Commedia*. Chapter Eight, "The Soul's Claim: Choose It or Lose It" is a personal essay that tracks the origin of my interest in Depth Psychology and in the poetic psyche. It includes some of my own poetry as illustration of this cross over between soul and aesthetic expression. Chapter Nine, "Humanities Education" explores Alduous Huxley's *Brave New World* to illustrate what degenerative effects losing a sense of the disciplines included in the Humanities canon has on individuals and cultures. It then discusses the value of both Humanities learning and poetic knowledge. Chapter Ten, " Poetics of Soul: *Revisioning Psychology* as Mythical Method" explores a few sections of James Hillman's valuable work to glean from them lineaments of the mythic method he employs in revaluing psychology as a disciplined and imaginal way of knowing. Chapter Eleven, "The Memorable Teacher: Father Zosima's Active Love and Learning in *The Brothers Karamazov*" enumerates many of the traits and qualities of character that comprise the effective and compassionate teacher. Like so many of the essays that precede it, this essay finds its way to the heart of imagination as the sterling quality that can soften one into a deeper way of knowing.

Learning is an affectionate enterprise. Stimulated by the imagination, as Berry so persuasively describes it above, learning opens to disclose what may be new, or to re-configure what is known, or to construct a synthesis of what needs to be known. But in all forms of knowing, the heart, not the head, is at the center of gnosis. To learn is to learn to love the matter at hand; it feels that affection and reciprocates. My hope is that a few new sprigs spring up in the field, a new dish makes its way to the table, perhaps biscuits covered with a checkered cotton napkin lying in a wicker basket. They are still warm. See which one calls to you. You can imagine what you find and find what you imagine, in these essays.

References

Berry, Wendell, "It All Turns on Affection." *The Progressive*. Vol. 76, Number 8. August 2012. 16-21.

Taylor, James S., *Poetic Knowledge: The Recovery of Education*. Albany: State University of New York Press, 1998.

I

Formal Essays

I

Psychic Energy's Portal to Presence in Myth, Poetry and Culture

But even so, amid the tornadoed Atlantic of my being, do I myself
still for ever centrally disport in mute calm; and while ponderous planets
of unwaning woe revolve around me, deep down and deep inland there I
still bathe me in eternal mildness of joy.

—Herman Melville[6]

I begin by acknowledging a debt to mythologist and literary critic, Joseph Campbell, who introduced the idea of energy and myth, especially in his naming "mythogenetic zones" as "the primary region of the origin of the myths."[7] In teaching a course on his work for the last several years, I discerned a pattern in his thought in the form of recursive ideas he continually spiraled back to in his explorations of world mythologies. These included the terms "energy fields," "power centers" around the globe where people were drawn on their life pilgrimages, myths as "energy-producing" agents, and embodied energy fields, often within the organs of the body that were in conflict or complement with one another, as he outlines this notion in *The Power of Myth*: "Myth is a manifestation in symbolic images, in metaphorical images, of the energies of the organs of the body in conflict with each other."[8] His focus on body energetics as well as Jung's exploration of "psychic energy" comprise the core of this essay.

6 Melville, Herman, "The Grand Armada," *Moby-Dick*, p. 416.
7 Campbell, Joseph, *The Fight of the Wild Gander*, p. 78.
8 Campbell, Joseph, *The Power of Myth*, p. 39.

9

The beauty of Campbell's thought moved me slightly to the left of considering myths as stories, shifting my focus instead to contemplate them as energy patterns of body and psyche that, when channeled through particular corridors of mind, have the power to redirect both matter and energy into new folds of understanding; one of these packets of understanding is of course narrative. But I wish to get behind the overt action of story and ask what essential power directs and affords narratives their libidinal energy in the life of an individual or that of an entire populace.

I have also been stirred by the anthropologist Robert Plant Armstrong's fine insights in *The Powers of Presence: Consciousness, Myth and Affecting Presence,* as well as his earlier title, *Wellsprings.* His argument in the later work is richly complex, told in sometimes quirky prose, namely, that artifacts, art objects make present through the acts of rites and rituals a particular brand of power, of energy, that vitalizes and animates an individual, a tribe, a people, or a race, and brings them into a deep remembrance of their origin—their own brand of the mythogenetic zone—even as it encourages them to celebrate their seen and unseen destiny. In fact, the very same artifact that lies dormant, without power in a box in someone's attic, can, when unwrapped and worn in a tribal ritual, bring the power of a living myth into that ceremony with the psychic force of a hurricane.[9] What emerges is the force and élan vital of a living mythos.

While it is too involved to enter into in this essay—in fact, I have presented almost enough material already to fill a small book—the other piece to be presented here is the power of *mimesis* laid out briefly but clearly and provocatively by Aristotle in his *Poetics* in the 5th.century BCE. My own thought, which I will mention and then discard here, is that the poetics of *mimesis* is at the heart of psychic energy and the very crux of the presence of a vital and engaging myth. Myth is powerfully mimetic; it is in the myth that works of poetry have their strongest ally and their most resonant being. Mimesis as a human action grows directly from our universal impulse to imitate. Imitating brings pleasure, believes Aristotle, and is the origin of all poetry.[10] Mimesis consists of an imitation of an action of life itself[11] and allows us to see by means of a re-presentation some formative principle unfolding in life, a universal action that as human beings we all participate in. Mimesis rests on a knowing by analogy, by correspondence and by likeness.

9 Armstrong, Robert Plant, *The Powers of Presence*, p. 7.
10 Butcher, S.H. *Aristotle's Theory of Poetry and Fine Art*, p. 15.
11 Butcher, *Aristotle's Theory*, p. 17.

It goes without saying that the unnamed source for so much of what has appeared in this essay already is the powerful chapter in C.G. Jung's *The Structure and Dynamics of the Psyche,* and what stirred my initial creation of this essay, his observations "On Psychic Energy." He is the unbidden shaman in the enterprise I now embark on. What Armstrong, Campbell and Jung share and what *mimesis* adumbrates, is a relation of movement, or perhaps better said, a relational motion, whose nature and structure is captured and embellished in metaphor. Jung's own observation is helpful here when he relates, early in his discussion of psychic energy, that in "the energic point of view..., some kind of energy underlies the changes in phenomena, that it maintains itself as a constant throughout these changes, and leads finally to entropy, a condition of general equilibrium."[12]

So I asked: how is it that cultures' energy fields ebb and flow? What is it in psychic energy that has the capacity to revitalize a people or an individual and what devastation accrues when that flow is end-stopped, no longer capable of providing nourishment to its eager recipients? What counter forces drain a people of their psychic prowess? Finally, what place does inspiration play in revitalizing one's energy? One's erotic or libidinal involvement with the world's matter in and through one's self?

These questions prompt me to speculate on energic fields, archetypal energy pockets, or in the language of Campbell, marsupial pouches, ways and means of energy flowing, abating, clogging, rushing, gushing variants in their alternating between poetry, anthropology, depth psychology and mythology. I am seeking something of the broad contours of these phenomenal fields which I find stubbornly elusive. For example: what energy field was created, which destroyed, when two commercial 737 jet liners hit and brought to collapse the twin towers of world commerce in New York city's Trade Center in 2001? Certainly a historical threshold was crossed and something new was made enormously present. A shift in the mythology of America was instantly ratified, even made permanent in the national psyche. History, moreover, this incident italicized, conveyed a mythic as well as a temporal structure.

A less dramatic example might be framed this way: what field of energy is created in the classroom, or in a lecture, such that each embodied psyche is exposed to a mythogenetic zone of thought, feeling and insight that may arouse further thought, deeper speculation as well as a variety of conclusions? What field of energy is evoked in reading a text, and even more so, in rereading it, especially the poetry of world

---

12 Jung, C.G., CW 8, ¶ 3. (Note CW refers throughout to the *Collected Works of C.G. Jung.*)

literature, such that they take on a reality even more intense and heightened than the quotidian world we co-inhabit? The space between myth and literature grows extremely thin in such moments of energy transfer back and forth because the sluices of psychic energy flow in two directions.

Conversely, what are the presences that arrest or mute a people or a culture by their government, their local leaders by their numbing slogans and enervating bromides under the admonition of being unpatriotic, or worse, a danger and an enemy of the common weal? It seems to me we are persuaded constantly by the force of energy fields working on us collectively and individually. The power of myth may reside then most poignantly in the folds of the metaphors that power the myth, that give it shape and form to augment its persuasive presence.

Certainly subatomic physics leads us in this direction, wherein patterns of consciousness, of reality, of knowing, are created by the mixing of matter, spirit and energy in psychic play.[13] Campbell, writing in July 1955 in Kyoto, Japan, identifies the "learning tension" that is so easily destroyed in an act like studying Japanese when even one classmate is intent in seeing it not form, or destroying it when it does coalesce, which in its congealing creates a bond of kinship around the subject matter, like a group of tribal elders gathering around a fire, to be warmed and illuminated by it.[14] These matters of making something present and in-tension are mythic in scope, mimetic in layering, psychological in design and imaginal in intent. Rituals help to promote such a reality and this is what I want to explore: what kinds of actions are rituals such that they galvanize an area, a field, an idea, an image and invest it with an experience that is both meaningful and memorable, a knowing that, recalled at various temporal junctures, reinvests the subjects with something of their original numinosity. Psychic energy, I propose, is the deep sluice of flow under the entire complex of relationships.

---

13 In correspondence that lasted decades, the physicist, Wolfgang Pauli and C.G. Jung argued and shared common insights on the nature of spirit, soul and matter. At one point Jung writes to Pauli: "The psyche...as a medium participates in both Spirit and Matter. I am convinced that it (the psyche) is partly of a material nature" (*Atom and Archetype* 100-101). See also the fine study by David Lindorff, *Pauli and Jung: The Meeting of Two Great Minds*. Foreword by Markus Fierz. Wheaton, Ill: Quest Books, 2004.

14 Campbell, Joseph, *Sake and Satori*, p. 194.

Metaphor and Mimesis

I sense that the existence and presence of metaphor, of symbol, is alive and present in such a manner that they enhance the reality one enters, invents, invests in, discovers, or creates in a poiesis, or a making and a shaping, of measured zeal. C.G. Jung writes of the core ingredient of "relations of movement" which require the energic standpoint."[15]

The psychologist van Grot first proposed this idea of psychic energy:

1. Psychic energy possesses quantity and mass, just like physical energies.
2. As various forms of psychic work and potential, they can be transformed into one another.
3. They can be converted into physical energies and vice versa by means of psychological processes.[16]

While Jung inserts a large question mark at the end of number three above, nonetheless, it seems to suggest that thoughts, images and beliefs may then congeal into behavior on an individual or collective level. They can, for instance, become foreign policy or Constitutional Amendments. Thus, from psyche to policy is worthy of study through the aperture of psychic energy. Now here is where things gather additional interest.

Jung believes there is a quantitative estimate of psychic energy—because the psyche possesses a well-developed evaluating system such that values may be understood as quantitative estimates of energy. He refers to this entire field as an *energic* approach to psychic events, for he assumes that "psychic energies possess quantity and mass, just like physical energies.[17] With values as his springboard he then asks how one determines the value of unconscious contents. My own thought is that metaphor is a way to access unconscious contents through the relation it sets up between unconsciousness and consciousness. Campbell, borrowing the structure from Kant's understanding of the unknown as the ultimate ground of a metaphor, constructs the following:

---

15 Jung, CW 8, ¶ 4.
16 Jung, CW 8, ¶ 11.
17 Jung, CW 8, ¶ 13.

A------B

As

C------X

(x is what cannot be known)[18]

Two elements are important to underscore here: 1. part of the content of the metaphor appeals to or intuits the contents of the unconscious in a value-laden way; 2. the power or energy field of the metaphor rests not in any one of its parts but in the dynamic relationship crafted between the relation A—B to the relation C—D. The unconscious contents, or more accurately, the fields that lie untrammeled in the unconscious, are activated through metaphor's relational properties. The relation of the parts resonate the relationship of the whole through its formal properties. Is then a metaphor a created complex with "a nuclear element and a large number of secondarily constellated associations" as Jung defines the complex?[19]

A metaphor is, as Joseph Campbell suggests, a transport vehicle—it allows movement from one reality field to another, to cross over, to transgress, and to violate boundaries in order to open up a new energy field of understanding.[20] If such is indeed the case, then is this the nub of how an individual or a culture forms values, or begins to value what it believes to be true? If a critical mass of a population accepts the constelled metaphor as a formidable and persuasive view of reality, does this become the agreed-upon way of seeing and interpreting the substance of experiences? The metaphor, in other words, becomes mimetic of the plot line of reality as generally understood. The power inherent in mimesis' presence is that it, according to Gunter and Wulf, "allows new thought, new creation, new syntheses to come into being."[21] Mimesis introduces the power of the analogical, the way in which consciousness finds analogies of its experiences in other forms of narrative. My own sense is that psyche is fundamentally mimetic, always seeking and befriending duplicates and representations of itself, an idea I hope to substantiate further. What seems plausible to suggest, however, is that myths have their genesis right here, in the shape of an analogy.

---

18 Campbell, Joseph, *The Inner Reaches of Outer Space*, p. 29.
19 Jung, CW 8, ¶ 18.
20 Campbell, *Inner Reaches*, p. 63.
21 Gunter and Wulf, *Mimesis: Culture, Art, Society*, p. 2.

Francis Fergusson, in his finely-wrought Introduction to Aristotle's *Poetics,* quotes the translator S.H. Butcher, who writes: The praxis that art seeks to reproduce is mainly *a psychic energy* working outwards."[22] Art is engaged in creating channels or sluices that are aesthetic in design and powerful in structure in order to construct and deliver psychic energy fields that have the capacity to transform consciousness. The imitation that *mimesis* engages touches on one or several of the infinite designs or patterns that the soul discovers and /or crafts of lived experience. Art constructs these likenesses in a range of aesthetic forms to guide the imagination to see more fully, with a greater orbit of awareness. Moreover, if, as Joseph Campbell believes, "metaphor is the native tongue of myth,"[23] then myths themselves grow from the above relation. A metaphor may then mirror or duplicate so as to represent a complex as well as a complex way of knowing, to reveal to the psyche a complexity and nuance in surprising associations and in new iterations. Such is the power of metaphor and *mimesis* for expanding one's circuit of knowledge.

I write the above in part because of Jung's grasp of a complex consisting of two components: 1. a factor determined by experience and causally related to the environment (exterior); and 2. a factor innate in the individual's character and determined by his disposition (interior). The combination of this very psychic and indeed, poetic arrangement would seem to lead Jung to ask: "But what means have we of estimating the energic value of the constellating power which enriches the complex with associations?"[24] The accumulated number of associations comprise the metaphors hidden in the energy, encompassed by the energy and created by psychic energy; the result is the manifestation of what Armstrong, bearing the weight of the same theme, refers to as "affective presence."[25] Once again, the fundamental quality of the psyche is to be relational, analogic, metaphoric, similetic, connected, symbolic and in accord with something greater than itself.

I digress from Jung's *Collected Works Volume 8* for a moment to cite what I sense is the heartbeat of depth psychology in the format with which I am exploring the nature of metaphor. It occurs in *Volume 9ii, Aion: Researches into the Phenomenology*

---

22 Francis Fergusson in introduction to Aristotle's *Poetics*, p. 8. NOTE: I engage this quality of motion outwards as part of mimesis in my essay, "Poetry's Mode of Knowing: Dante's Pilgrimage From Mimesis to Wisdom" (*A Limbo of Shards* 118-39).

23 Campbell, *Thou Art That*, p. 6.

24 Jung, CW 8, ¶ 20.

25 Armstrong, Robert Plant, *The Powers of Presence*, p.6.

of the Self. Here Jung, as I trust the translation, tucks this insight into an introductory adverbial clause, surprising for me because of the importance of his assertion: "Since analogy formation is a law which to a large extent governs the life of the psyche, we may fairly conjecture...."[26] His words resonate a poetic quality to psyche, that its language is metaphor, as is Campbell's *lingua franca* for myth. The suggestion I would draw out is that psyche is fundamentally mythic and metaphoric and that psychic energy is composed and coagulates primarily along these forms.

My thinking therefore runs this way: metaphors are clusters or knots of affects, of affective energy—what it allows perception to open to via imagination. Metaphors are fiercely rooted in the world of matter, but that matter contains its own spiritual, psychological and philosophical variants. A passage from a classic work of literature may further ground this idea. We might contemplate the words of Captain Ahab's musings on the quarter deck of the Pequod at the end of chapter 70, entitled "The Sphinx" in Herman Melville's *Moby-Dick*. The image of the Sphinx refers to the head of a whale decapitated and dragged up by chains to dangle along the side of the ship: "It was a black and hooded head; and hanging there in the midst of so intense a calm, it seemed the Sphinxes in the desert."[27] Alone, Ahab approaches and gazes at this marvel and then wonders what it knows as a consequence of having dove to the farthest depths of the sea.

He is, however, suddenly interrupted in his musings on the whale's hooded head by one of the crew, who shouts out from the crow's nest the sighting of another whale: "'Three points on the starboard bow, sir and bringing down her breeze to us.'" Ahab acknowledges this directive and then utters to himself the following reverie:

> Better and better, man. Would now St. Paul would come along that way, and to my breezelessness bring his breeze! O Nature and O soul of man! How far beyond all utterance are your linked analogies; not the smallest atom stirs or lives on matter, but has its cunning duplicate in mind.[28]

Something gathers in Ahab's philosophical way of seeing the world as he seeks in wounded vengeance to "strike through the mask"[29] of the material, phenomenal world in order to give voice to what is in the mind. In the mind appears a double

---

26 Jung, CW 9ii, ¶ 414.
27 Melville, *Moby-Dick*, p. 332.
28 *Moby-Dick*, p. 333.
29 *Moby-Dick*, p. 174.

of the world. Not mind over matter so much as mind mirroring matter, even mind mimicking matter. He sees something, a wall perhaps, dissolve between the world of matter and the matter of mind. I sense that at least at this moment he casts the shadow of a depth psychologist. Something of the whale's heady presence and his own heady thoughts congeal in a rich vision of the mirroring or duplication of the world and mind, another spin, I suspect, on the myth of Narcissus that seems to haunt the entire epic with its duplicating and at times duplicitous, mirror reflections. Perhaps seeing double—the appearance of matter and the mentation of mind—is our shared common perception, an "as-if" mode of knowing that self-duplicates and self-references at once.

I am suggesting that psychic energy enters to invest this observation of Ahab, to make of it a truth of Being itself, which is where I sense poetry's impulse wants to take us as often as we will yield to it. Ahab muses on a sense of relationship. He imagines metaphorically for a moment and in that respect duplicates the mind of Ishmael, the story's narrator—they are cross-over twins on many levels in the epic, refracting, reflecting and giving one another his due and duty on board this magical ship, which itself duplicates in its piecemeal construction aspects or pieces of whales hunted in its rich past as a warrior whaler of the seas. Jung, not incidentally, said this of Melville's whaling venture. Commenting on the important difference between psychological and visionary fiction, he names a few representatives of each nomenclature. He then designates as an illustration of visionary fiction: "I would also include Melville's *Moby Dick*, [sic] which I consider to be the greatest American novel, in this broad class of writings."[30]

Metaphors Matter

I am suggesting that psychic energy engages metaphor, perhaps makes metaphor matter, become material. Metaphors are then energy fields that bridge some quality between consciousness and the unconscious, and body-psyche. Metaphors open us to the symbolic realm; their poetic power consists in their ability to make and shape a new reality based on this initial relation. The relation exposes a pattern of consciousness which involves replication, repetition and similarity but couched most often in

30 Jung, CW 15, ¶ 137.

difference. When this connection of relationships, which D. Stephenson Bond offers, is always a mediating between culture and the environment, including individual interiority, "mythic form must fail as the moment passes," meaning that myths dehydrate, turn into dry husks when they know longer authentically embody the above relationship: "It becomes dysfunctional because it points to an adaptation that is no longer adequate." [31] I would add that the flow of psychic energy has diminished to a trickle or dried up, leaving no trace. The myth becomes de-eroticized and is no longer a vital force in the community or individual because its relational coherence has fled. To cling to it is to embrace a dogmatic, rigid belief that allows no flexibility. It sees only itself.

Michael Conforti, an early pioneer in this field of archetypal energy fields as they relate to the new physics, writes that the alchemists, like St. Francis, viewed all expressions of matter in the outer world as physical representations of eternal archetypal forms and processes. [32] Matter becomes psyche's attempt to make present in symbolic form the face of an archetype in image. This attempt is yet another form that *poiesis* may assume in the shaping of something into a coherent design or pattern.

If the nuclear element of a complex, therefore, has a constellating power corresponding to its energic value—i.e. it produces a constellation of psychic contents, giving rise to the complex, which is a constellation of psychic contents dynamically conditioned by the energic value, then it would seem that the constellating power of the nuclear element corresponds to its value intensity. I believe what Ahab felt in the scene described above, what he became present to affectively in gazing at the head of the whale hanging by chains over the edge of the Pequod's deck, is precisely this energy that we, by analogy, in reading a poem, an engaging novel, a short story, seeing a play performed or even gazing at a masterpiece in contemplation, sense: the nuclear element lying like a coiled snake within its form, where the power of the object or narrative stirs psychic contents in the viewer or reader, seeks and discovers a simulacrum of itself, and embraces a similar quality or tone or affect to which to adhere. Writing on the power of psychic energy, Jungian analyst M. Esther Harding reveals that,

---

31 Bond, D.S., *Living Myth*, p. 44.
32 Conforti, Michael, *Field, Form and Fate*, p. 6.

> The first exploit of the hero is to arouse the dragon, that lurks in the unconscious, so that he will come out and fight, for only by this manoeuvre can the treasure concealed beneath his great bulk be revealed.[33]

In addition, these psychic contents form patterns over time; it suggests that psyche is a pattern-making, pattern-discovering quality of consciousness wherein the patterns expose the imprint of the archetypes. Patterns uncover as well the field of archetypal presences. Into this jurisdiction the artist plunges in order to engage the design in the tapestry of consciousness, return with it as a boon, and shape it into a comprehensible communal form for us to navigate in reading or viewing. This shaping into a patterned reality in matter is the imaginal activity of *poiesis,* a making or shaping into a form that leads us back and down into the archetypal nether regions. Forms guide us by revealing the way. What Harding refers to as the hero above I call the artist; the task of the artist is to arouse the dragon. Otherwise the treasures remain inaccessible. That the images depict or resemble a deeper archetypal reality attests to the validity and power of the soul's mimetic capacity as well as its metaphoric way of knowing.

Jung leads us to such a conclusion when he writes specifically of the nature of metaphor:

> An archetypal content expresses itself, first and foremost, in metaphors. If such a content should speak of the sun and identify with it the lion, the king, the hoard of gold guarded by the dragon, or the power that makes for the life andhealth of man, it is neither the one thing nor the other, but the unknown third thing that finds more or less adequate expression in all these similes...yet remains unknown.[34]

We have seen such a phenomenon recently in the way energy gathers, waxes and wanes around this or that presidential candidate. They in turn wish to gather that nuclear element around themselves which energizes them, their ideas, their visions and dreams as well as all those who support them.

Furthermore, in his essay "On Psychic Energy" Jung postulates that "we cannot prove scientifically that a relation of equivalence exists between physical and psychic energy, we have no alternative except either to drop the energetic viewpoint altogether, or else to postulate a special psychic energy....[35] In this passage he encourages a way to speak of the power of metaphor, the force of symbol, indeed the power of myth

33 Harding, M. Esther, *Psychic Energy*, p. 243.
34 Jung, CW 9ii, ¶ 267.
35 Jung, CW 8, ¶ 28.

to gather or constellate energy-producing thoughts and actions. I conclude from this assertion that metaphor and myth congeal in poetic patterns as they gather psychic energy in their making and in their distribution and dissemination. When we engage it as active readers, we are shaped by the contents, yes, but more importantly, by the psychic energy released through the language and the mythos of the plot. The power of presence is unleashed in the unfolding of the plot. Released is what Jung refers to as its life energy, and psychic energy is part of, but does not contain, the whole story.

So, he writes: let us "call our hypothetical life-energy 'libido'" to distinguish from a concept of universal energy...."[36] He believes as well that even though the libidinal energy is not synonymous with bio-energy, it is related to it—highly probable, he argues, that the psychic and physical are not independent parallel processes but connected through reciprocal action which we do not know. [37]

Patterns of Psyche-Soma

Metaphors, I understand in this context, are bridges between psyche-soma energy fields; they reveal in their structure and by analogy a relationship of body and psyche that is indispensable to understanding. It may be that myths as well are bridges or complex interlocking networks on this same level of psychic energy and body energetics wherein myths are matters of both mind and soul. More specifically, the collaborative work of Stanely Keleman and Joseph Campbell on bios and mythos makes this connection abundantly plausible: "A mythic image is the body speaking to itself about itself....They are patterns of embodiment: they show us how to grow our inherited biological endowment into a personal form."[38]

I propose metaphors, then, as energy fields that bridge some quality between conscious and unconscious contents and body-psyche. Symbols and their formations are part of the discussion here as well, for they carry a linguistic and poetic power to both make and shape a new reality based on this initial set of relations. Words themselves have body, have an etymology (history) and can body forth psychic energy as both

---

36 Jung, CW 8, ¶ 32.
37 Jung, CW 8, ¶ 32.
38 Keleman, Stanley, *Myth and the Body: A Colloquy with Joseph Campbell*, p. 3.

stand-alone words as well as forceful combinations with other words to create star-tlingly new potent and persuasive realities.

Shortly after the above observation, Jung pushes further into libidinal energy in writing that, "nowhere can we see more clearly than in the relation of sexuality to the total psyche how the disappearance of a given quantum of libido is followed by the appearance of an equivalent value in another form."[39] The suggestion here is that some law of psyche is working itself out. The libidinal energy does not disappear; instead it migrates to another field. Such a further migration offers greater credence to how the psyche is fundamentally metaphorical and energic, or energically metaphorical.

Metaphor is closer, as I suggested above, to an energy transfer system, perhaps as well a psycho-poetic energy translation via *equivalence,* of one part of reality with and for another. Metaphor imbeds in itself a method of transferring libido from text to imagination, of story to imagination, of plot to body, so that it is experienced viscer-ally, even *consubstantially*, a word I borrow from the writing of Jacques Maritain.[40]

Moreover, the act of interpretation is itself an energy transfer phenomenon. When I suggest that metaphor is a method, I mean that it is an impulse of transferring libido from the text to imagination of the reader and a libidinal exchange from reader to the text. Here we can pose the question: What analogies in us are incited or provoked in the act of reading a poem or in engaging a passage like that of Ahab's above? The act of interpretation imaginally transfers energy from text to body's texture. This energy, or libido energy in Jung's' words, can disappear into the unconscious, to gestate and then to give birth to something the client, the reader or the culture is not yet aware of. So is it then hidden from all eyes and ears? Perhaps then the hero, or the heroic part of our own complexity, enters here to stir the dragon who sleeps atop the treasure.

To answer the question above, I want to lean a bit more on the nature of myths by suggesting that myths are bridges, or complex interlocking networks operative on the level of psychic energy and body energetics. These myths are repositories for certain narrative patterns necessary for the rich texture of life itself, like certain foods the body needs in its will to survive. The language of myth, as Campbell has asserted, is

---

39 Jung, CW 8, ¶ 35.

40 Maritain, Jacques, *Creative Intuition in Art and Poetry*, p. 259. Jacques Maritain's brilliant assessment of the poetic sense of poetry offers this analogy: "The poetic sense is to the work what the soul is to the person" (*Creative Intuition*, p. 191). Therefore reading poetry is very experiential, including the entire visceral and intellectual and emotional response of the reader.

metaphor. I propose that metaphors are energy fields that promote conversation and traffic between consciousness and the unconscious through body psyche. Symbols and their formation are part of the discussion as well, for they carry linguistic and poetic power in order to make and shape a new reality based on this initial relation. To consider metaphor in this manner is to engage reality as a relational complex that shifts its ground via the metaphors one lives by. As the "native tongue of myth," metaphors reveal the contours, if not the texture, of the personal myth one is living both in and out.

The "how" of each of our endeavors and desires to create meaning from lived events appears predicated on the metaphors that grow directly from the individual and collective mythos operating in the basement of our belief system. Lawrence Coupe's fine little book, *Myth,* assists us here. He writes: "myth-making is a primal and universal function of the human mind as it seeks a unified vision of cosmic order, social order and individual life order."[41] The impulse of which Coupe speaks seems a variation on Jung's belief in the *unus mundus*, that below the water line of differentiation lurks a unifying design that connects all apparent disparities. Myth's method of discernment, furthermore, is eloquently displayed in literary critic and mythologist Louise Cowan's understanding of mythic consciousness:

> For mythic consciousness is not only a basic need of the human spirit, but a characteristically human mode of thought, like imagination, memory and reason;.... it takes hold of a thing or a situation intuitively and wholly, so that motive and method are perceived simultaneously with the good to be served. It allows a person to grasp entire forms, discern the coherence of their parts, and apprehend the totality of their purpose.[42]

Myth, therefore, like poetry, offers its own form of knowing, a discernment of the patterns inherent in a thing or circumstance and a coherent form in the making, which may be grasped with the guidance of a prevailing myth.

---

41 Coupe, Lawrence, *Myth*, p. 6.
42 Cowan, Louise, "Myth in the Modern World," p. 6.

Oedipal Patterning

At this point, an illustration would help ground some of the above theoretical mus-ings. I have never tired of reading and teaching/being taught by, the *Oedipus Trilogy* of Sophocles. I pause here on a scene early in *Oedipus Rex,* just at the moment when Jocasta, the wife/mother of Oedipus, tells her king, husband and son what she knows of the circumstances of the slaying of Laius, the former ruler of Thebes. In her recol-lection she includes a description of the place where three roads meet, a powerful im-age on many levels. To be more geographically correct, however, we notice that there are in fact two roads, one leading from Delphi, the other from Phocis; when they meet they create the third terrain, the *tertium quid* of the highway, the third road that grows from the convergence of the two.

As she tells Oedipus of the scene, Jocasta suddenly sees a strange change cross the face of her husband-son—the latter relation she is yet to learn—and asks Oedipus what troubles him. His response is less certain, more musing than his earlier, more direct and even mathematically precise language: "Strange, /hearing you just now... my mind wandered/my thoughts racing back and forth."[43]

Now we don't want to miss the dramatic irony here. It is Jocasta's intent to put her king's mind at ease on his involvement with the death of the king by distancing him from the slaying of Laius. But her well-intentioned story has the opposite effect: it jostles in Oedipus' memory something dire, indeed terrifying. The act of relating the story transforms Oedipus' relation to place. Her story defines anew his remembered locale at the foot of Mount Cythera. Her description activates both his memory and his mythos. The drama heats up mightily at this juncture: the place where two stories meet—the one in telling, the other in listening and in recollection. Something not wanted, not invited, gains affective presence through the narrative details that find a new home in Oedipus' memory as it begins to create a third thing: his true identity. His wife's intention to distance him from any thought of guilt for the king's murder instead shapes in him an intimacy with the story's meaning.

Memory and imagination conspire to bring him closer to who he is, not more distant from such a troubling truth. Her intention becomes his aperture into his past behavior and identity, including the oracle's words that spawned it. In the history-myth of Oedipus, the story takes on new energy, a mimetic power to transform his

---

43 Sophocles, *The Three Theban Plays*, ll. 801-03.

past into the present with a new vitality, intimacy and meaning. Energy has invested the story with a new dynamic and its effect is to make the once more certain king wander in thought—straight toward who he is but has lived unconsciously his entire life. The dragon has been successfully roused.

Under the principle of equivalence that Jung develops through a discussion of psychic energy, he cautions that one watch for where a quantum of libido will reveal itself in unconscious activity, for example, with a patient in an intensification of certain symptoms, or a new symptom, peculiar dreams, or fleeting fantasies.[44] The primary task of the analyst is to bring to consciousness those hidden contents, which have not a few features in common with conscious contents that have since lost their energy. In the case of Sophocles' play, the energy has returned to find the murderer of the king after so many years because a blight has descended on the Theban landscape, making the discovery necessary and essential for the health of the natural and civic orders.

We might conjecture that in listening to the story Jocasta relates, Oedipus' past is re-energized; he senses the analogy of her story as it is placed beside his own history. Psyche has found its truth in the analogy of the narratives—one recounted by Jocasta, one remembered by Oedipus as a lived reality. The two roads, perhaps a rich metaphor for the binding quality of psyche's anthropology, have met once again to create a third thing: a new reading of the past through a current story recollected. Her narrative beds down with her son's recollection, now shaped anew by the story he hears. Bios meets mythos as Oedipus' full and authentic identity squeezes up from below ground, the terror of which will bring her to self-murder and him, with the aid of his mother's brooches from her apparel, to blind himself in shame, the latter an ironic tragic consequence of a profound insight. Jocasta's story is told at this juncture in time to send her son back to just such a place of recollecting his own slaying of a man who has, until now, remained anonymous and therefore without significance. But the pattern was and is now and it surfaces again seeking a story to shape. Part of the essential "mythogenetic zone" of Oedipus has found new energy and is now affectively present in his memory.

One last observation on this relation of metaphor as energy transfer system and the workings of libidinal energy: Jung quotes Carl Hartmann to the effect that "the quantity, or the extensity factor of energy is attached to one structure and cannot be

---

44 Jung, CW 8, ¶ 35.

transferred to another structure without carrying with it parts of the first."[45] If we continue to think of the power of a metaphor lying, in its relationship of parts to other parts, as configured above, and as an energy transfer system of psyche, then we discern that the way of metaphor occurs in carrying from one part of it to the other part or parts some of the energy imbedded in the first part, such that one's energy field is divided, then integrated through the metaphor, as a new thing, event, idea, emotion or insight. *Tertium quid* has been realized. Metaphor therefore makes conscious something hidden by means of its implicit energy transfer system. Such is what Jocasta valiantly attempted *not* to do in her description of the three roads meeting, yet her success was precisely in the opposite direction: she succeeded in arousing in her son an analogical experience of his own three roads' meeting there. Unknowingly, he slew a stranger, his father. By means of analogy and through the power of metaphor, he now knows vaguely and uneasily: through questioning, however, will soon know more precisely and terribly.

Patterns and Tradition

T.S. Eliot, in his controversial and remarkable essay, "Tradition and the Individual Talent," claims that tradition is moved by the energy of a creative voice which, working within the tradition, nonetheless brings with him/her enough truly new and creative expression—and can we add, psychic energy from the field of the collective?—to move the tradition forward, howbeit slightly. Such is the sign of a vital and organic tradition, imbedded in a coherent and organically alive myth, which sustains enough elasticity to both hold its values sacred while remaining open to accommodating change. Joseph Campbell is eloquent on this point: "Living myths are not mistaken notions, and they do not spring from books. They are not to be judged as true or false but as effective or ineffective, maturative or pathogenic. They are rather like enzymes, products of the body in which they work."[46] In other words, do they have the vitality to lead the individual or an entire culture towards greater maturity?

When Jung observes that there exists a psychological extensity factor which cannot pass into a new structure without carrying over parts or characteristics of the previous

45 Jung, CW 8, ¶ 37.
46 Campbell, Joseph, *Wild Gander*, p. xiv.

structure with which it was connected, he affords us different language for a similar or the same historical phenomenon: that a tradition—which I understand to be a congealing of myth as history and a historical placement of a myth—pulls forward into its future what sustains an individual or a people, while leaving in its wake what no longer serves, what, like old skin, needs to be shed and discarded as it pursues a new synthesis.

The force of drama inhabits this region: narrative's deep nature needs the libidinal energy inherent in its structure if it is alive and vital, to create a split, then a new amalgam; without the energy to realize this new synthesis is a psychic impossibility. The very nature of a dramatic narrative is to engage conflict, breakage, or stress to the point of permanent distortion and then breakdown, followed by some form of a consequential break-through, if not in the characters themselves, then at least in the reader as witness to the energy transferred from one idea, emotion, character, to another.

If the metaphor, a large elaborate construction that is the Tradition, is exhausted, depleted, made anemic, then it won't have the rich libidinal blood to successfully carry the psychic energy into a new form. Metaphors, like organic living things, can slip into the condition of cadavers. Cultural clichés in thought, language, point of view, or knowledge are no longer capable of carrying the energy in its vehicle. The engine is worn out, the tires bald, the gears stripped, the tank empty.

In addition, Jung's observation above suggests an essential element of metaphor: the body and soul of metaphor, which includes then the body in physical energy and the soul in psychological extension. Both sides are needed in this transfer system of psyche that is capable of leading one to new insights.

The above observation has a likeness to Campbell's idea of energy flow. But the questions raised include: what parts are carried over? what designates those parts from all others? who is responsible for making the cut? Early in his classic work, *The Hero With a Thousand Faces,* Campbell observes that in mythology the hero appears at those historical junctures when the energy flow between three realms—macrocosm, mesocosm, and microcosm—has dwindled or ceased altogether, like the flow of blood in an artery clogged with cultural and/or psychic placque.

The task, then, of the Hero is:

1. To hear the call out of necessity;

2. To heed the call;

3. To submit to the call

for the hero's goal is to move into that closed arterial blockage and to unstop the flow so that the circulation continues between these three connected domains.[47] I believe Ahab's reverie earlier touches on the same phenomenon—some duplicate or correspondence must be allowed to reveal itself in the flow—between cosmos, social constructions and the individual. The hero reinvigorates the motifs of the culture, even reinvents them if necessary, in order to restore the life force to the people suffering such a debilitating blockage. Such is the central task of artist as heroic presence.

The hero then, is the force that restarts and revitalizes the energy field—something akin, I believe, to what Barack Obama carries today in the collective psyche of America. He has, of course, his prototype in Oedipus cited earlier. What Sophocles reveals to us is that the pilgrimage to self-identity and to a fully realized self-consciousness is often a collateral form of suffering and ultimate benefit of the hero's essential task to remedy the pollution, dissipate the blight, unplug the blockage, so that the life blood of psyche can flow again through the communal body and in so doing serve as ballast for the ship of state. Said another way, the tradition of a people, its animating mythos, is retrieved by the heroic presence of energy that an extraordinary individual has the capacity to accept and implement and then share the fruits of his/her exploits.

I discern a connection here between Jung and Campbell in the following way: Jung stresses that the symbolic interpretation of causes by means of the energic standpoint is necessary for the differentiation of the psyche, "since unless the facts are symbolically interpreted, the causes remain immutable substances, which goes on operating continuously."[48] May then the task of the hero be to shift the collective point of view, its prevailing attitude, its locked-in way of interpreting life, by opening it to a new or revised manner of envisioning experience not just for him/herself, but for all its citizens? It seems to me that the heroic project, both from Jung and Campbell's perspectives, is to recover the symbolic order of being, a task that I believe poetry—indeed all the arts generally—have as one of their primary missions and intentions.

---

47 Campbell, *The Hero With a Thousand Faces*, pp. 49-59.
48 Jung, CW 8, ¶ 46.

Poetic Symbol

An individual as well as an entire culture can flat-line in their preoccupation with external stimuli, diversions and entertainments as well as those events that muster fear in the collective psyche to rob it of its freedom. Lost then is the symbolic order which carries the values of a people, what they hold most sacred as beliefs and as impetus for continuance. This is the mythic scaffolding that any people rely on for their health and vitality: the flow of blood into the communal body. Art serves this end, primarily, by offering an *aesthetic stimulus package* for the collective to redeem itself by.

Poetry expresses in due measure the non-normative forms of things, as in the following poem of mine, "Silent Places of the Body Under Siege,"[49] written while I sat in an oncology waiting room at a hospital in California. I was full of anxiety anticipating a dermatologist who would cauterize precancerous lumps on my chest and arms as well as biopsy others to see if skin cancer was to be part of my future. To relieve the pressure, I wrote the following:

> In the Cancer rooms of the clinic
> is a forest of words that terrify.
> Like beasts they move between us
> sitting on the quiet chairs,
> their lairs the slippery dark
> places of our flesh.
>
> Quiet green lighting is broken by the beasts
> describing *angiograms, endemas*—fluid
> in there that is not good—
> *thrombosis* and *metastasize,*
> the vocabulary of penetration.
>
> What is it to part the screen of the word
> Cancer
> and see, as above the lintel of Inferno:
> "Abandon all hope you who enter here"?

49 Slattery, Dennis Patrick, *Casting the Shadows*, pp. 25-26.

28

Invisible birds with sharp yellow beaks
fly through the halls unmolested
past the outbursts of laughter pouring
out of far
too cheery receptionists.

We sit in the antechambers of Hell
or by the lowest, widest spiral of
Purgatory with others peering
at us,
seeing into one another's ailments.

The man next to me breathes
with gurgled sounds from his hollow chest.
He looks over his glasses and stares at
my Levis as if they might have a heart
condition.

I wear deodorant today to beat back the stress
and cannot keep knives out of my mind.
A patient enters holding a bag of liquid
with a line snaking into her arm under
the long sleeve of her yellow blouse.

A snake bite of venom keeps her fluid in motion
and the rest of us sit thumbing magazines
looking for even a shred of our own stories
hidden in the pages full of healthy images
of young people whose teeth
are far too white and whose laughter
promises no contagion.

The poem directed the psychic energy outward, into a display of emotional images that helped to soothe my frayed interior. I chose not to ignore or deflect or suppress my emotional life, but to channel it into words, to relegate the experience into a new territory in a dynamic movement, not by jettisoning the past but transforming it by pulling it forward into a new energy field. To create a symbol, a metaphor, an analogy of a charged event is to shape the event into a formed experience—a poiesis of the original event that now, mimetically, mirrors the event through a formative principle. The libidinal energy of the original event in history is transferred into a mytho-poetic expression that gains presence in symbol. This shaping of history into a poetic utterance is a mythic act that encourages it to become what was before an unformed, frightening ordeal, affectively present.

Jung helps us deploy such a notion when he observes that "psychic development cannot be accomplished by intention and will alone; it needs the attraction of the symbol, whose value quantum exceeds that of the cause. But the formation of a symbol cannot take place until...the inner and outer necessities of the life process have brought about a transformation of energy."[50]

Psyche's fundamental poetic response to life reveals how it is constantly carrying, metaphorically, traces of character from the old to the new. My intention here is to develop an image of psyche as a metaphorical matrix of energy, located in a libidinal field constantly crossing and recrossing boundaries from history to myth and myth to history. The pivot or fulcrum in this exchange is the human body. The epic task of psyche is to interpret the facts or events of the world symbolically; otherwise, the facts remain immutable and continue operating without surcease. Keeping the symbolic energy transferring process that allows for energy's reciprocal motion is the best and most efficacious way to keep the status quo in place and in power.

Presencing as Psychic and Mytho-Poetic Phenomenon

As a teacher and writer, I am concerned with how to make something present: to make it vivid, alive, vibrant and fresh. In this attempt I try to reread the poetry and prose texts that I teach each year in the same course. Even while I have pages of typed

---

50 Jung, CW 8, ¶ 47.

notes on the poems, the likes of which include Homer's *Odyssey*, Melville's *Moby-Dick,* Toni Morrison's *Beloved,* and Dante's *Commedia*, as well as the prose works of Joseph Campbell and essays by C.G. Jung, I am compelled to return to *the experience* each work yields. But my response is that I never truly read the same work repeatedly; in fact, in all my years of stepping on board the Pequod of Melville's epic whale tale, for example, never has the same white whale breached twice. It is always a different whale carrying splinters of the previous leviathan in its fluky wake.

Nonetheless, what is it that makes something present, which is part of the intention of this essay. Look for a moment with me, for instance, at the following poem by one of my favorite poets, William Stafford, called "Our Story."

> Remind me again—together we
> trace our strange journey, find
> each other, come on laughing.
> Some time we'll cross where life
> ends. We'll both look back
> as far as forever, that first day.
> I'll touch you—a new world then.
> Stars will move a different way.
> We'll both end. We'll both begin.
>
> Remind me again.[51]

The poet wishes to bring something to his and our attention, perhaps even to his and our *intention.* What is it? By what means does he use language to make it attentional and available? However we ask these questions, I believe we can assume that some energy gathers around the images, about the sentiment and encircles our own histories to create a complex and nuanced energy field. I return for a moment to a writer mentioned earlier, for what he observes bears on Stafford's poem.

In *The Powers of Presence,* Robert Armstrong calculates the potency of Presentness, which I understand as another form or consequence of psychic energy. He distinguishes between two types of Presence: 1. works of identity or effective processes (management of the universe), i.e. an aesthetic of invocation; and 2. works bearing

51 Stafford, William, *The Way It Is: New and Selected Poems*, p. 49.

the presence of excellence, i.e., those dedicated to the management of energies of their own internal systems, not present of persons, but presence of qualities of internal significance,[52] what he refers to as an aesthetics of virtuosity. He further claims that while #1 is not present all the time, #2 is.[53] He goes on to delineate two moments, if you will, in an aesthetics of invocation: the physical thing, the mask is one; the power that under appropriate conditions infuses it is the second.[54] Therefore, when the object or event is in enactment, it is a work; when that same object or event is at rest, it is "not a work." Thus, when the object or event is not invoked—mask, statue, text, music, dance—then "what we call in our aesthetic 'the work' is in an aesthetic of invocation but an 'item' in the work.[55] Enactment may be one of reading a poem like Stafford's, meditating on it, carrying it into a classroom and noticing the various responses to it; all these are rites of presencing.

A work that is invoked as an aesthetic object has power; an item that is the work has no power. Armstrong suggests the line in the sand between the two is that the invoked work exists only in *performance*.[56] Now, when I pause for a moment in writing these words at the computer and glance around the room at the hundreds of books that line the shelves of my study, my gaze falls on some titles that changed my life and continue to alter my perceptions every time I enter their infused world and invoke as a reader the power of their ideas. The sentences in performance—in reading silently or aloud—and even more poignantly, if I teach that work in a classroom, something else is added: a spiritual, or numinous or extraordinary heightening of consciousness itself, so that our own orbit of understanding, our level of awareness, is magnified. I/ we become more, not less aware through the sentences and the images carried in the language as well as the beauty of the language itself, as in this passage from Toni Morrison's Pulitzer Prize novel, *Beloved*. It is a moment early in the plot when a runaway slave, Paul D., returns to 124 Bluestone Road after 18 years, there to find a woman, Sethe, who he loved much earlier but could never approach until now.

> Not even trying, he had become the kind of man who could walk into a house and make the women cry. Because with him, in his presence they could. There was something blessed in his manner. Women saw him and wanted to weep—to tell him

52 Armstrong, Robert, *The Powers of Presence*, p. 9.
53 *The Powers of Presence*, p. 10.
54 *The Powers of Presence*, p. 11.
55 *The Powers of Presence*, p. 11.
56 *The Powers of Presence*, (my emphasis) p. 11.

that their chest hurt and their knees did too. Strong women and wise saw him and told him things they only told each other: that way past the Change of Life, desire in them had suddenly become enormous, greedy, more savage than when they were fifteen, and that it embarrassed them and made them sad.[57]

The power inherent in the words surfaces as the presence of an energy field, of psychic energy, or perhaps better said, psycho-poetic energy. Some core of reality is evoked in the expression—and I sense that myth is created, its germination stage active right here—myth as the mucilage that holds the narrative together and guards it from collapsing around its own delicate presence. We as readers do not murder to dissect the parts, to analyze or to chew it up into bits and pieces and spit the pulp of what is irrelevant out. No, that is tyrannous reading. But in contemplation something else is alive, working, that invites presence to protrude. In this mode something of consciousness itself is at risk and fragile but forceful in its presence. Now a power enters that was not there prior to the book being opened, like a treasure trove that can only be gainsaid when the lid is lifted. The contemplative act, as Evelyn Underhill has written of the mystic's response to the transcendent, "has the capacity to alter consciousness."[58]

Energy gathers around the words, ignites them, and brings them forward to be contemplated in the full light of the reader's ability to glow from its presence. Actually, that is the point: the work has achieved an affective presence, for the presence is not without emotional torque. Some investment in the work has activated it like a sleeping page full of still words that begin, once evoked, to crawl all over the page and into the body of the reader to make consciousness gather itself on another level of awareness. Armstrong admits as much when he observes that "the work of affective presence—sharing psychological processes with persons—sometimes seems as much to apprehend its witness as its witness apprehends it."[59] He further suggests that in a mask, in music, or in a poem's language, "we know that something is abroad there, something akin to but yet not ourselves—something existent there, *something being.*"[60]

I like this idea very much: that the work itself has its own, or participates in a form of consciousness itself. It judges us, our reactions, our interpretations, our hunches,

---

57 Morrison, Toni, *Beloved,* p. 17.
58 Underhill, Evelyn, *Mysticism,* p. 62.
59 Armstrong, *The Powers of Presence,* p. 16.
60 *The Powers of Presence,* p. 16.

conjectures, and intuitions, even as we pass judgment on it. Only a work that has achieved or crossed the threshold of Affective Presence may dare make such a claim. And let's sidestep Projection at this juncture—the idea that we are merely hurling onto the work the dross of our own psyches. Rather to say that the work gathers into its own field, once it is welcomed by being opened, read, traced, copied, underlined, marginalized with script—that the work is analogous to a living person—perhaps whoever approaches it with some humility and not a little welcoming love. Then the work's own impulses reach out to soothe us in our pilgrimage through it, in the same way that in 19th century romantic literature, trees reach their branches down to caress a night traveler, or even to embrace so to protect the innocent in their shivering vulnerability.

What passes between the reader and the text are two distinct consciousnesses that relate, share ideas, counter one another, interrogate one another's motives, and seek always the hot nugget of the controlling mythos that governs the plot of each. Reading is then more like a mutual plotting of the imagination than it is a reader pouncing on dead meat to extract whatever nutrients may have been left behind. Both the foreplay and the moments following include a continual inter-penetration of the universal by means of the particulars and the upswing or uptick of the particulars by the larger force field of the universal in a constant rocking back and forth until the last lines of the narrative. Then something closes and what is left is the material for contemplation and reflection.

Armstrong leans on this interpenetration as part of its hermeneutics when he asserts that "the first power that invests the work of Affective Presence is the power of analogicity,[61] which he links to the body,[62] not just the body of the text but the body of the reader. Reading is incarnational, visceral, not simply heady but head-to-foot, which at the same time engages: 1. the power of subjectivity; 2. the power of the mythic.[63]

Perhaps most importantly is that it is an aesthetic response, tracking that oft- overused word to its root to mean *a showing forth* or *display*; what is displayed in what is made present, not neutrally, but with affect, with energy, with an erotic charge that attracts and thus invites lingering. My own sense is that affect is one way that psy-

---

61 Armstrong, *The Powers of Presence*, p. 10.
62 *The Powers of Presence*, p. 19.
63 *The Powers of Presence*, p. 19.

chic energy inhabits perception, makes it keener, more heightened and finally, more beautiful. It is analogous mythically to a double viewing in which both Aphrodite and Apollo are present in a double vision—both poetic, aesthetic and keen—by which I mean sharply-delineated.

Armstrong is helpful here. In *Wellspring: On the Myth and Source of Culture,* he observes early on that "in some cultures, the chief value of an Affecting Presence is that it directly bears power. Affective Presence directly presents affect;"[64] thus, form incarnates affect such that there is a universal aesthetic and—not to lose the other half of the equation, "variations can proliferate into a particular system of aesthetics."[65] By embracing what he labels "aesthetic pluralism" can we accept more easily how "the nature of aesthetics" cannot hold on to the idea that "great art is everywhere responsive to identical human needs and ought to be western."[66]

Now we touch on the field of pattern within variability. His assumption here was given earlier in his study: Anthropology believes that all human life is patterned;[67] these patterns coalesce to constitute culture. But what dynamics shape this coalescence? What determines the shapes? These are the questions Armstrong believes a new form of anthropology now must entertain in order to move one's studies along such corridors. He calls it Humanistic Anthropology,[68] which inflects its interest to the "quality of a situation, belief, experience with which he is concerned;"[69] further, it is interested in patterns and structures whose significance lies in human experience and is yet to be found.[70]

His concern and focus on works of art, and I am including poetry here to accord with my own interests, is based largely on the premise that works of art have beingness, are analogous in many respects to the beingness of a person, and might best be conferred a respect often reserved exclusively for persons. Further, the human being, the work of affecting presence and, by extension, a culture at large, all carry certain shared and fundamental "primary processes" that abide in the work and exist in all cultures under their own forms. He uses the term "vitality" to designate the values

64 Armstrong, *Wellspring*, p. 13.
65 *Wellspring*, p. 13.
66 *Wellspring*, p. 8.
67 *Wellspring*, p. 3.
68 *Wellspring*, p. 4.
69 *Wellspring*, p. 5.
70 *Wellspring*, p. 6.

that "give life to the consciousness as blood to the body, or as meaning is a value of a word, or as a particular number is the value of a symbol, so is affect the value of the rightness of the world; thus, all these processes are *in affect*—they are sources of affect. The powers of a work are essentially its enactments of affect and constitutes the sum total of its various powers "and is the equivalent of presence itself."[71] I think the above observations comprise the heartbeat of Armstrong's work as well as a rich repository in which Jung's studies of psychic energy may find a more vibrant home.

Conclusion: A Short Excursion into Rock Art and the Power of Analogy.

Several years ago, during a sabbatical, I took to the road for 5 weeks in order to visit and study rock art sites and cliff dwellings in the Southwestern United States. I explored dozens of sites of petroglyphs and pictographs as well as cliff dwellings in five states of the Southwest: Arizona, Utah, Colorado, New Mexico and Texas. I had sketched out 35 sites to visit, but saw only 25. It was during the months of April and May, before tourists had begun clogging the highways. Many of the sites then were only sparsely inhabited. It turned out to be a magnificent five weeks.

Any site, however, like Canyon de Chelly, where people were already swarming, I skipped. Several times I found sites where no one was present, which conjured at times a bit of fear as I was hiking back into canyons by myself in weather that was toasting up rapidly in anticipation of the coming scorching summer months. It occurred to me that if I wanted to feel, in a deeply affective way, the power inhabiting the intersection between nature and culture—this time of Native American peoples— then rock art and cliff dwellings were the artifacts to befriend and enjoy. Little did I realize the immense pockets of energy these sites contained and have harbored for thousands of years.

One site among many I still recall with fondness. It was in New Mexico. To get to the petroglyphs, I had to hike for over a half mile along the side of a mountain lipping a deep canyon. It was early in the day since I often tried to get to a site and back out before the heat of the afternoon whenever possible. I noticed and loved the desert be-

---

71 *Wellspring*, p. 22.

ginning to bloom: delicate little yellow and purple flowers peeking about from behind rocks along my path; the flowering cacti with their delicate purple and red blooms; fresh grass gathering where a small pool of water had collected.

I came on a site high above a snaking river below me and was amazed to see that some of the geometric designs carved into the varnish of the rock were uncanny duplications of the river's serpentine flow below. I sat down, took off my pack and listened and felt the breeze coursing up the canyon and passing me by, but not before stroking my face with wisps of winged breezes. I sat in front of the images as if they were on a screen in front of me, a chocolate brown backdrop with sandy colored images. A woman, along with her friends I had passed coming out of the canyon, warned me of a *pornographic image* of a woman carved into the rock. I told her I would be careful around it. When I did see the image she described as pornographic, I saw a figure giving birth: legs spread, a tiny figure by her, a smiling face on the delivering mother. Childbirth as pornography.

But I sat in silence, listening to the wind. I was alone. I could see my path along the side of the mountain and realized no one else was coming. I was in church, in an outdoor place of worship, old and fresh at once. The wall crawled with images, geometric designs, distorted beings, a figure on a horse, little lizards, groups of families surrounding something—perhaps a fire. I was in the presence of a civilization aesthetically realized in these icons of life in the tribe. Some figures could have been drawn under the influence of peyote or another mind-altering hallucinogen, which would not be unusual. I saw a figure that looked like a ghost, or a shaman—taller than the rest of the figures, perhaps a protective presence, an ancestor, a spirit of the place, a shaman, an apparition from the other world, perhaps the world that was just inside the rock face had made its appearance. The figure exhaled a deep mystery it was enough to gaze upon in wonder. I had no desire to interpret it or figure out what it meant. I simply sat in the powerful presence of this lush tribe of images.

But to be candid, the most dramatic part of the experience was the feeling of a benevolent energy emanating from the rock and its gathering of shapes. I felt their strangeness as well as their familiarity. I was in the presence of images that carried in their forms the psychic energy of the tribe, of an entire people. I also felt that these figures were very conscious of me being conscious of them. I was viewing a story the plot of which I could not grasp, but that I was not excluded from at the same time. I felt very palpably their affective presence; they were, like me, subjects on the wall of time and inhabited at the same time some universal space in the natural order. Theirs was a mythic presence.

Moreover, to back pedal into the language of Armstrong for an instant, I was in the presence of value and affect; that I was deeply affected is without question. Further, I was arrested, captivated by the power of the analogic; from my view, the power of the analogic is where one expression of psychic energy pools and conveys to the one experiencing it a deep sympathy and connectivity to the Otherness as similar, to the foreign as familiar, and to the strange pattern as intimate with my own designs on and in life. The sense of analogy between these figures and my own life was a principal engagement of a power transfer from me to the figures and the figures back to me. The energy of the collective psyche of this tribe gathered in these aesthetic images, carved carefully into the rock's varnish in order to make present the vitality of the tribe in history.

These moments conveyed to me the absolute necessity, a deep need in the psyche, to find the power of the analogic in order to grasp the sense of one's own world through the psychic power of the Other, then to convey it, and finally to know it. It is a hunger that this pilgrimage to rock art sites was finding fed and satisfied. Something basic and appropriate had been quenched. Is it at the same time too much to assume that the figures themselves, in their own beingness, found some additional satisfaction in being because they had completed something missing in me? If so, then I think I was sitting in a very unique and numinous place—namely, a confluence or convergence of where history and myth, nature and culture, aesthetics and the ordinary, body and image found a common heritage and grounding. What could possibly be more sacred than a moment such as this I could not fathom.

I now understand more fully what Armstrong means when he suggests that the work of Affecting Presence is an end-in-itself, that it is in addition "self-constituting,"[72] namely, that it has a nature of a self and has the capacity to "abide in a condition of self-awareness."[73] Some presence was aware of me even as I sat quietly that warm breezy morning in April in front of the petroglyphs of New Mexico. I felt seen as I witnessed these tribal figures out of history and a bit out of time. They contained a quantity of psychic energy that I could feel in their storied figures.

---

72 *Wellspring*, p. 32.
73 *Wellspring*, p. 32.

I end this series of musings, sitting there, absorbed in the figures, content beyond all measure while the sun worked itself above the rocks to warm still further the waters of the serpentine river making its spiralic way through this land of enchantment and deeply engraved mythic figures. Their presence embodied my own plot as well.

Joy suffused the silence; contentment bathed my viewing, and a cosmology made itself present across from me, in the face of a large rock, a meteorite, perhaps, from another planet, bearing a gift to contemplate, pornographic image and all.

References

Aristotle, *Poetics.* Trans. S.H. Butcher. Intro. Francis Fergusson. New York: Hill and Wang, 1969.

Armstrong, Robert Plant, *The Powers of Presence: Consciousness, Myth and Affecting Presence.* Philadelphia: U Pennsylvania P, 1981.

_____. *Wellspring: On the Myth and Source of Culture.* Berkeley: U California P, 1975.

Bond, D. Stephenson, *Living Myth: Personal Meaning as a Way of Life.* Boston: Shambhala, 1993.

Butcher, S.H., *Aristotle's Theory of Poetry and Fine Art: With A Critical Text and Translation of* The Poetics. London: MacMillan And Co, 1902.

Campbell, Joseph, *The Inner Reaches of Outer Space: Metaphor as Myth and as Religion.* Novato, California: New World Library, 2002.

_____. *Flight of the Wild Gander: Explorations in the Mythological Dimension.* Novato, California: New World Library, 2002.

_____. *The Power of Myth,* With Bill Moyers. Ed. Betty Sue Flowers. New York: Doubleday, 1988.

_____. *Thou Art That: Transforming Religious Metaphor.* Ed. Eugene Kennedy. Novato, California: New World Library, 2001

_____. *The Hero With a Thousand Faces.* Bollingen Series XVII. Princeton: Princeton UP, 1973.

_____. *Sake and Satori: Asian Journals—Japan.* Ed. David Kudler. Novato, California: New World Library, 2002

Conforti, Michael, *Field, Form and Fate: Patterns in Mind, Nature and Psyche.* Rev. ed. New Orleans: Spring Journal Books, 1999.

Coupe, Lawrence, *Myth.* London: Routledge, 1997.

Cowan, Louise, "Myth in the Modern World." *Texas Myths.* Ed. Robert F. O'Connor. College Station, Texas: Texas A&M UP, 1998. 3-21.

Eliot, T.S., "Tradition and the Individual Talent." *Selected Prose of T.S. Eliot*. Ed. Frank Kermode. New York: Harcourt Press, 1975. 37-44.

Gebauer, Gunter and Christoph Wulf, *Mimesis: Culture, Art, Society*. Trans. Don Reneau. Berkeley: U California P, 1995.

Harding, M. Esther, *Psychic Energy: Its Source and Its Transformation*. Foreword by C.G. Jung. Bollingen Series X. Princeton: Princeton UP, 1973.

Jung, C.G., "On Psychic Energy." *The Structure and Dynamics of the Psyche. Collected Works*, Vol. 8. Trans. R.F.C Hull. Princeton: Princeton UP, 1960. 3-66.

____. "Psychology and Literature." *The Spirit in Man, Art, and Literature. Collected Works, Vol.* 15. Trans. R.F. C. Hull. Princeton: Princeton UP, 1978. 84-108.

____. "The Psychology of the Child Archetype." *The Archetypes and the Collective Unconscious. Collected Works,* Vol. 9i. Trans. R.F.C. Hull. Princeton: Princeton UP, 1990. 54-72.

____. "The Structure and Dynamics of the Self." *Aion: Researches into the Phenomenology of the Self*. Second Edition. *Collected Works,* Vol, 9ii, Trans. R.F.C. Hull. Princeton: Princeton UP, 1970. 222-265.

Keleman, Stanley, *Myth and the Body: A colloquy with Joseph Campbell*. Berkeley: Center Press, 1999.

Lindorff, David, *Pauli and Jung: The Meeting of Two Great Minds*. Foreword by Markus Fierz, Wheaton, Ill.: Quest Books, 2004.

Maritain, Jacques, *Creative Intuition in Art and Poetry*. Bollingen Series XXXV, A.W. Mellon Lectures in the Fine Arts. Princeton: Princeton UP, 1977.

Meier, C.A., Editor. *Atom and Archetype: The Pauli/Jung Letters, 1932-1958*. Trans. David Roscoe. Princeton: Princeton UP, 2001.

Melville, Herman, *Moby-Dick; or, The Whale*. Norwalk, Conn.:The Easton Press, 1977.

Morrison, Toni, *Beloved*. New York: Random House, 1987.

Slattery, Dennis Patrick, " Silent Places of the Body Under Siege." *Casting the Shadows: Selected Poems*. Goleta, California: Winchester Canyon Press. 25.

____. *A Limbo of Shards: Essays on Memory, Myth and Metaphor*. New York: iUniverse, 2007.

Sophocles, *The Three Theban Plays*. Trans. Robert Fagles. Introd and Notes, Bernark Knox. New York: Penguin Books, 1984.

Stafford, William, "Our Story." *The Way It Is: New and Selected Poems*. St. Paul, Minnesota: Graywolf Press, 1998. 49.

Underhill, Evelyn, *Mysticism: A Study in the Nature and Development of Man's Spiritual Consciousness*. London: Methuen P., 1922

2

The Wonder of Wandering: Archetype, Myth and Metaphor in William Faulkner's "The Bear."

"I am a wanderer and mountain-climber, he said to his heart, I love not the plains, and it seemeth I cannot long sit still"

—Friedrich Nietzsche[74]

I still remember the occasion for an extended pilgrimage that held me out on the road wandering for three and a half months in the fall of 1998. I use that deeply disturbing and consciousness-expanding period and its subsequent backwash to begin this essay on the power and gravity of wandering.

Personal Wandering

In a bookstore in San Antonio, Texas many years ago, I was led by some impulse to the travel section where I pulled down a book on Ireland, origin of my family lineage, for I had dreams of returning to that ancient land. But with that book another, seemingly stuck to it, came tumbling out to land on my left shoe. I remember the leftiness of that drop for reasons that became more apparent as I entered into the writings of

---

74 Nietzsche, Friedrich, *Thus Spake Zarathustra*, p. 106.

popular mythologist, Joseph Campbell. But at that moment, I picked up the book and read its black title against a creamy yellow backdrop: *A Guide to Monasteries and Retreat Centers in the Western Half of the United States.* When I read it, I shifted my attention from the emerald isle to locales closer to home and decided on the spot that I would spend my first sabbatical wandering from monastery to Zen Buddhist retreat centers to sacred sites of meditation and renewal. My excitement made me giddy.

Life, however, had other plans. I left that teaching position and moved my family to Santa Barbara, California to begin full time teaching at Pacifica Graduate Institute. Then, after I had taught for four years in the Mythological Studies program, another sabbatical opportunity presented itself: to pursue sites listed and described in that initial foot-fall book. In August of 1998 I packed my Ford Ranger Pickup truck with camping supplies, clothes, a used laptop, more books than I could read in a decade, and set the compass north, up the California coastline. From then until December I drifted from site to site, often camping in state or national parks in between sacred places that included monasteries and retreat centers operated by Benedictines, Carmelites, Franciscans, Dominicans and other religious denominations, as well as two Zen Buddhist centers, all of which were spread throughout 8 states in the Western half of the United States.

During my stays I experienced the deepest depressions, severe bouts of loneliness, feelings of complete estrangement from everything I loved, bewilderment over who I was, mystical moments of profound spiritual growth and, in the process, shed 20 pounds in long walks through forest and desert landscapes while enjoying vegetarian meals in the process. I pilgrimaged through these landscapes of uncertainty and more than one moment of deep confusion as to my place in the world. I was accompanied, however, by one sustained companion that visited me early in the journey: wherever I visit and stay, I will meet people who have something important to transmit to me; moreover, I will meet people to whom I am directed to tell something they need. Not once was this untrue in the 12-13 different locales I made home for a several days or a week at a time. Having kept a daily journal of my experiences, I gathered them into a memoir that was subsequently published.[75] The experience of wandering alone for these months, along with the subsequent writing of its more poignant moments, renewed and redefined me at the deepest levels of my being.

---

75 Slattery, Dennis Patrick, *Grace in the Desert: Awakening to the Gifts of Monastic Life.*

Even earlier in my life, at the age of 20, with a secure job as a deputy bailiff at a municipal court, a new car, and part time college attendance, I nonetheless felt empty and restless. Soon, with a friend, I pursued avenues of escape, finding ourselves at one point at the Cleveland docks on the shores of Lake Erie hired on as mess boys on a German freighter, the SS Transamerica, owned by Poseidon Lines in Hamburg. We shipped out from Cleveland to Bremerhaven, Germany. We then meandered through Western Europe into Wales and the British Isles, resting finally with relatives in southern Ireland. Only the intensifying war in Vietnam (1965) and our revised status that made us eligible for the draft forced us home early. From both of these experiences I learned that the soul has an innate impulse, a need, to wander out of the familiar territory to renew and revive itself throughout one's life, so the personal myth one is living is renewed through new adaptations.

Wandering, I now recognize, has a hidden order, a unique flow of psychic energy, its own mythos, and when reflected upon, as I did a year after returning from my experience of being adrift for a time, reveals a series of patterns impossible to discern when in the experienced moment. I therefore begin with the observation that wandering and the wanderer carry in their respective backpacks a paradox: wandering is another form of being guided and directed towards a telos that feels in the process circumambient, tangential, slanted and not infrequently, disconnected. Only the act of imaginative reflection brings it to light with clarity of presence that is nothing shy of miraculous. Memory is at the heart of this myth-making discovery. C.G. Jung understood the intrinsic force of such experiences when he wrote of a religious experience, which "strives for expression and can be expressed only 'symbolically' because it transcends understanding. It *must* be expressed one way or another, for therein is revealed its immanent vital force."[76]

Thinking about it now, wandering feels more akin to a spiral than a haphazard squiggle; it carries in it a circling, a moving around and through something not yet identifiable. One feels as if one's travels and travails are aimless, without shape or form. It also carries a bit of a striptease wherein so much of what one felt essential is now discarded, shed, until what remains are only the clean bones needed for preservation. One may feel deeply the aura of being cast adrift, left only with the substantial self that may seem diseased, afflicted, inflected, infected, such that courage in a strong

---

76 In an essay by Murray Stein, "Symbol as Psychic Transformer," in *Symbolic Life*, p. 12.

heart is the best baggage one can maintain through it; that, and a faith in whatever it is that supports as ballast one's emotional and moral order.

I have written in another context the following observation that bears directly on wandering and the wanderer's shifting presence in the world:

> To be wounded is to be opened to the world; it is to be pushed off the straight, fixed, and predictable path of certainty and thrown into ambiguity, or onto the circuitous path, and into the unseen and unforeseen. One begins to wobble, to wander, and perhaps even to wonder not only about one's present condition, but also about one's origins. Circling the edges of the wound, so to speak, one's vision may clear, one's perception sharpens, and one may grasp for the first time what James Hillman describes...as that 'innate image' that lies at the heart of the acorn that is me,[77] that defines my heritage and my destiny.[78]

In this context I found helpful a fine article by Jungian analyst Steven Joseph, in which he explores the power of desert wanderings that salves the shattered psyche in biblical narratives: "Dwelling imaginally in the desert, listening carefully to the midrashic antitheses that characterize desert living and journeying, we may gain insight into the Real. We learn to see into the state of being always on the way, always betwixt-and-between, being a passer-over...."[79] Perhaps we have made too much of "centeredness" and mandala-inspired wholeness and balance, sacrificing in these moments of good will the fragmentation, aimless, drifting qualities of the psyche along the ragged margins and in the interstices of life that lead to where affliction offers its own form of blessed knowing.

It may also introduce us into an epistemology of uncertainty, which is akin to "incapacity," as Jung reveals in his own wandering outlined in *Liber Primus,* which, like the oft-cited term from the poet John Keats, "negative capability," relies on not grasping after certainty and surety, but instead warrants the ability to dwell in the circuitous circuits of being that wandering italicizes. Jung relates that "We cannot slay our incapacity and rise above it....Incapacity will overcome us and demand its share of life....The one who learns to live with his incapacity has learned a great deal. This

---

77 Slattery, *The Wounded,* p. 4.
78 Slattery, *The Wounded,* p. 13.
79 Joseph, Steven, *Journal of Analytical Psychology,* p. 397.

will lead us to the valuation of the smallest things, and to wise limitation, which the greater height demands."[80]

Historical and Literary Wanderers

When we turn to the literary traditions, we notice no end of wanderers in several of the great classics: Homer's *Odyssey* may be the most popular and well-known story of the wandering soul who is devastated by years of combat, disassembled, decentered, deconstructed, seeking home, but inevitably forced to wander for years until every vestige of the Trojan war is stripped from him—all but his memories and narratives of that brutal encounter. Sophocles' Oedipus experiences a moment of slippage from his calculating mind and precise questioning about the slayer of the former King, Laius, his father. When his wife/mother Jocasta attempts to eliminate all doubt from the king's growing obsession concerning his own possible involvement, he starts suddenly: "Strange/hearing you just now...my mind wandered,/my thoughts racing back and forth."[81] At the end of *Oedipus Rex*, after his own self-wounding, he wanders through the wilderness with his daughter Antigone for years before finally stumbling blindly into the sacred grove of Colonus, there to experience another journey wherein his pollutedness is transformed into blessedness.[82]

Just as an individual may wander, so too may a nation, as is the case with the Israelites seeking freedom from bondage; they wander in the Sinai desert with an image of a land of bounty to guide them, yet wandering seems a necessary condition in their destiny before they are gifted a place, a site, in which to prosper. George Williams writes of the wilderness in pre-Christian and Christian thought: "the wilderness is not only geographical but psychological. It can be a state of mind as well as a state of nature. It can betoken alternatively either a state of bewilderment or a place of protective refuge...as well as literally the wilds."[83] Religious leaders and spiritual guides have themselves engaged part of their calling in wandering: Jesus, Mohammad, Buddha, St. Theresa, Gandhi—as if to underscore that wandering is a mythic necessity in a life

---

80 Jung, *The Red Book,* p. 240.
81 Sophocles, *The Three Theban Plays,* p. 201.
82 *The Three Theban Plays,* pp. 282-388. P. 284.
83 Williams, George H., *Wilderness and Paradise in Christian Thought,* pp. 3-10, P. 4.

called forth and singled out, for service. Bereft by loss, the Sumerian hero Gilgamesh wanders through threatening landscapes seeking an antidote to his mortality; afflicted as he is by the loss of his beloved Enkidu, his wandering reveals the inevitability of sacrifice and finite boundaries. Dante's magnificent poem on individuation, his *Commedia*, begins with his pilgrim/poet, as himself, waking in a dark wood at midlife, conscious that somehow he has strayed from the right path and is now terrified and vulnerable in the obscure woods of uncertainty.[84] Faust too, as Jung identifies him in a letter written by Conrad Gessner of Zurich who, in denouncing the forbidden arts practiced still in his day, makes reference to the rise of "the wandering scholars, as they were commonly called. The most famous of these was Faust, who died not so long ago."[85]

Faust no doubt had a powerful pull on Jung; he returned repeatedly to Goethe's masterpiece for further refreshment. In his discussion of the hero cited earlier, he quotes a passage from the German play that bears on the wandering impulse of the soul. In a conversation with Mephistopheles, Faust is instructed to find the habitation of the Goddesses, powerful, threatening and formidable forces "named indeed with dread among our kind./To reach them you must plumb the earth's deepest vault." When Faust asks for directions, Mephistopheles snaps back: "There's none! To the untrodden/Unreadable regions—the unforgotten..../Through endless solitudes you shall be drifted./ Can you imagine Nothing everywhere?"[86]

A new form of research opens for Faust at such a terrifying revelation, as it does for any wanderer. One must be willing to risk landscapes that have not yet been imprinted by others, for there the treasure is to be found. Without the courage or heart-will to enter the unfamiliar and to live within it on its terms, the journey will not yield what is necessary for the soul. Where no path exists, that is the path assigned within the paradox of wandering. If the path is clear, the directions crisp and accurate, footprints already present, no wandering ensues. Moreover, as Joseph Campbell develops the theme of calling forth the heroic in us, he adds, that, "there are many ways in which the adventure can begin. A blunder—apparently the merest chance—reveals an unsuspected world, and the individual is drawn into a relationship with forces that are not rightly understood."[87] The blunder may be an archetypal short course in

---

84 Alighieri, Dante, *The Divine Comedy*, pp. 2-3.

85 Jung, CW, ¶ 154.

86 Jung, CW 5, ¶ 299.

87 Campbell, *The Hero With a Thousand Faces*, p. 51.

wandering. A blunder may initiate wandering, where other forces deflect us from the narrow path we had so carefully planned and adhered to.

Jung himself criticized the Western psyche's propensity "to turn everything into methods and intentions," according to the editor of *The Red Book*.[88] Jung himself realized in that text a quality of his soul's nature: "My soul leads me into the desert of my own self. I did not think my soul is a desert, a barren hot desert, dusty and without drink."[89] He senses the power of solitude when one enters the desert of the soul: "Solitude is true only when the self is a desert."[90]

Finally, another powerful influence on Jung was Nietzsche's *Zarathustra,* who we learn in the prophet's Prologue, left home when he was thirty years old "and went into the mountains. There he enjoyed his spirit and his solitude, and for ten years did not weary of it. But at last his heart changed."[91]

Psychology of Wandering

In many of these references there emerges a tension between the willingness to be guided and a powerful libidinal urge to wander off the path in search of something needed, perhaps to be discovered only by stepping into virginal territory or blundering into what is unfamiliar, where a part of the soul needing to be redeemed carries the necessary energy for the project.

To wander may then be a psychological necessity to restore the soul, as Jung intimates in an essay on poetry: "Loss of soul amounts to a tearing loose of part of one's nature; it is the disappearance and emancipation of a complex.... It throws him off course and drives him to actions whose blind one-sidedness inevitably leads to self-destruction."[92] Wandering may be the occasion for some dimension of the soul to expire, to be burned in the fire of uncertainty and ambiguity that attends the wandering person or the collective soul, for an entire people may lose their bearing and be cast adrift when the myth that has served them no longer contains the necessary psychic

---

88 Shamdasani, Sonu, *The Red Book*, p. 237.
89 *The Red Book*, p. 235.
90 *The Red Book*, p. 236.
91 Nietzsche, Friedrich, *Zarathustra*, p. 1.
92 Jung, CW 6, ¶ 384.

energy to congeal their collective identity in a cauldron of shared values and beliefs. Fragmented, the collective soul begins to wander and—to mix the metaphor—to lose heart.

In the same volume cited above, Jung meditates on the archetype of the wandering Jew, Ahasuerus, who is described as having been born as "a late Christian legend which cannot be traced back earlier than the thirteenth century."[93] As a part of the soul, Jung suggests, Ahasuerus represents "an unredeemed element in the unconscious"[94] that, frustrating the work of the Redeemer and which must be held in check by being chained and restricted, "is projected upon those who have never accepted Christianity....The restlessness of the wandering Jew is a concretization of this unredeemed state."[95]

It should be noted that Jung himself was not a stranger to the impulses of the wandering soul. In a section entitled "Soul and God" he observes: "I wandered for many years, so long that I forgot that I possessed a soul."[96] In a footnote on the same page, the editor, Sonu Shamdasani continues the quote: "I belonged to men and things. I did not belong to myself."[97] The editor notes in the same footnote: "In *Black Book* 2, Jung states that he wandered for eleven years."[98] Finally, following close by, the editor asserts that, "in 1912 Jung argued that scholarliness was insufficient if one wanted to become a 'knower of the human soul'"[99] and then leads us to a paragraph in *CW* 7, which I cite here:

> Therefore, anyone who wants to know the human psyche will learn next to nothing from experimental psychology. He would be better advised to [abandon exact science] put away his scholar's gown, bid farewell to his study, and wander with human heart through the world. There, in the horrors of prisons, lunatic asylums and hospitals...through love and hate, through the experience of passion in every form in his own body, he would reap richer stores of knowledge than textbooks a foot thick could give him....[100]

---

93 CW 6, ¶ 454.
94 CW 6, ¶ 454.
95 CW 6, ¶ 454.
96 Jung, *The Red Book*, p. 233.
97 *The Red Book*, fn. 48, p. 233.
98 *The Red Book*, fn. 48, p. 233.
99 *The Red Book*, fn. 55, p. 233.
100 Jung, CW 7, ¶ 409.

In another context, and one in which Joseph Campbell entertains and in fact could have been one of his inspirations for *The Hero With a Thousand Faces*, Jung explores the relationship of the heroic with wandering in "The Origin of the Hero." He conjectures that "The heroes are usually wanderers, and wandering is a symbol of longing, of the restless urge which never finds its object, of nostalgia for the lost mother....The heroes are like the wandering sun."[101] He continues to consider that the heroic in each of us "is first and foremost a self-representation of the longing of the unconscious, of its unquenched and unquenchable desire for the light of consciousness."[102]

Finally, to enter the heartbeat of this essay, I mention Jung's observation just before he quotes Goethe's play cited above, wherein he focuses on the power of the natural order in the heroes' wanderings:

> But consciousness, continually in danger of being led astray by its own light and of becoming a rootless will o' the wisp, longs for the healing power of nature, for the deep wells of being and for unconscious communion with life in all its countless forms.[103]

The wanderer is not always restless, but as an archetypal action as well as an archetypal figure, wandering as well as the wanderer seek to complete something missing in the soul, to redeem what has remained outside of redemption, to recycle a quality, attribute, or image that the soul needs to fulfill itself. Wandering grows from a lack, or from a test, an occasion for endurance, or situations that demand or evoke courage, where the heart has been suffering and seeks now the completion or further addition of the narrative that contains, buried within it, a sustained mythos seeking emergence and recognition. Now, more often than not, the individual, man or woman, is well on his/her life's path; we do not normally encounter a youth wandering. I have therefore chosen a young man, Isaac McCaslin in William Faulkner's chapter "The Bear," that comprises part of a larger epic narrative, *Go Down, Moses,* to explore the wandering healing motion of the journey into wilderness.

---

101 CW 5, ¶ 299.
102 CW 5, ¶ 299.
103 CW 5, ¶ 299.

The Bear and Isaac McCaslin

First published as *Go Down, Moses and Other Stories* by Random House in 1942, it was republished in 1949 under its current title, one that Faulkner much preferred. He claimed that "the unity of the work as a novel" was preserved with the original title, according to Nicholas Fargnoli.[104] Faulkner, one of our richest mytho-poetic American writers of the South, crafted an entire cosmos in his fictional Yoknapatawpha County, in which all seven of the interconnected stories that comprise *Go Down, Moses* occur. "The Bear," one of Faulkner's masterpieces, is the fifth story in the series. Of it, Faulkner scholar James Early has written that "'The Bear' brings in the tangled history of the McCaslin family and the South, relating a recognition of the evil of slavery to the death of the bear,"[105] Old Ben.

Go Down, Moses is unequivocally one of Faulkner's most mythic tales of the South, its anguished relation between history and myth, the witnessing of the dissolution of an old order and the encroaching machine into the garden of nature; it also deploys the ritual of initiation experienced by one young 16 year old man, Ike McCaslin, who is educated in his novitiate into the ways of the wilderness by his mentor, now an old man, Sam Fathers, "son of a negro slave and a Chickasaw chief,"[106] combining two worlds comprised of indigenous people and an enslaved civilization. A significant moment in his initiation into the wilderness will be Ike's solitary wandering into the woods one morning in anticipation of seeing this indomitable animal who has been hunted for decades every November by a group of men in a ritual enactment of connecting back to some primal qualities in themselves. That moment of decision to enter the woods alone will comprise the remainder of this essay.

Of the story and its significance, we might listen to Faulkner himself when he was interviewed in Japan in 1955 on its impact. To a question about the "symbolized feature of truth" in the story, Faulkner responded:

> The story itself, I hope and intended, told the truth. "The Bear," as a story, was a truth of the bears and animals, was a natural force which represented not a deliberate evil, not a satanic evil, but the quality of evil in sample size and force, which exists, which man has got to face and not be afraid of, that force itself has certain rights which

---

104 Fargnoli, Nicholas, (ed.), *William Faulkner: A Literary Companion*, p. 441.
105 Early, James, *The Making of Go Down, Moses*, p. 33.
106 Faulkner, William, "The Bear" in *Go Down, Moses*, p. 197.

must be respected. That force must not be reduced by trickery, it must be reduced by a bravery comparably as strong as its power.[107]

Faulkner's response takes the reader to the heart of myth and into the archetypal vessel that the natural world affords. He also outlines the place and value of the heroic heart in its refusal to shrink from this force's presence, but instead moves towards it, scared, but not afraid, as Sam Fathers instructs Ike as he contemplates his wandering into the wilderness.[108] It is also worth mentioning at the outset that Faulkner's observation above reaches back to a core value of his that appears in his "Address Upon Receiving the Nobel Prize for Literature" in Stockholm, December 10, 1950. It is a one page speech as eloquent as any statement of a world view or a people's collective myth as has been uttered; Faulkner shares those "verities" that sustained his life and writing. He is explicit about having as his audience young writers who share with him the anguish attendant upon the creative act: "to create out of the materials of the human spirit something which did not exist before."[109]

He then laments the fact that writers have forgotten "the problems of the human heart in conflict with itself, which alone can make good writing...."[110] For our purposes I call attention to one additional aspect of this magnificent document: the ability to remember what has been culturally forgotten, as well as the writer's responsibility to help the rest of us remember: "He must learn them again. He must teach himself that the basest of all things is to be afraid, and, teaching himself that, forget it forever, leaving no room in his workshop for anything but the old verities and truths of the heart," which he names to include: love and honor and pity and pride and compassion and sacrifice."[111] Absent them, nothing else seems worth writing about.

"The Bear" is a poetic witness to the fears of the heart being conquered in the breast of one young man who finds within himself the ability and courage to go it alone, and to enter a place of dissolution and revelation, what Campbell refers to as "the morphogenetic field into which the enraptured yogi lets dissolve his humanity and its world...."[112] and there to confront what has already loomed blur-edged and alone in

107 Meriwether and Millgate, (eds), *Lion in the Garden: Interviews with William Faulkner*, p. 120.
108 Faulkner, "The Bear," p. 198.
109 Faulkner, "Address Upon Receiving the Nobel Prize For Literature," pp. 119-120.
110 Faulkner, "Nobel Prize Speech," p. 119.
111 Faulkner, "Nobel Prize Speech," p. 120.
112 Campbell, *The Inner Reaches of Outer Space*, p. 80.

his imagination: "It loomed and towered in his dreams before he even saw the unaxed woods where it left its crooked print, shaggy, tremendous, red-eyed, not malevolent but just big, too big for the dogs...."[113] His imagination stirs with a reality that longing for the journey promises to satisfy, or at least intensify in its urges, for the bear is connected with a larger reality, one that breeds fear in the hearts of men who struggle to subdue it through conquest. This reality takes us to the fearful center of the story: "It was as if the boy had already divined what his senses and intellect had not encompassed yet: that doomed wilderness whose edges were being constantly and punily gnawed at by men with plows and axes who feared it because it was wilderness...."[114]

The courage of the human heart begins to loom like the phantom of the bear itself as a testing ground for a soul that must relinquish certainty, protection, and safety if it is to recognize on a deeper level the power of the numinous presence in the world, along with its fierce force to ravage any who come within its fateful grasp. The way to such a presence is not by means of a linear trajectory, but slant-wise, circuitous, a wandering in and through; then what one seeks will be offered, but on its terms, and as the narrative makes clear, only for an instant and in appearance closer to an apparition. Such is the wonder that can often attend wandering. The wandering soul must conquer or integrate the fearful heart in order to be worthy of the vision. Its reward is a moment of wonder at the ineffable, what cannot be described but which can be experienced.

Old Ben is the occasion for the men gathering for two weeks each November in the dreary shift of seasons to hunt him. While Ike has accompanied them many times already, beginning when he was ten, he had never seen the bear, only its ragged traces after the dogs had chased it without success. He stands in the wilderness with his mentor, Sam Fathers "in the great gloom of ancient woods and the winter's dying afternoon, he looked quietly down at the rotted log scored and gutted with claw-marks and, in the wet earth beside it, the print of the enormous warped two-toed foot."[115] Yet the bear has been in the human imagination from time immemorial as an archetype of animal guide as well as the occasion for courage and an embodiment of the numinous quality of the natural order that frightens those without courage or consciousness. Even the dogs suffer an initiation into courage's heartbeat when they return from their own confrontation with this animal force of nature. One of 11 that

113 Faulkner, "The Bear," p. 185.
114 Faulkner, "The Bear," p. 185.
115 "The Bear," p. 192.

hunted Old Ben returns quivering and torn up from its battle, wherein Sam "daubed her tattered ear and raked shoulder with turpentine and axlegrease"[116] as he muses out loud: "'Just like a man....Put off as long as she could having to be brave, knowing all the time that sooner or later she would have to be brave once so she could keep on calling herself a dog, and knowing beforehand what was going to happen when she done it.'"[117]

In June of the following year a few men return to the woods, bringing Ike with them. They are there to celebrate Major de Spain's and General Compson's birthdays,[118] but as the wandering Ike's foray into the wilderness will reveal, it is his birthing day into a consciousness that integrates the mythology of the bear into his being and allows the image to live within him for the rest of his life. A call, a presentiment, an invitation coaxes Ike into the woods alone with his new rifle, given to him as a Christmas gift, with the date 1878 engraved on it. All of the others assume he is out early hunting squirrels, but his mentor, Sam Fathers, begins to suspect the young man is after larger game.

The moment of initiation into the wilderness and its soul in the image of Old Ben commences in a slow circumambulating motion as Ike enters the woods with his compass and rifle and penetrates its interior, "green with gloom,"[119] in order to hunt the bear on his own terms. He wanders farther into its embrace as it opens to allow him entrance, then closes immediately behind him, embracing him fully. But his vision is limited by his equipment; he sees nothing.

Sam, now aware of Ike's motives, tells him on his return one morning: "'You ain't looked right yet.'"[120] What holds his vision back and makes impotent his searching is, according to Sam, his rifle. "*The gun,* the boy thought. *The gun.* 'You will have to choose,' Sam said."[121] The gun is both his protection and his impediment to the bear's presenting itself to him. He cannot have it both ways, so,

> He had left the gun; by his own will and relinquishment he had accepted not a gambit, not a choice, but a condition in which not only the bear's heretofore inviolable

---

116 "The Bear," p. 190.
117 "The Bear," pp. 190-191.
118 "The Bear," p. 196.
119 "The Bear," p. 196.
120 "The Bear," p. 197.
121 "The Bear," p. 198.

anonymity but all the ancient rules and balances of hunter and hunted had been abrogated.[122]

Equipped still with his compass, he now enters virgin territory, the "immemorial darkness of the woods."[123] He follows the directive of the compass for guidance in space but also with "the old heavy, biscuit-thick silver watch which had been his father's"[124] to order him in time. These technologies, however, impede him from slipping over the abyss of complete unknowing; they too will become greater hindrances than helps in his pilgrimage into the sanctity of the natural order, ancient, mysterious and oblique, which demands more a meandering than a methodical ordering of the self in space and time. "He stood for a moment—a child, alien and lost in the green and soaring gloom of the markless wilderness. Then he relinquished completely to it. It was the watch and the compass. He was still tainted."[125]

Fascinating in this moment of total abandon and unequivocal yielding is that Ike gives himself over to the soul of the wilderness, which has its own terms, autonomy and measures of engagement. What is free is to choose, give up, in, over or remain protected and limited in one's orbit of understanding because the wilderness has its own hermeneutic, its own laws that govern its revelation. What it will disclose of its numinous and ancient mysteries is in direct proportion to what one is willing to forego. What the wilderness demands of the young man, who is of an age to be initiated into a deeper dimension of his life, is abandonment, so to become completely lost, to turn himself over without reservation to presences and energies that are both anonymous and autonomous. Ike enters the deep terror of becoming lost and vulnerable without the knowledge that brings certainty and security. I briefly mark here Barbara Hannah's recollection of something Jung observed:

> In his essay on the transcendent function Jung says that to go back to nature in the primitive sense would be a mere regression, but to strive to reach it through psychological development is something quite different, for this time it means doing consciously what we previously did unconsciously, consciousness being 'continually widened through the confrontation with previously unconscious contents.[126]

---

122 "The Bear," p. 198.
123 "The Bear," p. 197.
124 "The Bear," p. 198.
125 "The Bear," p. 199.
126 Hannah, Barbara, *The Archetypal Symbolism of Animals*, pp. 4-5.

Entering the bear's field is the latter instance that Jung observed, for Ike. It is his initial initiation into the unconscious, to make it conscious, through his vulnerable disposition. Vulnerable wandering appears to be able to or invite a porousness the normally walled partition between consciousness and the unconscious prohibits. For the men who come to hunt Old Ben, the bear is an occasion for an annual ritual with the possibility of conquest; for Ike, his wandering into the woods is an occasion for confronting the archetype of the soul of wilderness and in the process, one of the deepest places in his own interior forest. Jung observes on this score that "archetypes are typical modes of apprehension, and wherever we meet with uniform and regularly recurring modes of apprehension we are dealing with an archetype, no matter whether its mythological character is recognized or not."[127]

Ike turns without hesitation and sets both compass and watch together on a nearby bush "and leaned the stick beside them and entered it."[128] Soon, however, he realizes he is lost, so he calls on the coaching of Sam Fathers as his Virgilian guide in the thick woods. He slows, he deliberates, he goes inward rather than seeking outwardly the technologies he has relinquished. From a psychological point of view, his movements are informative. He then begins to move in small circles in one direction in order to pick up where he had been when he crosses over that spot; when it proves at first futile, he "made this next circle in the opposite direction and much larger so that the pattern of the two of them [circles] would bisect his track somewhere, but crossing no trace nor mark anywhere of his feet or any feet, and now he was going farther though still not panicked...."[129]

In the moment unfamiliar time and unknown space coalesce around the young man to place him in a terrain both strange and alien; he has no analogies to pull from, no remembrances that will help make a connection to where the landscape is recognized. In fact, as he uses up the last of Sam Father's instructions on how to move in the wilderness with one's own wits and skills for tracking back and around, he inhabits a landscape that completely bewilders him. His space is both liminal and a *temenos* at once, for he now inhabits the inner sanctum of the wilderness, a sacred place of refuge and danger, open now to the unexpected and the wished for, a terrain of both terror and delicious anticipation. The former implicates and invites the latter.

---

127 Hannah, *The Archetypal Symbolism of Animals,* p. 6.
128 Faulkner, "The Bear," p. 199.
129 "The Bear," pp. 199-200.

Ike soon comes on a tree, which could be the one he passed earlier, he thinks; but no, "because there was a down log beside it which he had never seen before and beyond the log a little swamp, a seepage of moisture somewhere between earth and water."[130] He has wandered into the unknown, but in the strange paradox that may be an essential element of all wandering, he has also been guided by forces unnamed and unknown, invisible, mythic and eternally present. Not yet, however, can he discern such a reality until it appears to him as powerfully as any hierophany.

On the other hand, he invited these presences in to guide him by his act of humility and respect: relinquishment of stick, rifle, compass and watch. By doing so he exposes himself to the eternal and the numinous presence of Old Ben, archetype and architect of the natural order as well as steward of the wilderness that men packed with fear continue to gnaw into fragments in order to domesticate and dismantle its mystery.

Ike dwells now, in a last resort, for Sam Father's training has also been strained to exhaustion. I believe his mentor's training must also be shed, jettisoned, worn out and through before Ike is completely free in abandonment, isolation and alienated from all forms of the familiar scaffolding that has served him in the past. Now, between water and earth in the swampy region of the heart where it is moist, it nonetheless maintains solidity in the stew of the earth he will steward for the next 70 years of his life. Ike sits down on the log and immediately is guided in perception,

> seeing the crooked print, the *warped indentation* in the wet ground which while he looked at it continued to fill with water until it was level full and the water began to overflow and the sides of the print began to dissolve away.[131]

One might be inclined to say he has wandered into this moment, so close on the paw prints of the animal's presence. But it would be more accurate to entertain the idea that he has been guided here, at this instant, where the presentness of the bear has been replaced by a trace, in its absence, of its consequences in nature: the weighty indention of such a middle region between two elements, and their mixing to complete fullness in the "crooked print."[132] Its condition is also relevant to Ike's wandering, for its malformation imprints its identity of *this* bear in *this* region at *this* moment.

---

130 "The Bear," p. 200.
131 "The Bear," p. 200. (My italics)
132 "The Bear," p. 200.

Its crooked nature reminds me as well as the crooked lower jaw of the multi-scarred and marked white whale, Moby-Dick, into whose vicinity Ahab has wandered, his own Old Ben in the watery wilderness of the world's seas.[133] Both white whale and brown bear convey as natural symbols the presence of the *anima mundi*, the world soul, that each must meet on his/her journey and mark it through its jagged and malformed imperfection. Both their histories and the markings of their eternal presence are conveyed in the afflicted bodies that deploy their identities to the world.

Neither this paw print filling with water and already disappearing in another instant, nor the next, nor the next, would have manifested if Ike had not abrogated his control of the journey and allowed the reins of his life to fall slack so another force could take them up; from his perspective he is lost. From the perspective of the ancient other, he is about to be found: "Even as he looked up he saw the next one, and moving, the one beyond it; moving, not hurrying, running, but merely keeping pace with them as they appeared before him as though they were being shaped out of thin air just one constant pace short of where he would lose them forever and be lost forever himself,..."[134]

Then, from the wilderness, Ike finds he has been led into a little glade "and the wilderness coalesced...[where] the tree, the bush, the compass and the watch glinting where a ray of sunlight touched them."[135] So first, in his wandering he has been led back to those instruments of time and space that situate him in the world of the familiar. He has, in the lexicon of psyche's voyage, come full circle to where home is easily retraced. Then his vision of the bear, which carries qualities of a mystical union, a moment where one is in the presence of a god or goddess, a luminous force, a manna power beyond time, space or causality. Such is the gift often received by one who yields to the presences that remain invisible until one steps into their field and allows their persuasive pattern to become part of one's being:

> Then he saw the bear. It did not emerge, appear: it was just there, immobile, fixed in the green and windless noon's hot dappling, not as big as he had dreamed it but as big as he had expected, bigger, dimensionless against the dappled obscurity, looking at him.[136]

---

133 Melville, *Moby-Dick*, p. 437.
134 Faulkner, "The Bear," p. 200.
135 "The Bear," p. 200.
136 "The Bear," p. 200.

I recall in this description what Jung wrote in *The Red Book* that aids our understanding of what Ike has just become witness and disciple to. Jung discovers an essential truth early on in his quest in 1913 when he feels that he has lost his own soul: "If we possess the image of a thing, we possess half the thing. The image of the world is half the world. He who possesses the world but not its image possesses only half the world, since his soul is poor and has nothing. The wealth of the soul exists in images."[137]

I believe his insight helps to illuminate what has just happened to Ike in the bear's presence. He has carried this image of the bear for at least 6 years from the first time he was brought with the men in November to hunt Old Ben. He has been engaging the image of the bear imaginally for this long; now, following Jung's insight, he brings together the imaginal with the actual and, following the psychic logic of Jung's observation, he now possesses the whole world by yoking the two halves, the world and its image in a moment of symbolic comprehension. Writ small, the bear is the image of the world; as a symbol it can lead one to a fuller depth of participation in the world through one's yielding and imagining at once. Ike's wandering is complete, circular, mandala-like in design and completes the young man's search. Not a hunter of the bear but now one of its devotees, Ike's moment passes quickly: "Then it moved. It crossed the glade without haste, walking for an instant into the sun's full glare and out of it, and stopped again and looked back at him across one shoulder. Then it was gone."[138]

Old Ben takes on the tone and pressure of an apparition; it is a haunting presence that is neither fully flesh nor complete spirit but both in unison to reveal a full vision of the natural and supernatural realms in harmonic correspondence: "It faded, sank back into the wilderness without motion as he had watched a fish, a huge old bass sink back into the dark depths of its pool and vanish without even any movement of its fins."[139] Such is the motion of an apparition as it fades back into a timeless abyss the way dream images begin to dissolve as one wakens and lies for a moment in bed trying to remember and to discern their still disturbing traces. They are like liquid images, watery and solid, like the consistency of mercury, insisting on being both solid and liquid in the same momentum.

---

137 Jung, *The Red Book*, p. 232.
138 Faulkner, "The Bear," p. 200.
139 "The Bear," pp. 200-01.

Finally, there is an important correspondence between the freshly-initiated Ike and the more seasoned Zarathustra. In his experience as "The Wanderer," the title of one of Nietzsche's chapters, Zarathustra laughs to himself on his own solitary walks in the mountains where he wanders in thought and landscape, confiding to himself: "ever hast thou approached confidently all that is terrible. Every monster wouldst thou caress. A whiff of warm breath, a little soft tuft on its paw—: and immediately wert thou ready to love and to lure it."[140]

Ike too carries this profound archetype of the wanderer who comes to himself by confronting, within the "strong rapid little hammer of his heart"[141] *the mysterium tremendum* that Joseph Campbell believed contained "the energies of the deepest secret of our being."[142] Perhaps it is the most soulful moment of Ike's life, captured in the hunter-turned-aspirant, a vocation that Old Ben invites him into—the *sanctum sanctorum*—to realize through a vision captured within a glade brightly, one which allows a luminescent moment to illuminate his soul for the succeeding 7 decades.

Note

This essay was awarded the Jan Lee Prize for Analysis and the Arts for the best paper published in UK Psychoanalytic and Jungian Analytic Journals in 2011 that demonstrates a creative approach to the arts from an analytic perspective. See www.janleeprize.co.uk

---

140 Nietzsche, *Zarathustra*, p. 105.
141 Faulkner, "The Bear," p. 200.
142 Campbell, Joseph, *The Mythic Dimension*, p. 82.

References

Alighieri, Dante, *Inferno*, in *The Divine Comedy of Dante Alighieri*, trans. Allen Mandelbaum (New York: Bantam, 1982).

Campbell, Joseph, *The Inner Reaches of Outer Space: Metaphor as Myth and as Religion* (Novato, California: New World Library, 2002).

Campbell, Joseph, *The Hero With a Thousand Faces*, Bollingen Series XVII (Princeton, NJ: Princeton University Press, 1973).

Campbell, Joseph, *The Mythic Dimension: Selected Essays 1959-1987* (Novato, California: New World Library, 2007).

Early, James, *The Making of Go Down, Moses* (Dallas: Southern Methodist University Press, 1972).

Faulkner, William, "The Bear" in *Go Down, Moses* (New York: Vintage Books, 1970).

Faulkner, William, *William Faulkner: A Literary Companion*, Fargnoli, Nicholas, (ed.) *William Faulkner: A Literary Companion* (New York: Pegasus Books, 2008).

Faulkner, William, "Address Upon Receiving the Nobel Prize For Literature," Stockholm, December 10, 1950 in James Meriwether (ed), *Essays, Speeches, and Public Letters by William Faulkner* (New York: Random House, 1962?).

Hannah, Barbara, *The Archetypal Symbolism of Animals: Lectures Given at the C.G. Jung Institute, Zurich, 1954-1958,* David Eldred (ed.) (Wilmette, Illinois: Chiron Books, 2006).

Joseph, Steven, "Desert wanderings: pathways for whole, broken and shattered psyches," *Journal of Analytical Psychology* (2000).

Jung, C.G., *The Red Book: Liber Novus*, ed. Sonu Shamdasani, trans. Mark Kyburz, John Peck and Sonu Shamdasani. Philomen Series (New York: W.W. Norton and Company, 2009).

Jung, C.G., *Alchemical Studies*, vol. 13 (1967) of *The Collected Works of C.G. Jung*, trans. R.F.C. Hull, ed. H. Read, M. Fordham, G. Adler, Wm. McGuire, 20 vols. (Princeton, NJ: Princeton University Press).

Jung, C.G., *Symbols of Transformation,* vol. *5* (1967) of *The Collected Works of C.G. Jung,* trans. R.F.C. Hull, ed. H. Read, M. Fordham, G. Adler, Wm. McGuire, 20 vols. (Princeton, NJ: Princeton University Press).

Jung, C.G., "The Type Problem in Poetry," in *Psychological Types,* vol. *6* (1973) of *The Collected Works of C.G. Jung,* trans. R.F.C. Hull, ed. H. Read, M. Fordham, G. Adler, Wm. McGuire, 20 vols. (Princeton, NJ: Princeton University Press).

Jung, C.G., "New Paths in Psychology," in *Two Essays on Analytical Psychology,* vol. *7* (1973) of *The Collected Works of C.G. Jung,* trans. R.F.C. Hull, ed. H. Read, M. Fordham, G. Adler, Wm. McGuire, 20 vols. (Princeton, NJ: Princeton University Press).

Melville, Herman, *Moby-Dick,* ed. Harrison Hayford and Hershel Parker (New York: W.W. Norton, 1967).

Meriwether, James B., and Michael Millgate (eds), "Interviews in Japan, 1955" in *Lion in the Garden: Interviews with William Faulkner, 1926-1952* (Lincoln, Nebraska: University of Nebraska Press, 1964).

Nietzsche, Friedrich, *Thus Spake Zarathustra,* trans. Thomas Commons (Mineola, New York: Dover Publications, 1999).

Slattery, Dennis Patrick, *Grace in the Desert: Awakening to the Gifts of Monastic Life.* Foreword by Thomas Moore (San Francisco: Jossey-Bass, 2004).

Slattery, Dennis Patrick, *The Wounded Body: Remembering the Markings of Flesh* (New York: SUNY Press, 2000).

Sophocles, *Oedipus the King,* in *The Three Theban Plays,* trans. Robert Fagles (New York: Penguin Books, 1984).

Stein, Murray, "Symbol as Psychic Transformer," in *Symbolic Life: 2009, Spring 82* ed. Murray Stein *(A Journal of Archetype and Culture),* Fall, 2009.

Williams, George H., "The Wilderness Theme," in *Wilderness and Paradise in Christian Thought: The Biblical Experience of the Desert in the History of Christianity* (New York: Harper and Brothers, 1962).

3

Mytho-Poiesis: The Shared Ground of Psyche's Dreaming and Poetic Impulse[143]

Sometimes we accomplish our greatest deeds in dreams.

—C.G. Jung[144]

I am new at making any observations about the dreaming soul; nonetheless I want to explore in an initial way some notions that have been haunting me these past two years and to which I offer some beginning observations on the relation between poetic and dream images. I sense that, while different, they share a common or originating ground of creation and of emanation.

I have spent my professional life teaching perduring poems primarily within the Western Canon. They have come to be more than poetry of various historical periods. More to the point, they have been psychic and spiritual guides of my own and my students' lives, creating, narrating and forging identities that sustain and deepen a meaningful life: Homer's *Iliad* and *Odyssey*, the Sumereian epics *Inanna and Gilgamesh,* the Oedipus plays of Sophocles, Aeschylus' *Oresteia*, Dante's *Commedia*, Milton's *Paradise Lost,* Melville's *Moby-Dick,* Dostoevsky's *Crime and Punishment,* Toni Morrison's *Beloved*, to name several, as well as a host of poets from antiquity to the present. I have

---

143 A shorter version of this essay was presented to the San Diego Friends of Jung, 16 April 2010.
144 Jung, C.G., *The Red Book*, p. 242.

recently completed a fourth volume of poetry and have published a first novel, *Simon's Crossing* with my co-author, Charles Asher. The subject matter for the latter, as with so many of my own poems, came to me in a waking dream or reverie. I felt at those moments that I was called, in the manner of how a vocation calls one, to do a work, to complete something that wishes to move through me into the world. These promptings and studies over decades have led me to write this essay on the kinship between two kinds of images: poetic and oneiric.

In addition, about 20 years ago I began rising at 4 a.m., compelled by the fact that there were simply not enough hours in the day to perform my professional duties and include time to read and write on subjects that, like a lodestar, attracted me. At this hour, I am still sleepy and drowsy as I enter my study and look squarely at the black glass of the window. Its shiny surface holds back the world until dawn. This is the cocoon I enter to feel a joy in reflecting, in writing in my journal, in allowing reveries to reign, a time to compose poems, to welcome ideas that often rise unbidden from the dreaming body I still am.

At this hour the world is dark, silent and deliciously still. Ghosts hover in the corner; ideas and images limpidly circle the chair in which I repose. Even the birds are still resting. Deer graze peacefully on our front lawn in the Hill Country of central Texas, just north of San Antonio. On occasion I have looked up and to my right from my study chair to see a deer, its nose almost against the glass, staring with large black liquid eyes at me, wondering, I like to imagine, what is so important to be up this early to pursue? Their presence and their gaze always lift my spirits.

I set the scene in just this way because I want to entertain for a short time how dreams, like poems, come from the body—either the body of nature, or the body I am, or the communal body of the world. Moreover, when I read or compose poetry at this early morning hour, I still have one foot in the dream realm of sleep and the other a bit unsteadily in the waking life of consciousness. The images that I read and sense or the images and narratives that emerge into poems come from the *metaxis*, the Greek word for in-between, the cracks, the gaps, the bardo place of opening that is a small yaw between yawns and insights, between fatigue and discoveries such that my conviction grows that the space between, where the soul has room to move, is the locus of dream and poetry's intimate arrangement and powerful engagement with one another. I believe it is the place, not exclusively, but nonetheless a central place of psychic energy's gathering to engage what I wish to call mytho-poiesis.

Joseph Campbell thought that myths emerged out of the energies of the organs of the body in conflict or in complement with one another.[145] He intuited that myths have a somatic reality and many of his insights are gathered in a book of conversations with Stanley Keleman on myth and the body.[146] Marie-Louise von Franz suggested as well that dreams originate from Nature; they are, for her, natural phenomena carrying with them "a superior intelligence, a wisdom, a guiding cleverness. They show us where we are wrong."[147] My own sense is that in the interstices of myth and dream, poetry is born, borne forward, if not directly conjured, as one might invoke the image of a lost, but still intensely animated, Love.

I must make one distinction here. In this exploration I have found extremely influential Jacques Maritain's *Creative Intuition in Art and Poetry* (1953), essentially a series of lectures he delivered at the National Gallery of Art in Washington, D.C. in 1952. Early in his musings over the poetic process, Maritain offers some provocative insights that have guided my own imagination on the nature of poetic creativity. In a chapter entitled "Poetry, Man, and Things" he offers this observation:

> Art and poetry cannot do without one another. Yet the two words are far from being synonymous. By Art, I mean the creative or producing, work-making activity of the human mind. By Poetry, I mean, not the particular art which consists in writing verses, but a process both more general and more primary: that intercommunication between the inner being of things and the inner being of the human Self which is a kind of divination (as was realized in ancient times: the Latin *vates* was both poet and a diviner. Poetry, in this sense, is the secret life of each and all of the arts; another name for what Plato called *mousike.*[148]

Poetry, from Maritain's consideration, appears to be muse-driven. I question as well whether dream images are also stirred by muses, inspirations of a creative impulse in the personal and collective unconscious of a dreamer to analogize one's life through a second story, a corresponding narrative or an imaginal "double talk" with its roots in both the unconscious and in waking life. Jung's own belief was that "analogy formation is a law which to a large extent governs the life of the psyche...."[149] The law of analogy is of primary shared importance in both dream and poetic image creation.

145 Campbell, J., *The Power of Myth.* p. 44.
146 Keleman, Stanley, *Myth and the Body*
147 von Franz, M., *The Way of the Dream*, p. 10.
148 Maritain, Jacques, *Creative Intuition in Art and Poetry*, p. 3.
149 Jung, *Aion*, ¶ 414.

Mytho-Poiesis

It suggests what Herausgegeben von H. Vaihinger, the 19th century German philosopher and explorer of the nature of fiction in the psyche, called "The philosophy of as-if" in his *Die Philosophie des Als Ob* (1877). In that work he suggests that the movement of the psyche is one of constant making and elaborating of fictions. G.R.S. Mead, commenting on Vaihinger's philosophy, believes that "the whole system of the *as if* philosophy is intended to prove that such fictions are not only permissible, but indispensable."[150] This "as if" quality of reality is shared, I sense, by Jung, by the dream and by poetic utterance in that all share a sensibility that analogy formation—an *as if* mode of knowing—is at the core of psyche's constructing a world of meaning.

To return to Maritain for a moment: he believes that the intercommunication between the inner being of things and the inner being of the human Self carries both a mythic resonance and a poetic certitude. I would think Jung's high regard for the law that seems to invest the psyche's creation of analogies is relevant to Maritain's insight. However, the deeper connection to it and dream did not fully descend on me until some years ago while teaching at Eranos in Switzerland for Pacifica Graduate Institute.

The history of this place, a melting pot of ideas from a myriad of disciplines, began in 1933 through the efforts of Olga Froebe-Kapteyn of Ascona, who believed that C.G. Jung and others should have an annual and permanent meeting place to share their new thoughts and works with others from many disciplines. Both C.G. and his wife Emma pilgrimaged annually for decades and where Jung himself presented many of his new insights into the life of the soul and world in the lecture hall that became famous in Europe and the United States.[151]

A Jungian Dream Room

In 2008 Pacifica began a Legacy Tour that, in addition to visiting sites in Zurich, Kusnacht and Bollingen, included a week of lectures at Eranos, followed by a week-long writing retreat that I co-taught that year with Marion Woodman and in 2009 offered it again on my own. During the time I was there both summers for periods of two

---

150 Mead, G.R.S., *Vaihinger's Philosophy of As If*, p. 251.
151 Robert Hinshaw has performed a vital service to the legacy of Eranos by creating *Eranos: Yearbooks Jahrbucher Annales* listing all the talks and the year that each was presented from its inception until 1988 (no date given, Daimon Verlag. See www.daimon.ch.)

weeks, I was given the large bedroom in Casa Gabriella that C.G. and Emma slept in when they stayed at Eranos in the Canton of Ticino, no more than a mile from Ascona on the Swiss-Italian border.

I include this personal story because until these summers, I had not been one to remember, let alone record my dreams; I could recall very few of them. When I did recollect a dream, I did not bother to write it down and so it slid quickly from memory. Some dreams, however, that repeated themselves found a home in my recollections and surfaced in waking life at unexpected moments. But sleeping in that bedroom in Casa Gabriella, something changed: I began to have and to recollect the most vivid dreams of my life with rhythmic consistency. When I awoke in the morning, the first face I saw was a penciled drawing of C.G. Jung, framed and sitting atop a large armoire in my room, looking down on me with patience and a comforting peace in his eyes. He was portrayed puffing gently on his pipe, a western Queequeg gazing at the more anxious and homeless Ishmael waking beneath him. I would rise early and immediately pilgrimage to the large Victorian couch next to the double doors that led out to the patio and a view of Lago Maggiore lapping gently against the side of Casa Gabriella. There I recorded my dreams each morning. I continued this writing meditation daily for that summer into the present day. Never before in my life had I been gifted on such a regular basis with the dream scape of my oneiric life. But at the same time, I could not help wonder: what is my conscious life doing to the original dream image in the act of recalling it? Was it shaping the dream's narrative and imagery in the conscious crafting, in effect doing to the original material what a poet might do to an original vision or insight, in order to give it a coherent shape and form in the act of poiesis, making and shaping it into a particular coherence and significance?

Only then did I begin in earnest to consider the narrative line of dreams, their storied power and the night energy they carried into morning consciousness as well as their relation to the poetic impulse that each of us carries as deeply as the dreaming rhythms and impulses of the psyche. More specifically, I began to wonder about the dream image and its relation *to* as well as its distinction *from*, the poetic image. I also wondered if the same mythic impulse gave rise to both of these image reservoirs, even a workshop of sorts, where psyche in its crafty and crafting way selects and shapes from both personal and collective domains a rich source of hammered wisdom?

Poetry, Dream and the Archetypal Leaf

I want to offer a comparison here, a further analogy of sorts, fresh from reading a figure whose own work both influenced Jung and set him on his aesthetic course[152] that may have then surfaced with fury in the often enigmatic but always beautiful paintings contained in his *Red Book*. I mention Johann Wolfgang von Goethe (1749-1832) here, less for his aesthetic theories than for his magnificent writings on Botany. In his formidable Introduction to Goethe's work on plants, Charles J. Engard relates how Goethe's love for the fan palm brought him to discover what he believed was an underlying unity in many types of plants. Goethe writes:

> Because they may be grouped under one concept, it gradually became clearer and clearer to me that the concept could also be valid in a higher sense: a challenge which hovered in my mind at that time in the sensuous form of a supersensuous plant archetype.[153]

These are Goethe's own words, which Engard furthers by citing the poet/botanist's conviction that what all forms of this fan palm shared originated in one archetypal structure: the leaf. He goes on to cite the botanist's observation as he developed "the doctrine of metamorphosis—the modern concept of homology,"[154] which led Goethe to write: "Everything is leaf, and through this simplicity the greatest diversity becomes possible."[155]

My intention in bringing this organic image into the discussion is to suggest an analogous living relation between poetic and dream imagery stemming from a similar leaf archetype: the reservoir of psychic or libidinal energy in the unconscious that surfaces through the same structural sluices that allow what is unconscious in location, metaphoric in structure and mythic in form to give rise to the images that we discover in dreams and that we entertain in reading poetry. My thinking runs this way: metaphors are clusters or knots of affects, of affective energy—what it allows perception to

---

152 I mention here the excellent two volume work by Paul Bishop, *Analytical Psychology and German Classical Aesthetics: Goethe, Schiller and Jung* (2008, 2009) that deepens our understanding of the origin or Jung's aesthetic and psychic sense, especially through Goethe's powerful influence on him.

153 Goethe, *Goethe's Botanical Writings*, p. 6.

154 *Goethe's Botanical Writing*, p. 7.

155 *Goethe's Botanical Writings*, p. 7.

open to via imagination. Metaphors are fiercely rooted in the world of matter, but that matter contains its own spiritual, psychological and philosophical variants, its own sets of *as if* clauses and comparisons. Psychic energy engages metaphor, perhaps makes metaphor [into] matter, become material. Metaphors are not unlike energy fields that bridge some quality between consciousness and the unconscious, and body-psyche.

Metaphors, by extension, open us to the symbolic realm; their poetic power consists in their ability to make and shape a new reality based on this initial relation. The relation exposes a pattern of consciousness, which involves replication, repetition and similarity couched in diversity. Jung assists us in making such a conclusion when he observes that "an archetypal content expresses itself, first and foremost, in metaphors."[156]

Gretchen and the Mimetic Turn

Moreover, Jung's own work in "The Analysis of Dreams"[157] offers a further lead when he chose to use Gretchen's song in Goethe's *Faust* as a way into dream interpretation. He first cites her song, which Jung suggests, carries "the hidden thought [which] is Gretchen's doubt about Faust's fidelity." The song, unconsciously chosen by Gretchen, is what we have called the "*dream material,* which corresponds to the secret thought." As Jung develops this moment in the poem wherein Gretchen sings a song that carries and constellates her doubt about Faust's fidelity, he suggests that, "Her dream—in reality, her song—expresses in a disguised form *the ardent desire of her soul.*"[158] I must admit that in reading Jung's discussion, I was more excited about his using a poetic narrative and imagery to elucidate the unconscious desire of the young woman than I was his actual interpretation, for in his illustration poetry and dream coalesced in such a powerful way that one might explore further the revelation of the poem's power as much for what it says of dream's canny presence in Gretchen's song.

In this brief discussion by Jung, he marries poetic image to a dream image and implicitly reveals some cunning similarities that push my own thought a bit deeper. I want to concentrate here on what the dream and poetic image share: a common

156 Jung, CW ¶ 267.
157 CW ¶ 69.
158 CW 4. ¶ 69.

impulse of *mimesis,* a term first given elucidation by Aristotle in the 5th century BCE in his treatise, the *Poetics,* where he explores the presence and power of mimetic impulse. There he suggests that poetry originates in two natural causes: "our proneness to imitate and our delight in harmony and rhythm—and intrinsic pleasure found in imitation."[159] O.B. Hardison's fine commentary on Aristotle's thought reveals that, "Aristotle's imitation is not the same as Plato's idea of imitation as a copy. He points out that, yes, there exists a certain pleasure in comparing a good likeness to the original,[160] but this does not afford the pleasure Aristotle has in mind. Rather, he refers to the fact that imitative works, if they are well done, reveal generic qualities—the presence of the universal in the particular—and that the spectator or audience learns from this.[161] One is reminded of Goethe's assertion that "everything is leaf" and that from a simple unity multiple levels of diversity ensue.

My sense is that Aristotle was already working towards the archetypal imagination in his theory of mimesis, which he refers to as an action of the soul that reveals a sense of itself in the making, in poiesis. "The object of imitation—action—gives the poem its form, its plot, which is also called its soul."[162] Hardison extends Aristotle's observation in suggesting that "imitation is something instinctive."[163] Mimesis is both an action *of* the soul and an action *on* the soul, for in it the soul discovers correspondences with its own emotional, intellectual and instinctive life; it discovers the *as if* quality of its being through things of the world, others and itself in relation to both. It also accounts for how each of us can be so "moved" by a play, a novel, a short story, a piece of music or a painting, because we have the capacity to enter into the work mimetically wherein the soul is affected and at times altered by its own awareness through the work contemplated.

Let's fast-forward to our own time and heed the voice of James Hillman, who in one of his most insightful works, *Healing Fiction* (1983), retrieves Aristotle's notion and offers it a further advancement for therapy and for plotting case histories. In a discussion of Freud's theories early in the book, Hillman suggests that Freud wrote in a "double style" which was required of him because of what he was trying to accomplish with our subject matter here:

---

159 Hardison in *Aristotles's Poetics*, 1968. p.91
160 *Aristotle's Poetics*, p. 93.
161 *Aristotle's Poetics*, p. 93.
162 *Aristotle's Poetics*, p. 96.
163 *Aristotle's Poetics*, p. 97.

What was plot and myth on one level was theory and science on another....Freud's one plot is named after a myth, Oedipus. With this move, Freud too placed mind on a poetic basis. He understood that the entire narrative of a human life, the characters that we are and the dreams we enter, are structured by the selective logic of a profound *mythos* in the psyche.[164]

Let us take one more step into this realm of theory, plot and myth in the life narrative of an individual or of an entire people. Hillman further praises Freud's insight into myth by locating the Oedipal narrative at its center, for Freud located psychology at the very beginning of poetics, with Aristotle's use of mythos in his *Poetics*,.... "wherever 'plot' appears the original Greek word is mythos. Plots are myths. The basic answer to why in a story, are to be discovered in myths.... To be in a mythos is to be inescapably linked with divine powers, and moreover to be in mimesis with them."[165]

From this position and following deeply in the grooves of this logos, Hillman concludes by observing that "the poetic basis of mind suggests that the selective logic operating in the plots of our lives is the logic of mythos, mythology."[166] I do not believe this is very far afield from Jung's own insight that

If we wish to understand what alchemical doctrine means, we must go back to the historical as well as the individual phenomenology of the symbols, and if we wish to gain a closer understanding of dogma, we must perforce consider first the myths of the Near and Middle East that underlie Christianity, and then the whole of mythology as the expression of a universal disposition in man. This disposition I have called the collective unconscious....[167]

Jung ends the paragraph with the observation that there exists "certain complex thought-forms, the archetypes, which must be conjectured as the unconscious organizers of our ideas."[168]

Now I may or may not be on completely solid ground to carry his thought over to Joseph Campbell's insights on myths and dreams, but I wish to briefly in order to convey what I sense to be the bedrock of psyche's motion, which is fundamentally

164 Hillman, J., *Healing Fiction*, p. 11.
165 *Healing Fiction*, p. 11.
166 *Healing Fiction*, p. 12.
167 Jung, CW 9i, ¶ 278.
168 CW ¶ 278.

mimetic, metaphoric and meaning-crafting—the three "Ms" of a "narrative identity," to borrow Paul Ricoeur's phrase.[169] Writing in his last work before he died, *The Inner Reaches of Outer Space*, Campbell, in a work that succinctly sums up a host of his life pursuits regarding mythology and its marriage to both history and to psychic energy, claims that "myths and dreams...are motivated from a single psychophysiological source, namely, the human imagination moved by the conflicting urgencies of the organs (including the brain) of the human body, of which the anatomy has remained pretty much the same since c. 40,000 B.C.[170] And then this revelation, which he repeats often in his earlier writings and is germane for my weaving of several strands of embodied consciousness into the imagery of poetry and dreams: "Accordingly, as the imagery of a dream is metaphorical of the psychology of its dreamer, that of a mythology is metaphorical of the psychological posture of the people to whom it pertains."[171]

Campbell's insight here is profound, most importantly because it helps us to grasp the connection of metaphor to mimesis and by means of it, the origin and development of a mythos. Francis Fergusson, in his fine Introduction to Aristotle's *Poetics*, quotes the translation of S.H. Butcher, who writes: "the praxis that art seeks to reproduce is mainly a psychic energy working outwards."[172] Art, and here for our purposes, poetry, is engaged in creating channels or sluices, aesthetic in design and powerful in structure, to craft and deliver psychic energy fields that transform consciousness.

The imitation that mimesis engages touches on one or several of the infinite designs or patterns that the soul hires in making sense of lived experience. Art constructs this in aesthetic forms "to guide the imagination to see more fully, with a greater orbit of awareness," as I have written elsewhere in "Psychic Energy's Portal to Presence in Myth, Poetry and Culture."[173]

Archetypal psychologist Michael Conforti has written originally on psychic field theory and the force of psychic energy in relation to the new physics. His thesis is that all expressions of matter in the outer world are physical representations of eternal archetypal forms and processes.[174] From his insights I suggest that matter becomes psyche's attempt to make present in symbolic form the face of an archetype in image.

169 Sipiora, *Archetypal Psychologies*, p. 134.
170 Campbell, J., *The Inner Reaches of Outer Space*, p. xiv.
171 *The Inner Reaches of Outer Space*, p. xiv.
172 Butcher, S.H., *Aristotle's Poetics*, p. 8.
173 Slattery, "Psychic Energy's Portal to Presence in Myth, Poetry and Culture." p. 442.
174 Conforti, Michael, *Field, Form and Fate*, p. 6.

This attempt is another form that poiesis can assume in the shaping of something into a coherent design or pattern.[175]

What dream images and poetic images share, therefore, is a mimetic impulse to capture psychic energy in the imagery, to reproduce by means of the power of analogy a reality that appears perhaps to be other, but in fact is another face, physiology and frame of ourselves in metaphoric guise, perhaps an expression of the supreme fiction of a self. A dream is thus a mimetic model, a reproduction carrying the force and energy of a reality that is germane to our further development as individuals. This power derives from the mythos in the psyche that guides, arranges and shapes its contours, its underlying and energy-directing poiesis. As Michael Taussig suggests in his fine study, *Mimesis and Alterity*, mimesis is an imperfect reproduction, yet it acquires the power of the original. "The task to which the mimetic faculty is here set is to capture that very same spirit power...."[176]

In his recent book, *Dream Tending*, Stephen Aizenstat suggests that "dreams are alive and embodied"[177] and should be afforded these two qualities through three methods for meeting and exploring the dream image: association (personal), amplification (historical) and animation (poetic).[178] He advocates that one deflect the tendency to find meaning in the image, at least initially, but better to approach and engage the dream in an attitude of not-knowing[179] so it may reveal itself.

I find his suggestions immensely helpful in working with poetic images as well. The most important hermeneutic both sets of images might be met with is that of being present in a state of wonder rather than one of muscling the image to fit a prescribed idea, agenda or ideology, or worse, the geography of depth psychology!

I end this essay by offering to the reader two dream images/narratives and a poetic image/narrative, followed by a series of possible queries. In considering them, the reader may wish to send me any observations both on this essay and on the two creations below.

---

175 Slattery, "Psychic Energy's Portal to Presence in Myth, Poetry and Culture." p. 447.
176 Taussig, M., *Mimesis and Alterity*, p. 17.
177 Aizenstat, Stephen, *Dream Tending*, p. 24.
178 *Dream Tending*, pp. 22-23.
179 *Dream Tending*, p. 27.

Dream Image #1- 9 January 2010 - Dennis Patrick Slattery.

Place: a garage inside and outside

What: two cats: black and tan

When: afternoon

I am alone. A black cat close to the open garage I frighten when I approach. It fears me. Then I come across it once more, this time in the garage. The garage doors are open. When I approach the garage, I hear great commotion. I then see two full-grown cats, one black, one tan. But the black one is so startled; it leaps in the air, knocking over some wood on a work table. It then runs and hides behind boxes in the back of the garage, against the wall.

The tan cat is there but much calmer in demeanor. It watches the black cat carefully, who is skittish and frightened. The black cat keeps a close watch on me and on every gesture or movement I make. The dream ends on this note.

Dream Image #2 - 5 March 2010 - Dennis Patrick Slattery

Place: A school room in a large house.

What: a young girl, age about 5 years, upset and crying.

When: afternoon.

I am in a child's play room at a school in a large house at the edge of a town. The children, about 4-6 years of age, are in a circle responding to the teacher. I cannot see her, but only hear her voice. I can see only the children from where I am standing close to the classroom door. Attention focuses on one or another child as the class progresses.

One young girl (5 years old), blonde, pretty and in the circle, suddenly leaves it and begins to run, crying. She runs very close to me standing in the back of the room, close to the door. I instinctively reach out and pick her up. She cries in my arms as I try to calm and sooth her. She does not struggle to get down but remains relaxed in my arms. The dream ends here.

Poetic Image: Tree Skin

For Dianne Skafte

Listen then deeply into the tree's skin
below the cragged black bark and deep patient
rhythm of age rough-hewn and weathered from
ten thousand sunrises and
deeper still into the whorls of sandy-colored
shy moist pulp,
the deep place where slowly in time its rings
move out to find the light and to mark its time.

If you must wound the tree, first
touch its skin with your palm face out.
pause for a moment with the iron axe blade or
Steel saw resting quietly by your side;
try with eyes gently closed to discover where
your flesh ends and its skin begins.

Imagine the moist pulp hidden deep within
holding water from another age.
You may then sense in that instant that
you are now a branch full of leaves
of what you wish to bring down.

Your feet and toes have already begun to bud
themselves into the loam beneath you.[180]

When we experience both of these images or sets of images,

---

180 Slattery, *Twisted Sky*, p. 123,

- what might we say about their structure and their coherence?

- What is it that they share?

- What makes each distinct and different?

- What of the crafting of the expression of them out of an initial experience or insight?

- What occurs in the shaping of the remembrance, that of a dream or a personal experience in waking life that language then forms into an identity that I have been calling an act of poiesis, or better, mytho-poiesis?

- What does this dream say to the poem and what is the poem's response to the dream? I did not select the poem in any conscious way to accord with the dreams, but several remarkable observations have been offered to me on Dream #2 by two fine Jungian analysts who work dream imagery in depth: Katherine Sanford and Charles Asher.

I leave the discussion here and invite the reader into the image/narratives to comment on either or both the dream image and the poetic image(s).

References

Aizenstat, Stephen, (2009*). Dream Tending*. New Orleans: Spring Journal, Inc.

Aristotle, (1961). *Aristotle's Poetics*. S.H. Butcher (Trans.). New York: Hill and Wang.

_____. (1988). *The Power of Myth*. With Bill Moyers. Betty Sue Flowers (Ed.). New York:, (1968).

_____. (1968) *Aristotle's Poetics*. Leon Golden (Trans.) O.B. Hardison (Commentary). Englewood Cliffs, NJ. Prentice-Hall

Bishop, Paul, (2008, 2009) *Analytical Psychology and German Classical Aesthetics: Goethe, Schiller and Jung* Two volumes. London: Routledge.

Campbell, J., (1986/2002). *The Inner Reaches of Outer Space: Metaphor as Myth and as Religion*. Novato, California. New World Library.

_____. (1988). *The Power of Myth*. With Bill Moyers. Betty Sue Flowers (Ed.). New York: Doubleday.

Conforti, Michael, (1999/2003). *Field, Form and Fate: Patterns in Mind, Nature and Psyche*. Revised Edition. New Orleans: Spring Publications.

Goethe, Johann Wolfgang von, (1952/1989). *Goethe's Botanical Writings*. Bertha Mueller (Trans.). Woodbridge, CN: Ox Bow Press.

Hillman, J., (1983). *Healing Fiction*. Woodstock, CN. Spring Publications, Inc.

Hinshaw, R., (n.d.). *Eranos: Yearbooks, Jahrbucher Annals.* Einsiedeln, Switzerland: Daimon-Verlag Publishing.

Jung, C.G., (1961/1985). *Freud and Psychoanalysis*. In *CW* 4. Princeton, NJ: Princeton University Press.

_____. (1959/1970). *Aion: Researches Into the Phenomenology of* the *Self. CW* 9ii, Princeton, NJ: Princeton University Press.

_____. (2009). *The Red Book. Liber Novus*. Sonu Shamdasani (Ed.). Trans. Mark Kyburz, John Peck and Sonu Shamdasani. New York: W.W. Norton and Company in the Philemon Series of the Philemon Foundation.

_____. (1959/1971). *The Archetypes and the Collective Unconscious.* In *CW* 9i, Princeton, NJ: Princeton University Press.

Keleman, S., (1999). *Myth and the Body: A Colloquy with Joseph Campbell.* Berkeley: Center Press.

Maritain, J., (1953). *Creative Intuition in Art and Poetry.* Bollingen Series XXXV-1. New York: Pantheon Books.

Mead, G.R.S., (1913/2002). *Vaihinger's Philosophy of 'As If'.* New York: Kissinger Publishing.

Sipiora, M., (2008). Myth and plot: Hillman and Ricoeur on narrative. In Stanton Marlan (Ed.), *Archetypal Psychologies: Reflections in Honor of James Hillman.* New Orleans: Spring Journal Books, 133-51.

Slattery, D., (2010). Psychic energy's portal to presence in myth, poetry and culture. In Riccardo Bernardini and John van Praag (Eds.) *The Legacy Tour of Zurich and Eranos, Ascona, Switzerland.* Einsiedeln, Switzerland. 435-474.

_____. (2010). *Simon's Crossing. A Novel.* With Charles Asher. New York: iUniverse Publishing.

_____. (2001). "Tree Skin". *Casting the Shadows: Selected Poems.* Kearney, NE: Morris Publishing Company, 71.

_____. (2007). *Twisted Sky: Selected Poems by Dennis Patrick Slattery.* Goleta, California: Winchester Canyon Press.

Von Franz, M., (1994). *The Way of the Dream: Conversations on Jungian Dream Interpretation with Marie-Louise von Franz.* Fraser Boa (Ed.). Boston: Shambhala.

Taussig, M., (1993*). Mimesis and Alterity.* New York: Routledge.

4

Thirteen Ways of Looking at a *Red Book*: C.G. Jung's *Divine Comedy*

I do not know which to prefer,

The beauty of inflections

Or the beauty of innuendoes,

The blackbird whistling

Or just after.

Wallace Stevens, "Thirteen Ways of Looking at a Blackbird"
1922. Harmonium 75.

One does not approach *The Red Book* of C.G. Jung without some combination of courage and awe, fearlessness and humility, for in its scope and in its powerful *physical presence* it evokes nothing less than the epic impulse in the soul to pilgrimage down and in and to see Big. Journeying through it as a reader, we realize that we are immediately transported into an epic pilgrimage of the soul towards a greater consciousness of the myths that define its trajectory. No theme could be more germane to the epic imagination, a term I will say more about shortly. *The Red Book* is a witness to the mythopoeic quality of Jung's own imagination.

My first felt experience when it arrived in the mail October 2009 was its luxuriant beauty. I wished simply to enjoy the calligraphic pages and the elaborate and detailed paintings before engaging the text itself. *The Red Book* has made even more palpable not just the reality of the psyche but also the reality of Jung's stature as epic pilgrim and poet through his courage to enter a path taken by no one else, and then to give it mytho-poetic expression in the 16 years it demanded of him. No wonder he turned to Goethe, Dante, Ovid, Nietzsche, Melville, and Thomas a Kempis, among others, for some of his visionary sustenance; his generic stature is epic and, I hope to develop in this essay, comic, in the spirit and pattern of Dante's *Divine Comedy*, which Jung knew well. From the angle of literary genre, which is the portal of entry, Jung carries in *The Red Book* the qualities of comic epic.[181] My intention is less to reveal, as in matching, or in outlining a direct correspondence how *Liber Novus*,[182] *Liber Secundus*,[183] and *Scrutinies*[184] might reveal resonances with Dante's three canticas—*Inferno, Purgatorio* and *Paradiso*—of his 14th century *Commedia*. Nonetheless, the pattern of the journeys into the Spirit of the Depths to confront and converse with the dead is a shared reality of both poems and quite often part of the fabric of epic.

On this score, the editor, Sonu Shamdasani's immensely helpful Introduction reveals the two fictions that perhaps evoked in Jung's imagination the formative principles he needed to navigate his own *descensus ad inferos*.[185] In 1914 Jung read Nietzsche's *Zarathustra* carefully, Shamdasani writes: "it strongly shaped the structure and style of *Liber Novus*.... But whereas *Zarathustra* proclaimed the death of God, *Liber Novus* depicts the rebirth of God in the soul. There are also indications he read Dante's *Commedia* at this time, which also informs the structure of the work."[186] If

---

181 I believe there is sufficient material both here and in his subsequent writings that cite directly or allude to Dante's *Commedia* to warrant a full-length study of the relationship between Dante's comic epic of the 14th century and Jung's *Red Book*.

182 Jung, *The Red Book*, pp. 227-256.

183 *The Red Book*, pp. 257-330.

184 *The Red Book*, pp. 331-359.

185 Such a descent, Jung makes clear, which, "consciously or unconsciously, is an *opus alchymicum*" (Jung 1953/1974, CW 12, ¶ 42). See also his discussion of the Christian nekyia in ¶ 178. Moreover, David Miller writes in *Hells and Holy Ghosts*: "The descent of Christ into hell leads theology toward a descent into mythology, a mythological way of seeing and thinking, a way that is nonliteral (2004, pp. 24-25)." This same insight can be applied to Jung's mythic journey rendered in *The Red Book*.

186 *The Red Book*, pp. p. 202.

there is one large generating theme that both Dante and Jung share, both as pilgrims on their own journey, and as poets rendering a formed shape to their deeply felt imaginal experiences, it is this rebirth of God in the soul. The theme becomes especially poignant when we consider that Dante wrote his poem in exile and that what informed his often acerbic denunciations of historical figures was what Giuseppe Mazzotta calls his "exilic imagination.[187] No less is it so for Jung, who, in the middle of his own life, and beginning with his exile from Freud as well as his own divorce, or split, from himself, began *The Red Book*. Both writers were drawn to the depths, not only of their own souls, but to the *Zeitgeist* of their own historical periods at moments of great upheaval. Dante crafted his poem towards the end of what had been the sustaining Christian mythos of the medieval worldview, while Jung was on the edge of the outbreak of WWI. Moreover, both writers shared what Jung was to write about in *Psychological Types:*

> So in Eckhart, we are confronted with new ideas, ideas having the same psychic orientation that impelled Dante to follow the image of Beatrice into the underworld of the unconscious and that inspired the singers who sang the lore of the Grail.[188]

Shamdasani, however, points out an important and dramatic distinction between the two writers who were separated by approximately 640 years. Dante lived from 1265-1321. *Liber Novus* depicts Jung's descent into Hell. But whereas Dante could utilize an established cosmology, *Liber Novus* is a heroic venture to shape an individual cosmology.[189] He then draws a brief comparison between Jung's guide, Philemon, the guide Zarathustra in Nietzsche's work and the classical poet Virgil as moral and poetic guide for Dante.

Epic Genre

What I seek in this essay are the patterns and large contours of epic that I believe informed Jung's poetic creation. I understand *The Red Book* to be an occasion for furthering a discussion of Jung as a poet, as an artificer and crafter of mythic movements

---

187 Mazzotta, Giuseppe, *Dante: Poet of the Desert*, p. 147.
188 Jung, CW 6, ¶ 410.
189 *The Red Book*, p 202.

of the soul in literary form, and to view him as an epic poet. Furthermore, I can easily see the possibilities of teaching *The Red Book* in literature courses on epic and most specifically in conjunction with Dante's *Commedia*. The former is as much a literary text in the tradition of epic poetry as it is a complex and demanding exploration of Jung's own *descensus ad inferos* that spirals out to include the larger historical psyche.

To give a context through texts, I mention several poems that conform to the patterns of epic: both Sumerian epics, *Inanna* and *Gilgamesh,* the latter finding a new form in the figure of Izdubar in *Liber Secundus,*[190] Homer's *Iliad* and *Odyssey,* Virgil's *Aeneid,* the Indian epics *Mahabharata* and the *Ramayana,* Dante's *Divine Comedy,* John Milton's *Paradise Lost,* Shakespeare's History Plays, the Russian *Lay of Igor's Campaign,* the Anglo-Saxon *Beowulf,,* the African *Mwindo Epic,* Leo Tolstoy's *War and Peace,* the Germanic *Nibelungenlied,* Herman Melville's *Moby-Dick,*[191] James Joyce's *Ulysses,* William Faulkner's *Go Down, Moses,* Derek Wolcott's *Omeros,* and Toni Morrison's *Beloved.* Films such as *Braveheart, The Lord of the Rings, Star Wars, Avatar,* as well as the television series *Star Trek* and the more recent *The Tudors* fall within the class of epic poems. Generally speaking, epic is a reconciling genre that moves in its action to realign the epic hero, and by extension his/her people with the large realms of: the Gods, the natural order, the underworld and the masculine-feminine coniunctio.

The character of epic as a literary genre generally and the Middle Ages specifically occupies Jung at various points in his work. In fact, *The Red Book* might be called *works* for it appears to me as two related stories paralleling one another throughout. Leaving aside the paintings as magnificent aesthetic renderings of characters and psychological forces[192] of the narrative's specifically plotted movement, the major text is

---

190 *The Red Book*, p. 277, n. 96.

191 I want to underscore the importance of *Moby-Dick* for Jung. In his penetrating essay on the creative process of the poet, Jung distinguishes between psychological and visionary fiction and proclaims that Melville's 19th century epic illustrates the latter form of poetic expression: "I would also include Melville's *Moby Dick,* [sic] which I consider to be the greatest American novel, in this broad class of writings. (1930/1966 CW 15, ¶ 237).

192 An exciting comparison might be made between both the composition of Jung's paintings with those of William Blake's that accompany his *Marriage of Heaven and Hell* to better understand the intimacy between word and image in the creation of a text to deploy a thicker texture of meaning. A second level of exploration might include Blake's renderings of scenes from Dante's *Commedia*, as for instance figure 19 in *CW* 12, *Psychology and Alchemy*, which depicts the soul guiding Dante in *Purgatorio* IV, (61).

Jung's own writing as he enters through a rich and sustained quest and a questioning of his own soul within the historical background of one of the most dramatic moments in modernity: World War I. The war's imminent destructive presence evokes the epic enterprise of a search for the Grail of the self. The second narrative resides in the on-going episodic plot of the notes that appear at the bottom of practically every page; they offer us a hermeneutic journey literally below the main plot as they comment on, correct, amplify, and further its main themes. These two narratives are in constant dialogue, with us as readers in between, stitching the two stories together within our imaginations as our own personal myths are activated through the dual drama of discovery.[193]

Epic Memory

I make this observation with knowledge of the insight Jung offers on the act of reading: "Know that you attain yourself from what you read in a book. You read as much into a book as out of it."[194] Reading itself is an epic quest.

On the last page of *Liber Secundus*,[195] Jung's observation made in 1930 further underscores by implication the importance of Dante's poem:

> A movement back into the Middle Ages is a sort of regression, but it is not personal. It is a historical regression, a regression into the past of the collective unconscious. This always takes place when the way ahead is not free, when there is an obstacle from which you recoil; or when you need to get something of the past in order to climb over the wall ahead.[196]

---

193 An area of exploration needing more space is Aristotle's idea of *mimesis*, or the imitation of an action that the plot reveals, which is outlined in his *Poetics*. The plot, for Aristotle, "is the arrangement of the incidents" (*Poetics*, date original/1902, p. 25), but the action is an imitation "not of men, but of... life, and life consists in action, and its end is a mode of action, not a quality" (p. 27). The place of art as an imitation in aesthetic form that offers us a glimpse of what is universal and unchanging should be addressed through *The Red Book*. S.H. Butcher's study, *Aristotle's Theory of Poetry and Fine Art*, is excellent on art as a mimetic rendering of organic form.

194 *The Red Book*, p. 244, n. 145.

195 *The Red Book*, p. 330, n. 354.

196 *The Red Book*, p. 330.

An essential quality of the epic enterprise includes a looking back, a remembering and then, a retrieval of what remains valuable for the future of a people, both personal and collective. The action of epic and the task of the epic hero is one of reversion, reversal, retreating back, there to gather up or harvest what still remains significant and valuable of the prevailing myth for an individual, and through that personage, for an entire people within the cultural-historical field that sustains them or a civilization—the true subject matter of epic—and to transport it forward through the present in song, story or drama. Such an enterprise involves a creative act of reshaping the myth that guides, confers value and thereby coalesces a people's most cogent ideals and beliefs.

I have suggested elsewhere of epic that "without memory, there can be no epic, since it is from memory that the mythology of a culture, if not the mythic impulse itself, is fashioned. And without remembrance, the establishment of a sense of place disappears."[197] Epic is the genre, among three others—lyric, tragedy, and comedy outlined by Aristotle in his *Poetics,* what he refers to as "kinds" of poetry, which is most inclusive of the others as well as the genre that most forcefully presents itself between myth and history.[198] These four poetic structures the literary theorist Louise Cowan delineates as the four generic landscapes in which the soul expresses itself mytho-poetically. Her grasp of genres as four gestures of the soul led her to affirm the power of the *mundus imaginalis...,* a cosmos of the imagination [which] is a realm not of pure spirit, but of matter permeated by spirit....[199] This world of the imaginal possesses an order that guides the interpretation of individual works and of whole families of works. The large forms of lyric, tragedy, comedy and epic comprise her "genre wheel" of the poetic cosmos; they embody certain complex attitudes of the soul, constituting complete worlds in themselves.[200]

---

197 Slattery, *The Epic Cosmos*, pp. 332-33.

198 While it is too vast a topic to enter here, Louise Cowan's organic understanding of genres as guiding forms of a literary work is relevant: "To be oblivious of the large generic metaphor governing the climate of a work and hence the very atmosphere in which its characters live and breathe is to remain unaware of its deepest meaning and hence its power." (1984, 8). As a student of Dr. Cowan for many years, I sense in her grasp of the organic form of poetry many crucial affinities with Jung's depth psychological comprehension of both imagination and psyche's structure.

199 Cowan, Louise, *The Terrain of Comedy*, p. 9.

200 *The Terrain of Comedy*, p. 9.

Literary genres, I would add, belong to that category Jung called "archetypes of transformation. They are not personalities, but are typical situation, places, ways and means, that symbolize the kind of transformation in question...They are genuine symbols precisely because they are ambiguous, full of half-glimpsed meanings, and in the last resort inexhaustible."[201] To enter into the terrain of epic, for instance, is to engage a particular symbolic order characteristic of that generic field and to forge in that imaginal landscape a distinct response of the soul to life.

In developing these four generic terrains of the soul's imaginal life, Cowan addresses the shape of their artistic creation that reflects a depth psychological cast of mind. In its formation, she suggests, "the mysterious process that produces any genuine work of art brings with it *ab ovo* a pattern and identity, so that the kind of poem, its genre, is already determined at the moment of fertilization."[202] An "ontological pattern" guides the work, a form of "genetic imprinting" that establishes a work's identity.[203] Her sense of each of the genres having its own poetic imprint and pattern, specific thematic inflections, time, space and movement of the soul, what Dante was to call a "moto spiritale," namely, a movement-of-spirit,[204] is especially crucial in epic, which in its movement 'activates a full and complete cosmos."[205]

Most important for *The Red Book* and Jung's epic odyssey within it that relies for structure, in part, on Dante's poem, is the close intimacy with which epic narratives connect the human with the Gods, as if a wall or partition was momentarily dismantled so that the two realms are able to communicate on a profound and sustained level. Such dissolution occurs in both Dante's pilgrimage through the terrain of "*animarum statem post mortem*," the state of souls after death, and Jung's journey through the realms of the dead. What links both ventures is the figure of Christ's own *via dolorosa* as backdrop of both epics; Christ's journey from crucifixion to descent to

---

201 Jung, CW 9i, ¶ 80.

202 Cowan, *The Epic Cosmos*, p. 3.

203 *The Epic Cosmos*, p. 3.

204 Francis Fergusson introduces S.H. Butcher's translation of Aristotle's *Poetics* by citing the latter: "'The praxis that art seeks to reproduce is mainly a psychic energy working outwards.'" Fergusson adds: "It may be described metaphorically as the focus or movement of the psyche toward what seems good to it at the moment—a 'movement-of-spirit,' as Dante calls it (1961, Aristotle's *Poetics* 1961, 8). This motion of the soul outwards is relayed through the various poetic creations of the four genres.

205 Cowan, *The Epic Cosmos*, p. 3.

resurrection structures the action of comedy in its three moments that Dante poetically develops: infernal, purgatorial and paradisal, and that Jung's *The Red Book* recovers once again from history.

Comic Epic

For example, in infernal comedy the ego is dissolved, dismantled and decentered as it witnesses through this landscape's often grotesque and malignant imagery, a fuller sense of its own shadowed nature. In purgatorial comedy, the landscape is less isolated, more communal; figures move to blessedness in hope; the souls that inhabit this region are, as Cowan observes, both "imperfect and weak."[206] In paradisal comedy, grace is most present and efficacious as it guides the soul toward the Primal Love, as Dante calls it, to a vision at once mystical and firmly grounded in the body. In the famous but controversial letter to his benefactor, Can Grande della Scala, Dante offers that, "A comedy begins with some adversity but its subject ends prosperously, as is seen through Terence in his comedies" (2010, "Excerpts from a translation by Nancy Howe www.web.whittier.edu/people/WebPages/PersonalWebPages/furman-adams).

Dante's *Commedia* I believe influences Jung's structuring the three realms of comedy as both a literary genre and as a psychic disposition. Nathan Schwartz Salant offers psychological language to this pilgrimage in writing on *The Red Book* of Jung's own experience of madness and disorder: "'becoming a wave' may represent an emergence of Jung's experience of chaos as rhythmic, here oscillating between order and disorder. This rhythmic experience of opposites is characteristic of a potentially positive outcome in which a new form of order, such as an ego-self relationship, becomes stable."[207] On an epic scale, the hero is often in conflict with values that are disintegrating at the same time that the sprouts and shoots of a new mythos begin to make themselves felt through parched soil to revitalize both the individual and the community that gave rise to the epic impulse. *The Red Book* is a redemptive epic text, comic in trajectory and Medieval in design that follows in part the structure of Dante's poem.

---

206 Cowan, *The Terrain of Comedy*, p. 13.

207 Along with this essay by Schwartz-Salant, I recommend others in the same volume by John Beebe, Ann Belford Ulanov and Robin van Loben Sels gathered, edited and introduced by Kathryn Madden in *Quadrant*, vol. xxxx: 2, Summer 2010, p. 21.

Both works share an elaborate journey that mytho-poetically tracks and remembers the soul's pilgrimage by giving it an organic form in order to render it intelligible both to the writer and to us readers.[208]

The Red Book begins in exile, yet with a firm conviction that in addition to the ephemeral spirit of the times, there is a deeper myth at work," the spirit of the depths" and to that geography Jung is drawn.[209] *Liber Primus* begins with the structure of a "Medieval manuscript, numbered by folios instead of pages."[210] While we are told he discards this model in subsequent sections, he nonetheless attunes his ear to listen to the spirit of the depths, not unlike an epic calling, which prepares him for the solitude of the desert.

At the same time, Jung is engulfed by a vision in October, 1913 in which he imagines a destructive flood "that covered all the northern and low-lying lands between the North Sea and the Alps. It reached from England up to Russia.... I saw yellow waves, swimming rubble and the death of countless thousands."[211] The image, while certainly apocalyptic, is, within this discussion, epic in grandeur and range. It sickens him with its brute force and clarity as well as its sheer geographic magnitude.

Then, on the fourth night of his journey, he cries out: "To Journey to Hell means to become Hell oneself. It is all frightfully muddled and interwoven."[212] The expedition, *descensus ad inferos,* and/or into the Underworld is a hallmark of the epic journey; it is the locale of both horror and wisdom as well as contact with the largest population, the dead. One of the most notable illustrations is in Homer's *Odyssey*. Odysseus enters his Nekyia and there confronts the shade of the prophet Tiresias who predicts his future, but then tries futilely to embrace the insubstantial shade of his mother, who died of a broken heart as a result of her son's long absence, and then finally witnesses all the wives and daughters of the Greek warriors who died at Troy.[213] He returns to

---

208 In a recent essay I explore how myths are "repositories for certain narrative patterns necessary for the rich texture of life itself.... The language of myth, as Joseph Campbell has asserted, is metaphor. I propose that metaphors are akin to energy fields that promote conversation and traffic between consciousness and the unconscious through the body psyche (2010, 451).

209 Jung, *The Red Book*, p. 229.

210 *The Red Book*, p. 229. n. 1.

211 *The Red Book*, p. 230.

212 *The Red Book*, p. 240.

213 Homer, *The Odyssey*, Book 11, ll. 140-229.

Circe changed by his meeting with the dead. I think it is important to recognize that this incident occurs midpoint in the *Odyssey*'s action and is relevant to the midpoint in life that opens Dante's epic poem as well as the midpoint in Jung's life when he enters the same psychic terrain. Dante's own epic begins with:

Nel mezzo del cammin di nostra vita (A)

mi ritrovai per una selva oscura, (B)

che la diritta via era smarrita. (A)

Ahi quanto a dir qual era e cosa dura (B)

Esta selva selvaggia e aspra e forte (C)

Che nel pensier rinova la paura! (B)[214]

When I had journeyed half of our life's way

I found myself within a shadowed forest,

For I had lost the path that does not stray.

Ah, it is hard to speak of what it was,

That savage forest, dense and difficult,

Which even in recall renews my fear:

This passage that begins the poem Jung had underlined in his copy.[215]

---

214 Alighieri, *Inferno*, I, ll. pp. 1-6.

215 I have placed letters at the end of each of the lines in Italian to reveal a hallmark of epic that Dante ingeniously creates a new rhyme scheme to convey, which he called terza rima, or third rhyme. It consists of a poetic pattern of three, a number which governs the entire poem as the presence of the Trinity. The first and third lines of a poetic "foot" rhyme. The middle term then becomes the first and third terms of the next terza rima, which then begins over again when Dante comes to the end of the alphabet and repeats the A-B-A structure. He sustains this rhyme scheme for the more than 14,000 lines of the poem. The movement of epic is a retrieval of the old that is reshaped into the new. It reveals in linear fashion the spiralic return to what was, but is never exactly retrieved, because when one journeys to the middle term and then backs up, one is changed such that the originary rhyme is "like" but not an exact copy of the first time. So the spiral captures the movement of epic more faithfully than does the circle. For an extensive discussion of this important structural element in Dante (and by implication) of the action of Jung's *Red Book*, see my essay," Dante's Terza Rima in *The Divine Comedy*: the Road of Therapy" (2008).

The effect of this beginning may be expressed in a footnote to *Liber Novus* in which Jung writes: "Life is an energetic process, like any other.... From the middle of life, only he who is willing to die with life remains living. Since what takes place in the secret hour of life's midday is the reversal of the parabola, the birth of death....."[216] The paradox inherent in his observation that reverts back to Dante's initial verse to inaugurate his pilgrimage as well as his poetic journey of transcribing his adventures, is part of Jung's methodology: less contradiction than paradox appears as a governing pattern of the soul's motion.[217]

The *Commedia* in *The Red Book*

In *Liber Primus,* two passages from Dante's *Purgatorio* are highlighted. Just before their presence in a footnote, Jung writes of the third night witnessing two serpents, one darkly coiled, the other white. "Both serpents curl about themselves, one in light, the other in darkness."[218] He relates this image to Elijah, who, in the spirit of Virgil, leads Dante up to a summit, in geography reminiscent of *Purgatorio's* mountain: "I follow. On the peak we come to some masonry made of huge blocks"[219] and then into a courtyard where an altar to the sun sits in the middle. Soon thereafter, "Elijah transforms into a huge flame of white light."[220]

Jung writes then, that, "My longing led me up to the overbright day, whose light is the opposite to the dark space of forethinking."[221] Footnote 213 then refers to lines he

---

216 *The Red Book*, p. 274, n. 75.

217 Robert Johnson's *Owning Your Own Shadow* (1991, pp. 85-94) is excellent in delineating the distinction between contradiction and paradox. Paradox is a condition or disposition that rests at the heart of poetic construction as well as being at the core of psyche's motion. James Hillman suggests as well that "the very fiction of the archetypes is that they posit themselves to be more than personal and human, because the psyche is both immanent in persons,...and also transcends persons" (*Revisioning Psychology* 1976, p. 151). The paradox that fiction carries in its bones is predicated on the paradox of the archetypes themselves as both/and.

218 *The Red Book*, p. 251.

219 *The Red Book*, p. 251.

220 *The Red Book*, p. 252.

221 *The Red Book*, p. 252.

copied into Black Book 2 from a German translation of *Purgatorio* 24: "And I to him: I am one who, when love/Breathes on me, notices, and in the manner/That he dictates within, I utter words."[222] In Dante's poem, Virgil and Dante meet Forese Donati, a friend of Dante's from Florence, in the realm of the Gluttonous. Forese offers Dante myriad examples of Gluttony to highlight its ubiquitous presence in the soul. Dante has just responded to Forese's curiosity when the latter asked if he, Dante, is the one who has brought a sweet new style of poetry forward (il dolce stil nuovo), by quoting from one of Dante's earlier poems which begins: "Ladies who have intelligence of love (Donne ch'avete intelletto d'amore),"[223] a line that appears immediately above those that Jung copied.[224] It is a signal moment in the development of the poem because it witnesses a new poetic manner of expression: the power of love as a way of knowing. Here in the realm of excess in Purgatory appears for the first time the new spare and eloquent poetic style that gives new form to love itself.[225]

Almost immediately following appears the second passage Jung copied from *Purgatorio* 25, the realm of the Lustful: "And then, in the same manner as a flame which follows the fire whatever shape it takes,/The new form follows the spirit exactly."[226] Here the Roman epic poet Statius, who lived in the period between Virgil and Dante and thus bridges their two poetic traditions, offers the poets a discourse on generation, the nature of the shades and "aerial bodies."[227] It helps as well to know the lines Statius speaks immediately following those Jung copied: "Since from that airy body it takes on/its semblance, that soul is called 'shade': that shape/forms organs for each

---

222 Alighieri, D., *Purgatorio XXIV*, ll. 52-54.

223 *Purgatorio XXIV*, l. 51.

224 This is one of the famous lines from poem XIX (1295/1973, 32) of *La Vita Nuova*, a series of courtly love poems with commentary that Dante wrote to his beloved, and in the process, concluded that his theme of love needed a much larger poetic container for its exploration. His insight led to the composition of the *Commedia*.

225 What Dante and Jung share in their respective epic journeys of the soul is the place of love as a powerful force for good or ill. In *Purgatorio* XVII Virgil instructs Dante on how all acts that embody the 7 sins are indeed acts of love: "'From this you see that—of necessity—/love is the seed in you of every virtue/and of all acts deserving punishment" (150, ll. 103-05), either love in excess, in scarcity or in distorted form. From these forms of loving arise the soul's manner of knowing: either in excess, diminishment or distortion. So to love "in due measure" is to know in that same disposition. Eros and epistemology are of a piece.

226 *Purgatorio XXV*, ll. 97-99.

227 *Purgatorio XXV*, ll. 49-96.

sense, even for sight."[228] The "new form that follows the spirit exactly" is the shade which allows Dante to know them as airy nothings who have appearance but lack substance.

Both passages share a keen interest in love: love as inspiration and love as excess in gluttony and lust. The sense here is that Jung was drawn to love as a force of inspiration that one might follow as he, Love, dictates what is to be said. These important and related set of passages reveal a shared poetic inspiration by Jung and Dante in that they each sought a new style or manner of expression that is both mytho-poetic and more in accord stylistically with their respective subject matters.[229]

Jung's own manner of elaboration with paintings that reminds one of illuminated medieval manuscripts, gives his writing a tangible intimacy with Dante's medieval world, deployed in a new poetic utterance: the terza rima rhyme structure. Finally, both poets have a sustained interest and desire to explore the complexity of Christ's own journey, motivated, one could say, by a selfless love that transcended individual interests. Each of these poets, Dante and Jung, elaborate and amplify mythopoetically the Christ narrative through their creations.[230] Ann Ulanov offers a fine insight on this dimension of the work when, in writing of the polytheistic population of so many Gods in *The Red Book,* she concludes, "Jung's searing experience, his imitation of Christ, being Christ, which does not mean he becomes God but that God is born 'through the spirit of men as the conceiving womb of God'"[231]

Jung as epic poet and as mythmaker is born in *The Red Book*'s creation; he adopts a style of working psychological material in the spirit of Dante's fierce mytho-poetic expression of his own soul towards a vision of wholeness in *Paradiso* that ends in an inclusive image of God's transcendence and human imminence. The epic journey is,

---

228 *Purgatorio XXV*, II.100-102.

229 Susan Rowland has contributed significantly to Jung's rhetorical style that demands more space than allowed here: *Jung as a Writer* (2005) and more recently, *C.G. Jung in the Humanities* (2010), especially her insightful chapter 2: "Jung the Writer on Psychotherapy and Culture" (pp. 27-46).

230 The complexity of the Christ narrative as metaphorical and symbolic quest so deeply in accord with Dante and Jung's respective epic journeys that culminate in a resurrection of sorts, is offered in Michael L. Cook's *Christology as Narrative Quest* (1997), especially within one of his initial observations that "Jesus continues to energize the imagination" ("Introduction, 7).

231 Ulanov, Ann, "God Climbs Down to Mortality: Jung in His Red Book," p. 72.

for Dante as for Jung, the pilgrimage of penning their respective visions, i.e. the creative process to give form via imagination. The formed rendering is as much a part of the epic enterprise as is the journey, as for example the *Gilgamesh* epic reveals when the hero returns and writes his story on the bricks of the city walls to fix it in the communal memory.

The Realm of the Dead

Both poets also share a sustained regard for the dead, for the ancestors, whose death does not relegate them to the past and to historical insignificance; rather, in many cases their presence intensifies as they become more prominent citizens of history. Both Dante and Jung saw the wisdom in reestablishing contact with the dead, for their presences live within both poets.

One important text among many that guides *Liber Secundus* to its end is Thomas à. Kempis' (1380-1471) *The Imitation of Christ*, first published anonymously in 1418 and later attributed to Thomas. Still generally agreed as the most read spiritual text after the Bible, its reputation remains today because of its "soul-building optimism about the benefits of aspiring to a Christ-shaped life."[232] Its importance for Jung is that it assisted in shaping his understanding of both Christ and the dead: "It belongs to the way of Christ that he ascends with few of the living but many of the dead. His work was the salvation of the despised and lost, for whose sake he was crucified between two criminals."[233] The dead and their restoration is part of the epic hero's charge, not just the historical dead, but as the short rotund professor who Jung meets in a hall by a "large gate,"[234] observes, "all the images you took in the past, which your ongoing life has left behind.[235] What *The Imitation of Christ* reveals is the love Christ had for the widest range of human persons, including the lowest and highest qualities and impulses in every individual.

This theme of love is dramatically developed then in *Scrutinies,* which carries the action of *Paradiso* in its folds as the figure of Christ and his narrative become more

232 Kempis, Thomas, *The Imitation of Christ*, Introduction, p. xx.
233 *The Red Book*, p. 297.
234 *The Red Book*, p. 295.
235 *The Red Book*, p. 296.

predominant. *Scrutinies* is the segment of the journey wherein one accepts in love "the hollow nothing that I am"[236] as Jung converses with his "I" who is "damned to haul you through a purgatory so you will become somewhat acceptable."[237] Shortly after the inception of this conversation with the I, one of three shades who appears to Jung, a feminine soul from the realm of the dead insists: "But love is: to bear and endure oneself. It begins with this...you are not yet tempered: other fires must yet come over you until you have accepted your solitude and learned to love."[238] Almost immediately thereafter appear images of the last supper and Christ's words to his apostles, remembered and uttered by this same shade:

> "Come drink the living blood, drink your fill....
>
> "Take, eat, this is the body that lives for you. Take, eat, drink, this is my blood, whose desire flows for you."[239]

Accustoming oneself to sacrifice, of self-offering in service to others and to honor and integrate the dead are all essentials of epic action. This section resonates many of the aphorisms and teachings of Thomas a Kempis that Jung appears to weave very skillfully into the complex carpet of *Scrutinies*. Thomas writes, for instance, in a chapter "Of The Zealous Amendment of Our Whole Life": "If Jesus crucified would come into our hearts, how quickly and fully should we be taught!"[240] Earlier he had written: "Thou must learn to break down thine own self in many things, if thou wilt have peace and concord with others."[241] The spirit of *The Imitation* pervades the latter part of *Liber Secundus* and informs in large measure the action of *Scrutinies*.

Scrutinies is Jung's *Paradiso* in ways that tolerate further amplification. Suffice it to mention here that the elements closest to the heart beat of the *Commedia*, however, would include the place of Christ's presence as a paradoxical figure both human and divine, his sacrifice, his death that initiates his resurrection, as well as the full extent of what Dante refers to as the Primal Love's presence in a human life and the image of the Pleroma.

---

236 *The Red Book*, p. 333.
237 *The Red Book*, p. 333.
238 *The Red Book*, p. 341.
239 *The Red Book*, p. 342.
240 Kempis, *The Imitation of Christ*, p. 43.
241 *The Imitation of Christ*, p. 23.

The purgatorial action is gathered in *Liber Secundus*: "Every step upward will restore a step downward so that the dead will be delivered into freedom,[242] which describes in the latter part the action of purgation in each soul ascending the mountain. Second, and in accord with Dante the pilgrim's struggle through his pilgrimage to blessedness is Jung's admonition: "learn to be with the dead—then you will discover the worth of the living companions,"[243] Finally, on the nature of sacrifice, which in conjunction with the resurrection in the Christian myth is "the law of love:" "Therefore you should have reverence for what has become, so that the law of love may become redemption through the restoration of the lower and of the past...."[244]

Love In The Paradisal Realm

First, the Pleroma, which we learn in the first sermon of Philemon to the dead in *Scrutinies*[245] is comprised of Nothingness and fullness: "In infinity full is as good as empty. Nothingness is empty and full."[246] In a lengthy footnote,[247] the word *Pleroma* is accounted a term from Gnosticism. Jung is quoted in 1929 as observing that "The Gnostics expressed it as Pleroma, a state of fullness where the pairs of opposites, yea and nay, day and night, are together, then when they 'become' it is either day or night."[248] In *Answer to Job* he continues: "What exists in the Pleroma as an eternal 'process' exists in time as aperiodic sequence, that is to say, it is repeated many times in an irregular pattern."[249]

---

242 *The Red Book*, p. 296.

243 *The Red Book*, p. 297.

244 *The Red Book*, p. 297.

245 *The Red Book*, p. 346.

246 *The Red Book*, p. 346.

247 *The Red Book*, p. 347, n. 82.

248 *The Red Book*, p. 347, n. 82.

249 For An insightful and thorough discussion of the Pleroma, see Kathryn Wood Madden's *Dark Light of the Soul* (2008). There she explores the work and influence of the German mystic, Jacob Boehme on Jung. She observes: "If, as I contend, a unitary reality underlies all psychological experience, then as clinicians we ignore the 'spiritual realm and the divine' at the risk of the totally psychic health of those in our care" (2008, 99).

The editor observes in the same note that Jung equated the Pleroma with the notion of the *unus mundus* of Gerhardus Dorn "to express the transcendental postulate of the unity underlying the multiplicity of the empirical world."[250] Without in any of this discussion seek out a match or a univocal correspondence of Jung's journey with Dante's, there nonetheless exists in the last image in *Paradiso* XXXIII a unity that surprises and perplexes the medieval poet. Yet it leaves him with a feeling of sublime harmony with the created order, imaged as a grand book of creation, its central metaphor, with its one author, God.

Led by Mary, the Mother of God, to this final vision, Dante then watches her retreat into the celestial rose, as he observed Beatrice earlier, leaving him exalted and exhausted in the presence of a growing light with three dimensions:

> In the deep and bright
>
> Essence of that exalted Light, three circles
>
> Appeared to me; they had three different colors,
>
> but all of them were of the same dimension;
>
> one circle seemed reflected by the second,
>
> as rainbow is by rainbow, and the third
>
> seemed fire breathed equally by those two circles.[251]

He senses that this vision exceeds both his understanding and his ability to express it adequately; nonetheless, he pushes further into it, beyond his normal capacities, by addressing God as the circle in the geometry. He continues to gaze on the three circles of three colors until a new image grows into his awareness:

> That circle—which, begotten so, appeared
>
> in You as light reflected—when my eyes
>
> had watched it with attention for some time,
>
> within itself and colored like itself,
>
> to me seemed painted with our effigy,
>
> so that my sight was set on it completely....[252]

---

250 *The Red Book*, p. 347, n. 82.
251 Alighieri, *Paradiso*, par. XXXIII, ll. 114-20.
252 *Paradiso* XXXIII, ll. pp. 127-32.

> I wished to see
>
> the way in which our human effigy
>
> suited the circle and found place in it—
>
> and my own wings were far too weak for that.[253]

The wings of his poetic abilities are inadequate for lift off. The image is beyond logic and even beyond poetic insight and expression. Dante nevertheless gives himself over, in an act of faith, to a stroke of light that flashes across his consciousness in such a manner that he realizes his mind had "received what it had asked:"[254]

> Here force failed my high fantasy; but my
>
> desire and will were moved already—like
>
> a wheel revolving uniformly—by
>
> the Love that moves the sun and the other stars.[255]

In the triple mirror of his own imagining, he gazes on the image of humanity—perhaps Christ and himself both, an image constellated in the reflected image of the Godhead, the source of the Primal Love whose energy creates and motivates the movement of Creation. The mirroring leads to the paradox that the Primal Love that moves the entire created order is at the same time within him, reflected in a Trinitarian way within his human nature and guiding his own impulses of love. Our human being is tri-partite, this image suggests, and yet a unity in the paradox that defines the mystery of our human-divine nature. The image in its force and comfort seems to recalibrate the final movement of Dante's soul so that he feels completely in accord with the mysterious mystical nature of Being and being conscious.

Jung writes in the last pages of *Scrutinies*: "Only fidelity to love and voluntary devotion to love enable this binding and mixing to be dissolved and led back to me that part of myself that secretly lay with men and things. Only thus does the light of the star grow, only thus do I arrive at my stellar nature, at my truest and innermost self, that simply and singly is."[256] One's stellar nature in conjunction with love comprises the last line of Dante's epic, here in Italian:

---

253 *Paradiso*, ll. 136-39.
254 *Paradiso*, l. 141.
255 *Paradiso*, ll. 142-45.
256 *The Red Book*, p. 356.

L'amor che move is sole e l'altre stele.[257] As the word "stele" is the final word of *Inferno* and *Paradiso,* so here it ends the entire poem with the soul of one being, including Jung's own "stellar nature," as part of the motion of the created order without and the eternal cosmos within each person. The entire poem is comprised of three stars. Unity and diversity exist in both images. In addition, one God is plural and one effigy is haloed in three circles of three colors. The paradox is that the *unus mundus* is itself a diverse plural creation that sustains the tension in both.

The epic closes a few pages later—Dante in accord with the circles and the created order, Jung within the twin images of Christ and the serpent—both inhabitants of the garden.[258] Both "were raised on the tree," as Philemon reminds him[259] so that "whoever hosts the worm needs his brother."[260] Both epics, Dante's 14th century *Commedia* and Jung's 20th century epic mimetically patterned in its vision and in its organic form, resolve nothing; better actually, they underscore the poetic power and presence of paradox as the authentic and sustained stance of the soul. In my mind Jung breaking off both his transcription as well as the Epilogue[261] does not leave anything unresolved. Something may appear complete, but the work is never truly finished. Such is the paradox of the images with which both epic poets conclude.

References

Alighieri, Dante, 1981 *Inferno. The Divine Comedy of Dante Alighieri.* Trans. Allen Mandelbaum. New York: Bantam Books.

_____. 1983. *Purgatorio. The Divine Comedy of Dante Alighieri.* Trans. Allen Mandelbaum. New York: Bantam Books.

_____. 1984. *Paradiso. The Divine Comedy of Dante Alighieri.* Trans. Allen Mandelbaum. New York: Bantam Books.

_____. 1973. *Dante's Vita Nuova.* Trans. Mark Musa. Bloomington: Indiana University Press.

---

257 *Paradiso,* l. 145.
258 *The Red Book,* p. 359.
259 *The Red Book,* p. 359.
260 *The Red Book,* p. 359.
261 *The Red Book,* p. 360, n. †.

Aristotle, 4th century/1961. *Aristotle's Poetics*. Trans. S.H. Butcher. New York: Hill and Wang.

Butcher, S.H., 1902/1934. *Aristotle's Theory of Poetry and Fine Art, with Critical Text and Translation*. London/New York, MacMillan and Company Limited, 1902.

Cook, Michael L., 1997. *Christology as Narrative Quest*. Collegeville, MN.: The Liturgical Press.

Cowan, Louise, 1984. Introduction: The comic terrain. *The Terrain of Comedy*. Ed. Louise Cowan.1-18. Dallas: The Dallas Institute of Humanities and Culture.

_____. 1992. Introduction: Epic as cosmopoesis. *The Epic Cosmos*. Ed. Larry Allums. 1-26. Dallas: The Dallas Institute of Humanities and Culture.

Furman-Adams, W., 2009. Dante's letter to Can Grande della Scala: Excerpts from a translation by Nancy Howe. web.whittier.edu/people/WebPages/PersonalWebPages/furmanadams/LettertocanGrandeExcerpts.HTM

Hillman, James, 1975. *Revisioning Psychology*. New York: Harper and Row.

Homer, *The Odyssey*. Trans. and Ed. Albert Cook. Norton Critical Edition. 1-356. New York: W. W. Norton and Company.

Johnson, Robert, 1991. *Owning Your Own Shadow: Understanding the Dark Side of the Psyche*. San Francisco: Harper San Francisco.

Jung, C.G., 2009. *The Red Book: Liber Novus*. Ed. Sonu Shamdasani. Trans. Mark Kyburz, John Peck and Sonu Shamdasani. New York: W.W. Norton and Company in the Philemon Series of the Philemon Foundation.

_____. 1957/1969. *The Structure and Dynamics of the Psyche*. CW 8. Note: References to *The Collected Works of C.G. Jung* are cited in the text as CW, volume number and paragraph number. *The Collected Works* are published in English by Routledge (UK) and Princeton University Press (USA).

_____. 1968. *Psychology and Alchemy*. CW 12.

_____. 1930/1966 *The Spirit in Man, Art and Literature*. CW 15.

_____. 1934/1968. *The Archetypes and the Collective Unconscious*. CW 9i,

_____. 1923/1990. *Psychological Types*. CW 6.

Kempis, Thomas à., 1418/2005. *Wellsprings of Faith: The Imitation of Christ.* 1-247. New York: Barnes and Noble.

Madden, Kathryn Wood, 2008. *Dark Light of the Soul.* Great Barrington, MA: Lindisfarne Press.

Mazzotta, Giuseppe, 1992. *Dante: Poet of the Desert.* Princeton: Princeton University Press.

Miller, David, 2004. *Hells and Holy Ghosts: A Theopoetics of Christian Belief.* New Orleans: Spring Journal Books.

Rowland, Susan, 2005. *Jung as a Writer.* New York: Routledge.

_____. 2010. C.G., *Jung in the Humanities: Taking the Soul's Path.* New Orleans: Spring Journal Books.

Schwartz-Salant, Nathan, The Mark Of One Who Has Seen Chaos: A Review of C.G. Jung's *Red Book. Quadrant,* volume xxxx:2, Summer 2010.11-40.

Slattery, Dennis Patrick, 2008. Dante's terza rima in *The Divine Comedy:* The Road of Therapy. In *The International Journal of Transpersonal Studies.*, vol. 27, Fall. 1-10.

_____. 2010. Psychic energy's portal to presence in myth, poetry and culture. In *Eranos Yearbook, 2006/2007/2008.* Ed. John van Praag and Riccardo Bernardini. Einsiedeln, Switzerland: Daimon-Verlag. 435-474..

_____. 1992. The narrative play of memory in epic. *The Epic Cosmos.* Ed. Larry Allums. 331-352. Dallas: The Dallas Institute of Humanities and Culture.

Stevens, Wallace. 1997. *Collected Poetry and Prose.* New York: The Library of the Americas.

Ulanov, Ann, 2010. "God Climbs Down to Mortality: Jung in His Red Book." pp. 61-78. Quadrant XXXX:2 Summer 2010.

5

Mimesis, Neurology and the Aesthetics of Presence

*In the intense instance of imagination, when the mind, Shelley says, is a
fading coal that which I was is that which I am and that in possibility I
may come to be.*

—Stephen Daedalus[262]

A deep affinity exists between poetic knowledge and psychological knowing. Such a relationship allows these two fields of experience and their expression to share a common ground. That shared base consists of analogy, metaphor, symbol, mimetic similitude as well as an aesthetic sense. Singly or combined, these elements comprising a knowing by indirection are what make possible an act of imagination which I define here as a presencing into form. Both psyche and poiesis have the capacity to discover relationships in an imagination that is analogical by design and creative in intent.

I wish to develop here the idea of psycho-poetics, wherein psyche is engaged in creating simulacra of its experiences, often with an aesthetic design, through poetry, to articulate in language—setting aside for the moment other creative forms—an appeal to others who seek to enter this same experience by analogy. Such a creation engages a movement that is both spiralic and creative, forging new iterations of itself that persuasively convey the deep texture of its multi-laden experiences. Psycho-poetics

---

262 in James Joyce's, *Ulysses*, p. 187.

is the means for conveying an original form of knowledge. James S. Taylor deploys something of this form of knowledge when he writes: "Poetic knowledge is a kind of natural, everyman's metaphysics of common experience. It is a way of restoring [restorying?] the definition of reality to mean knowledge of the seen and unseen."[263] The literary theorist Louise Cowan calls such a form of knowledge "a shaping force in culture" and concludes that we have abdicated poetry as the basis for this power to shape both the imagination of an individual as well as that of an entire culture. Poetry, she continues, "carries a self-organizing quality so that the material has a chance to find its own shape and can change shape with each reading."[264]

The poetic response is shape-shifting and thus able to accommodate new information and multiple levels of interpretation; its natural motion is analogical, a fundamental impulse in the soul to seek similarities within difference. Analogies, then, as forms of knowing by indirection, carry within them a tension and a psychic energy between what is like and what is dissimilar in order to successfully hold the two in a field of meaning.

C.G. Jung conveys a similar sentiment in his own understanding of the psyche's basic motion when he asserts that "Since analogy formation is a law which to a large extent governs the life of the psyche...."[265] The motion or action of psyche, one could add, is towards imitation, representation and duplication in another register, of an original event, person, object or image. A brief description of a concrete experience may serve to ground this speculation and reveal the fundamental analogical quality of psyche's poetic motion. This experience assisted me in becoming conscious of my own lived experience first through the embodied action of a literary classic wherein analogy formation surfaced to deepen a personal event. I will also engage the creation of three of my own poems to explore further this transfer of energy from events recollected to poetic responses to the events' invisible but no less palpable presences.

---

263 Taylor, J., *Poetic Knowledge*, p. 4.
264 Cowan, L., 2006. Lecture, University of Dallas.
265 Jung, CW ¶ 414

From Experience to Poetic Expression

My wife and I live on 5.5 acres of thickly wooded land in a rural area of Texas 40 miles south of Austin and the same distance north of San Antonio. It is 5 p.m. on a late February afternoon. The sun is low in the sky, shining more with a dim glow through the live oaks and mountain laurels that populate our property. Its light breaks up on the front lawn, soaking down to the road some 40 yards from where we now sit. Few vehicles pass by our house; when they do we both wave to one another.

After a few minutes' conversation, my wife Sandy and I sit in silence. I rise to put more branches into the fire I started in the chiminea on our front deck. We sip our drinks and settle into the placid, still air that surrounds us now that it has calmed down after my movements. Overhead, two turkey vultures coast on the updraft rising from the Guadalupe River below us—a 20-minute walk down a serpentine road that leads to its banks. The fire, now newly-replenished, spits and cracks and flames up, then slowly relaxes into a calm but intense burn that warms our legs. The wood turns a grayish white and rises up when a pocket of air is unexpectedly sucked into the chimenea's elongated opening.

I look up and around. The trees are beginning to darken, preparing themselves, I like to imagine, for their night's slumber. The air is soft and light on my wife's face. I feel the welcome glow of warmth from the belly of the clay vessel before us. But mostly it is the light, in broken clots and streams slicing through and settling on and between the darkening forest of trees, that gives rise to an analogous emotion in me. I say out loud: "How beautiful this is." And, in the same instant, I am overcome by a recollection: it is a transformative scene from Herman Melville's epic whale tale, *Moby-Dick,* relayed by Ishmael, the young isolato, who has chosen to deflect impulses of suicide by signing on a whaling vessel as a crew member.

As he sits comfortably with his newly-acquired friend and primal brother, Queequeg, son of a chief from the island of Kokovoko, together they turn the pages of a book by the fire of Peter Coffin's inn as the winter wind howls outside and ice crusts ever thicker on the window, with "phantoms gathering round the casements, and peering in upon us silent, solitary twain; the storm booming without in solemn swells; I began to be sensible of strange feelings." And then Ishmael's epiphany settles over him:

I felt a melting in me. No more my splintered heart and maddened hand were turned against the wolfish world. This soothing savage had redeemed it. There he sat, his very indifference speaking a nature in which there lurked no civilized hypocrisies and bland deceits.[266]

I feel the power of the lines evoked by a corresponding feeling: a melting in me: the air, the light, the fire, my wife of 43 years sitting close by. In this scenic serenity a transformation of attitude takes place: my senses are doubled to include not just the present moment of graceful joy in the fire and the fading light, but the additional formed experience that Ishmael relates, given to me in memory as a poetic imitation of a like experience that orders and deepens my own sensibilities, embodied, affective and transformative.

The power inherent in mimesis' presence, according to Gebauer and Wulf, "allows new thought, new creation, new syntheses to come into being."[267] Mimesis as an imaginative representation, thus introduces, even evokes, the power of the analogical, the way in which consciousness discovers analogies of its experiences in other forms of narrative.[268]

The poet James Joyce, in another context, referred to such an experience as a moment of "esthetic arrest" where, for a brief time, life is held in suspension in the presence of beauty, of a power of energy that makes something present in perceptual and affective splendor.[269] For an instant time stops and an intuitive apprehension beyond the confines of the quotidian allows a presence through a powerful affect.

Campbell amplified this experience of "esthetic arrest" earlier in the same volume on Joyce when he cited the work of John Weir Perry, who uses the term "affect image."[270] Such an image "immediately evokes in the observer *equivalent sentiments* and emotional impulses," which observation Campbell quickly equates with what he himself had defined earlier in his own writing: an effective mythological image is "an energy-evoking and energy-directing sign."[271] Such a memory flooding into my embodied felt sense of a moment of complete contentment sitting on the deck of our home as twilight approached shifted my experience onto a mythic level; such is the

266 Melville, *Moby-Dick*, p. 56.
267 Gebauer and Wulf, *Mimesis*, p. 2.
268 Slattery, *A Hudson View*, p. 442.
269 Campbell, J., *Mythic Worlds, Modern Words*, pp. 19-25.
270 *Mythic Worlds, Modern Words*, p. 3.
271 Campbell, *Thou Art That*, p. 86.

power, or energy force, of myth in its ability to elevate a human event into a formed mythopoetic expression through an innate impulse in the psyche to find equivalences, in this instance, from Melville's novel. Deck image calls to poetic image and something new is created as a response.

The current work of Nancy Mellon has developed further the healing quality of particular stories on certain organs of the body. She writes that, "each [organ] is a gateway of spiritual activity with its own intelligent mind-soul that is very sensitive to whatever is going on in our lives."[272] Recounting the history of one woman suffering from leukemia who mustered the courage to tell of abuses in her past in narrative form, Mellon writes: "In a meditative reverie, she told in metaphor the story of recurrent physical abuse that had occurred several years before the onset of her illness."[273] The healing power of the story was conveyed by "speaking at the imaginative level [which] helped her to remember her real life story and to speak openly through pictures about the traumatic experiences she had endured."[274] When Mellon later read the woman's story back to her, the latter beamed and said that it was "not a bad story!" Her delight in hearing her own narrative read back to her helped to modulate the traumatic events recollected.

Mellon surmises this outlet channel, converting the events of the woman's past into a narrative of the experience, aided her in the eventual cure of her deadly cancer. My sense is that something is transferred in the poetics of story's structure and story's voicing; psychic energy is channeled along different corridors that has the capacity to assist one less in being cured of the past than in being reconciled to it. Through story's aesthetic and emotional presence, past wounds may be given a new form, a formed meaning, and be redeemed in a crucial way to allow one to be liberated from their tidal devastations.

C.G. Jung is very informative here when he reflects on a dream that he and his small seminar were working on.[275] In the discussion he suggested that, "an archetype belongs to the structure of the collective unconscious, but as the collective unconscious is in ourselves, it is also a structure of ourselves. It is part of the basic structure of our instinctual nature."[276] Dreams, he observes further, are guides to helping indi-

---

272 Mellon, N., *Body Eloquence*, p. xviii.
273 *Body Eloquence*, p. xvi.
274 *Body Eloquence*, p. xvi.
275 Jung, C.G., *Dream Analysis*.
276 *Dream Analysis*, p. 129.

viduals return to "an archetypal situation" they have fallen out of, because there "you are in your right instinctive attitude in which you must be when you want to lie on the earth's surface; in your right atmosphere with your right food, etc."[277] He follows this observation with a keen insight that is pertinent for my discussion of mimesis: Jung observes that, "the old priests and medicine men understood the importance of one's moving back into and reclaiming this natural attitude that the archetypal situation renders. He calls on the example of a man bitten by a snake and how he would be treated today under the medical model: "We would give him serum, but the old Egyptian priest would go to his library and get down the book with the story of Isis, take it to the patient and read to him of the Sun God, Ra."[278]

Jung relates the story of how Ra's wife, Isis, placed a sand-viper in her husband's path as he journeyed on foot. The worm was placed just below the sand so that when Ra approached it, the viper bit him. Mother Isis was called in to cure him, but with limited success. So Ra had to surrender his powers to a younger god. This story was related to the man who was bitten by a snake. Jung defends this kind of medical means of curing with story: "they had good results with these methods, so they used them, it was 'good medicine.'"[279] It is as if a co-conspiracy developed between the man's physical wound and the mythic wound in the narrative to create a curative third event. Like may then cure like poetically as well as physiologically; Jung has perhaps discovered here a poetics of the body.

Jung's story is another variation on what the Greeks discovered in mimesis, an imitation of an action that a story carries that resonates invisibly in the soul of the audience, as my earlier story that engaged a scene from *Moby-Dick* resonated in me as a mythopoetic correspondence of the emotional condition I was enjoying sitting on the deck of our home. It also includes the story of the woman suffering from leukemia who placed her past into a narrative form and successfully created mimetically the abuse that had remained for years poisonously invisible and thus self-incarcerating.

Writing on Plato's understanding of mimesis in the *Timaeus*, Stephen Halliwell reveals that this Socratic dialogue suggests, "mimesis is a key to the structure of the world and of reality, which is to be comprehended in terms of correspondences and interrelations between mimetic subjects and objects."[280] More deeply, he senses that

277 *Dream Analysis*, p. 129.
278 *Dream Analysis*, p. 129.
279 *Dream Analysis*, p. 129.
280 Halliwell, S., *Aristotle's Poetics*, p. 118.

mimesis suggests "everything created is a correspondence to what is invisible, a higher order or paradigm of existence."[281] The motion of psycho-poetics includes a synthesis or a constellation of the visible and invisible realms that narratives have the capacity to unite to make our lives' past events into formed and coherent experiences that integrate these two realities, one more attuned to the facts of our past, the other to the mythopoetic truth of our histories. The nature of story-crafting includes a persuasive narrative structure that creates a likeness, an "as if" quality to assist one in regaining a rightful place within an archetypal constant that re-orders one's life. Stories, both told and heard, are transport vehicles that assist us in reentering the archetypal space that Jung pointed to earlier. I believe this re-ordering or re-organizing principle is the substance of myth.

Moreover, in his commentary on Aristotle's *Poetics*, O.B. Hardison reminds us that poetry originates in two natural foundations: Our proneness to imitate and in our delight in harmony and rhythm."[282] He observes that "Aristotle refers to the fact that imitative works, if they are well done, reveal generic qualities: the presence of the universal in the particular, and that the spectator or audience learns from this."[283] What he calls "universal" seems analogous to the archetypal situation Jung described earlier, which emerges or gains visibility through the particulars, in the case above, the snake bite treated with the *narrative* of Ra's snake bite, a poetic venom, so to say, that may hurt in the hearing but which realigns the man bitten in a curative way. In the story is a healing, a right ordering, a mimesis that is medicinal, metaphoric—in short, an analogy of the man's snake bite now expressed in mythopoetic form. I would suggest further that imitation contains a calculus of inspiration; by means of it some curative energy is released to bring one back into right relationship through an imaginal knowing, by way of the power of narrative presence. Energy is reorganized and rebalanced. If Campbell is accurate in calling metaphor "the native tongue of myth,"[284] then this rhetorical and mythopoetic figure, in its expression of a relationship of two unlike things via their likeness, carries within its structure a healing component.

In his fine study of poetic knowledge, James S. Taylor reveals how, for Plato and Aristotle, music, both in the rhythms and harmonies of song and lyre, as well as in the rhythm and harmony of words, must be one of the essentials of learning, for it

281 Halliwell, S., *Aristotle's Poetics*, p. 117.
282 Aristotle, *Aristotle's Poetics*, p. 92.
283 *Aristotle's Poetics*, p. 93.
284 Campbell, J., *Thou Art That*, p. 8.

offers to its audience both pleasure and beauty. For our discussion, moreover, here is the important codicil he adds: in the process of education, "a direct appeal to the sensory-emotional life of the human being is held to be necessary and essential *knowledge.*"[285] He then cites directly from Aristotle's *Politics:* "All men by nature desire to know. An indication of this is the delight we take in our senses...we do not regard any of the senses as Wisdom; yet surely these give the most authoritative knowledge of particulars."[286] From the particulars are gleaned a sense of the universals imbedded in the finite structures of experience. In addition, trusting Plato's *Timaeus,* in the particulars both what is eternal and invisible are invited to shine through.

When we recall Jung's story of the man bitten by a snake, it seems clear that to bring his now-wounded nature back into alignment with an archetypal situation that rightly orders the soul and body in its instinctive nature, narrative becomes an efficacious pathway to healing. In addition, it is not just the content of the story, but the process of its aesthetic ordering, that reclaims both order and balance. When Taylor quotes Socrates' famous insight—"the object of education is to teach us to love what is beautiful"—it includes, as he affirms, "the beauty of 'right judgments,' the 'delight in good dispositions and noble actions,' the pleasure of virtue itself,'"[287] all of which form the container for ancient education. I understand in his observations and in Socrates' insight a parallel or analogy to Jung's sense of "the right instinctive attitude,"[288] that comprises inhabiting an archetypal situation. This right instinctive attitude has its further analogy in Taylor's reading of both Plato and Aristotle in which both agree that "the senses, of their own nature, make a proportionate selection of what is pleasant, what is the 'mean,'....This 'just right' is poetic knowledge, the judgment of the senses, without which all higher learning tends to become dehumanized and increasingly destructive."[289]

---

285 Taylor, J., *Poetic Knowledge*, p. 22.
286 *Poetic Knowledge*, p. 22.
287 *Poetic Knowledge*, p. 21.
288 Jung, *Dream Analysis*, p. 129.
289 *Dream Analysis*, p. 23.

Aesthetics and Poetic Knowledge

Aisthesis includes a shining forth or a showing of itself in its appearance. It carries the sense of exposition, exposure, and expression. It is a moment of anticipation and fulfillment. *Aisthesis* engages a noticing and being noticed by. Its simple design reflects its complex grandeur. It is an instant of a sudden making, which is the original sense of *poiesis,* a shaping into a form that can be comprehended and shared, as was the story of Ra available for healing the snake-bitten man earlier, a poetic move into sunlight and public view that reveals good intentions and silences desires that consume one in the fires of one's own cravings. In its orbit we indeed are transformed such that, in Joseph Campbell's lexicon, we may become transparent to transcendence, absorbed by the wholly other that is us, especially when we tell a story by dropping into the metaphorical "as if" mode of our lives, the fiction in the fabric of our ordinary world, as did the woman suffering from leukemia. She realized herself on a deeper level of being through the narrative she crafted of her past. Her story was an effective form of myth-making. Campbell sheds light on this process when he writes: "And what the myth does is to provide a field in which you can locate yourself."[290] Stories would seem then to help us, either in the crafting, hearing or reading and then recollecting them, to recreate a field in which our identities may be given back to us on fuller richer levels than our awareness had heretofore allowed.

James Hillman writes beautifully about aesthetics: "what the Greeks called aesthesis," which is "the way the world gets to us...through sense perception."[291] In the health of a city's soul life, Hillman links aesthetics to ethics, which we will see shortly, is close to another writer's sense of beauty and justice. Aesthetics is not decoration, or an add-on, after the functions of a thing have been satisfied. It is more primal and imaginal than that and thus necessary for the survival of the soul life of both citizen and community, of consciousness, conscience and even commerce.

To bring some of the above theory to ground, I will use a poem of mine to illustrate how mimesis operates in the soul to achieve at least partially a right ordering through a sensate experience to uncover what might lie below consciousness, and to coax it into a more full and vibrant presence. The creative process informs and promotes a creative healing by forming into a coherent shape what might otherwise be

---

290 Campbell, J., *Pathways to Bliss*, p. xvi.
291 Hillman, J., *City and Soul*, p. 148.

only a fading experience that eventually exits our memory. The psychic energy that attends such an occasion carries with it healing properties.

A few years ago I gave a talk at a *Friends of Jung* group in a southern state. My topic was pilgrimage as soul journey, a subject I developed in a recently published book describing a lengthy pilgrimage of my own.[292] After the presentation, as often happens, a member of the audience, on this occasion, a woman dressed in a rainbow of bright colors, approached me. No sooner did she start telling me why she decided to attend the talk then she began to weep. When I asked her what upset her, she related to me without any hesitation, that her cat of 19 years had died a year ago the weekend of my presentation. It was her only family and now she was about to complete her first year living alone. The anniversary was too much for her and she wanted to share her loss, her grief and this important anniversary with me. I was both moved and honored. I did what I could to comfort her; I told her my wife and I had enjoyed the company of our own pet cats for all the years of our marriage. I told her I would be thinking about her and her beloved pet on Sunday.

That night I dreamed of this woman in her bright multi-colored regalia, her loss, her grief and her willingness to share such an intimate part of her life with me, a complete stranger. In the morning the following lines began to assemble themselves in the following way:

Orange Is the Color of the Grieving Wound

She did not look silly, not at her age.
Wrapped in the colors of fall—yellow
straw hat, orange shawl, the lightness
of filigree, a red blouse and lips the
color of a maple leaf along a road
in Vermont.

She asked of tattoos and what stories

---

292 Slattery, D., *Grace in the Desert.*

might be snagged in the skin of stains of
a riot of ink, she
a tattoo herself, a bright flare against
a drab horizon.

I liked her spunk, alone, unafraid in
the crowd of far younger folk wearing
shadows of clothes, no light from within.

Until her faced changed, grew dark
and far away just an instant before
tears began to bleed the yellows and
orange and reds into a fine and thick
commotion of grief:

"I have such deep wounds in my heart,"
she wept. "My cat, my only family for
19 years, died last year this Sunday.
What am I to do?"

Her question had the gravity of
a thousand leaves zigzagging down
from the great tree of life all at
once.

Buried in the branch of decay I could
not answer. She wept and I faced
the wounds in her heart, now visible,
beginning to speak, beginning to purr
in a ritual chorus of hard wood and stones.

The air grew cold between us. I saw just
above her yellow hat a sun setting on her
70 years.
A blue norther of approaching
winter snows.

Her grief grew bright orange until I could
no longer see her, there, falling
in front of me, my legs rooted in the soil
of her loss.[293]

The impact of her grief in loss was too powerful to disremember. It needed a formed receptacle to contain it, to fix it in words, so it would not be forgotten. There are so many experiences we have that come and go; but when one of them finds its way into our life in uncompromising particularity that refuses to be denied, coupled with a universal power to change us, then it must be codified in a ritual of some sort, as poetry encourages: to seek out some adequate and proper analogies to convey the mystery in the moment, here of another's grief that could no longer be contained. My talk struck something in her—even if only the time of the year I presented it—to discharge the grief she felt. I in turn, moved by her memory and her dread of spending the first year's weekend marking her pet's passing alone, felt both her grief and loneliness as my own. The rhythm of her grief had struck a chord in the cadences of my own losses, beloved pets included. Together, we created a community of loss, of expectation, of anticipation and of annihilation, standing as two merged into one among the crowd of people socializing around us. Her loss and my awareness of it now felt deeply, found common soil in the poem.

Writing of her experience for myself, I felt a healing, a closing of a wound and a strong presence of compassion for the suffering of another. It insisted, moreover, on a public expression of an internal condition, a right—even a rite—ordering in this moment of learning and leaning into her grief that was essential. Her bright clothing, full of radiance, was her grieving uniform, capturing in its sunny brightness and the colors of fall the memory of her pet of almost two decades. She had dressed the part, had made the weekend into a celebration and a dirge in dress that recalled her pet and

293 Slattery, D., *Just Below the Water Line: Selected Poems*, pp. 154-55.

then offered it to me as a gift as we stood by the podium. She, moved by something I had said, and I emotionally shaken by her narrative of loss, was like a snake bite that woke me into a consciousness of another's grief.

I wrote the poem in part to commemorate the moment, the agony of her anticipation of a lonely anniversary and her parti-colored clothes that re-membered the joy of so many years together with her family member whose passing was akin to an affliction opening up before me like a flower blooming in fall. Her own colorful showing forth was a celebration in fabric and design of what she had enjoyed for so many years with her family of one.

Robert Armstrong, writing on the powers of presence in works of art, suggests that the "presence achieved in a work is a sum total of all the powers that excited it, quickening it from its core to its flanks, charging it with significant perusals—the affirmation and interrogations of consciousness."[294] Not one impulse but a constellation of affects feed into what excites both wonder and astonishment that can give form to the experience and relay it thereby to others to feel in a visceral or connatural way. I appreciate Campbell's insight "that the metaphorical languages of mythology and metaphysics are not denotative of actual worlds or gods, but rather connote levels and entities within the person touched by them. Metaphors only seem to describe the outer world of time and place. Their real universe is the spiritual realm of the inner life."[295]

Neuroscience and Mirror Neurons

What Aristotle called mimesis and Jung referenced as finding a right instinctive attitude, Neuroscience designates as mirror neurons. While its complexity admits of only a short mention here, I do believe it crucial as well as provocative to acknowledge the work of this exciting new field, especially neurobiology, and specifically the work of Daniel Siegel on mindfulness, meditation and resonance with the world through specific areas of the brain. My intention is not to reduce the above illustrations to a scientific analysis, but rather to explore analogies between Siegel's discoveries that pertain to the discussion above. In his more popular book, *The Mindful Brain*, he outlines

294 Armstrong, R. P., *The Powers of Presence*, pp. 15-16.
295 Campbell, J., *Thou Art That*, p. 7.

the nature and structure of mirror neurons, which, among other duties, allow us to become aware of awareness itself as well as attend to *intention* that he outlines in Appendix III in a section of the same name.[296]

Within what he and others label our "social brain" is a mirror neuron system. Part of its workings allows each of us to "perceive the intentional goal-directed actions of others and link this perception to the priming of the motor systems to engage in that same action."[297] We, in effect, prepare to mirror in our own actions the behavior of others as one effective way to gain mindfulness towards them by attuning ourselves to their behavior. One of the results of such action is an increased awareness of the other through compassion. In the act of mirroring the other, we attune ourselves more cogently and directly with the other and in an imaginal way become the other, what Campbell calls "*tat twam asi*," "thou art that."[298]

Siegel labels this action the building of a "resonance circuit,"[299] which "directly involves the mirror neurons"[300] that promotes or fosters "imitative action" through the developed neural and affective condition of "resonance."[301] I hesitate to call his discovery a physiological mimesis, yet as Stephen Halliwell observes, the classical notion of mimesis "described a number of types of correspondence."[302] Halliwell goes on to discuss how Aristotle's guiding principle of mimesis is of "enactment;"[303] both enactment and narrative are two modes of mimesis. Mirror neurons seem to be inflected most emphatically in enactment; my poem above based on the woman's grieving, is closer to a narrative form of mimesis.

To return to Siegel: he then cites two other neuroscientists working on how we are able to empathize with others and ourselves: "Empathy is not a simple resonance of affect between the self and others. It involves an explicit representation of the subjectivity of the other."[304] Such a condition implicates the neural activity of "the ventral prefrontal cortex, with its strong connections with the limbic system, dorsolateral and

---

296 Siegel, D., *The Mindful Brain*, p. 347.

297 *The Mindful Brain*, p. 347.

298 Campbell, J., *Thou Art That*, p. 26.

299 Siegel, *The Mindful Brain*, p. 350.

300 *The Mindful Brain*, p. 350.

301 *The Mindful Brain*, p. 353.

302 Halliwell, S., *Aristotle's Poetics*, p. 111.

303 *Aristotle's Poetics*, p. 128.

304 Siegel, *The Mindful Brain*, p. 354.

medial prefrontal areas...."[305] Most fascinating for me in his discussion in Appendix III[306] is the work of two other researchers, Decety and Chaminade (2003) who have discovered that,

> Neuroimaging studies strongly support the view that during the observation of actions produced by other individuals, and during *the imagination of one's own actions*, there is specific recruitment of the neural structures which would normally be involved in the action generation of the same actions.... In this model, perception of emotion would activate the neural mechanisms that are responsible for the generation of emotions. Such a mechanism would prompt the observer *to resonate with the state of another individual*, with the observer activating the motor representations that gave rise to the observed stimulus....[307]

From these observations on Neuroscience, I wonder if the ancient Greeks grasped something of this physical phenomenon in their discovery of mimesis, wherein, for example, the action of Sophocles' *Oedipus Rex* performed on stage could elicit a similar set of emotions, including compassion, for the spectacle unfolding before them, and that this new discovery of mirror neurons less explains the phenomenon so much as it further delineates the ability of each of us to place ourselves in the emotional field of another with such force and authority that we are transformed in our own lives through empathy and compassion. The poem I wrote as a response to being with the woman whose pet had died was a mimetic response to being in her grief with her the evening before.

In his *Poetics*, Aristotle called it pity, along with fear, but we might want to shift it and call it compassion or empathy. He writes: "For the plot ought to be so constructed that, even without the aid of the eye, he who hears the tale told will thrill with horror and melt to pity at what takes place."[308] I would concentrate on his observation that "the plot ought to be so constructed," for it locates what has an analogous affect in the audience through the mirroring neurons that allow us as witnesses to participate affectively by analogy, in the mythos that underscores the logos of the drama. The plot's very structure finds an invisible correspondence in the patterns of our own psyche.

---

305 *The Mindful Brain*, p. 354.
306 *The Mindful Brain*, pp. 337-362.
307 *The Mindful Brain*, p. 353. (My italics)
308 Aristotle, *Aristotle's Poetics*, (336 BCE/1961) pp. 78-79.

In a section entitled "The Origin of Poetry and the Growth of Drama" Aristotle observes: "Speaking generally, the origin of the art of poetry is to be found in two natural causes: for the process of imitation is natural to man from childhood on: Man is differentiated from other animals because he is the most imitative of them, and he learns his first lessons through imitation...and all men find pleasure in imitation.[309] The impulse to imitate is of the instincts, and, as Siegel's work as well as others would confirm, it is neurobiological through mirroring neurons that in their behavior give rise to empathy and compassion through resonance and attunement to the other. Jung's story earlier of the man bitten by a snake being offered an analogous story of a god bitten by a snake seems to rest on the same root belief: by being offered a mimetic mirror in narrative form, the consequence might well be a healing through that narrative as it resonates within the field of his own affliction. As Greek scholar, S.H. Butcher, affirms in his classic study of Aristotle's theories of art, and that Francis Fergusson cites in his Introduction, "the praxis [the action] that art seeks to reproduce is mainly a psychic energy working outwards."[310] Fergusson adds immediately following: "It may be described metaphorically as the focus or movement of the psyche toward what seems good to it at the moment."[311]

Such is the case, I suspect, in our emotional life as well. What, I asked myself, has been the presence of resentment in certain life circumstances I have suffered? What would resentment look like poetically if I were to give it a voice, shape and form? In what manner would it appear if I were to remain faithful to its affective presence in my life? I had read about resentment from a psychoanalytic format, but would it be the same if I offered it an occasion to have its own voice? The following poem is one response to the question:

Zone of Resentment

Thick with the sludge of
a thousand wounds

---

309 *Aristotle's Poetics*, (1968) p. 7.
310 *Aristotle*, 1961/1969, p. 8.
311 *Aristotle*, 1961/1969, p. 8.

carried in pouches, bags
and a velvet valise

portable, permanent and
more precise than the budding of
a cactus in April

the zone of moans and
scratches of torn fabric

knees worn to the bone
from constant surrender.

In the zone of resentment
joy is murdered, disallowed
banished in twilight.

The zone harbors contrary
energies of a past packed
like crushed boxes in a garage whose
door must never be opened
never spoken.

Harpoons of past wounds
twisted into spirals push out
of the hide of horrid memories

corkscrews of pain that ooze
the past's permanent pillages.

The zone bursts with laborious
feats of painful punctures
to the heart.

> But others cannot hear its
>
> whispers of pain
>
> so they assume that one's life
>
> is absent regret.[312]

I was surprised at such a turnout. I cannot explain the images any more than I can do justice to the complexity of a dream. But one thing I feel certain about: the images emerged and arranged themselves from the deep recesses of the emotion that can dismember one, steal one's freedom and leave one hardened and envious; but externally it may not be detected. Inwardly it can act as "corkscrews of pain" that are always present, always spiraling into the flesh of joy, contentment and serenity.

So rather than explicating the poem, I want to recall what happened in its making: it was as if I opened to resentment not as something to rid myself of, but rather to invite it to be heard for the first time on its own terms. I never feel as if I am in control of the process; the impetus and the energy herd together someplace else and descend to the pen or the keyboard. The process is closer to a moment of recollection of an event that metamorphoses into a shaped set of images, sometimes with a narrative line, but just as often with juxtaposed images that coalesce into one another to shape coherence through the power of making something present that did not exist before. Resentment assumes a new face in the creative process, an original disposition. In the engagement I deepen my felt sense of Resentment's power and persistence.

In the process, some hold of this emotion on me is loosened, is less contagious and toxic. I have, for whatever worth it may possess, created a mimetic form of Resentment; it represents something of the devastating and debilitating sense of resenting someone or something, but it has now acquired an aesthetic face that transcends the mere emotional feeling of resenting some presence in my life. I also sense that in the poem I have mythologized Resentment; it is mine and yet larger, more universal. The metaphors that visited Resentment may have offered this eroding emotion a new energy, to be contemplated by readers who can test its veracity off their own experience of resentment.

---

312 Slattery, D., *Hudson View Poetry*, pp. 62-63.

Mimesis, Beauty and Justice

A final and extremely helpful voice to round out this topic is Elaine Scarry's small elegant book, *On Beauty and Being Just*, which contains crucial insights into the mimetic mode, learning and aesthetics. Her keen views on the nature of beauty are not unrelated to either Aristotle or Siegel's discoveries cited earlier. "Beauty," she writes in an early meditation, "brings copies of itself into the world. It makes us draw it, take photographs of it, or describe it to other people,"[313] which is what I wished to express of my own experience of being in tune with the closing of the day or entering the grieving circle of the woman whose loss of her pet profoundly altered her life or establishing a new relationship with Resentment. All of these comprise experiences that are both aesthetic and mimetic in nature. Scarry continues by observing that beauty "sometimes gives rise to exact *replication* and other times to *resemblances* and still other times to things whose connection to the original site of inspiration is unrecognizable."[314]

From her insight above I gather the following:

1. A sense of abundance attends beauty's presence.
2. Beauty affords or makes possible a moment of largesse, which may take the form of compassion through a suffering-with.
3. Beauty can issue in forgiveness. In the moment of beauty's presence I sense an opportunity to forgive others and myself.
4. In the presence of beauty wounds can heal, or at least close a bit further than they had previously been allowed or invited to.

Scarry continues her own attunement to beauty by suggesting that there exists a willingness by others to "continually revise one's own location in order to place oneself in the path of beauty. She suggests that "first, beauty is sacred....Second, beauty is unprecedented....Something beautiful fills the mind yet invites the search for something beyond itself, something larger or something of the same scale with which it needs to be brought into relation."[315]

---

313 Scarry, E., *On Beauty and Being Just*, p. 3.
314 *On Beauty and Being Just*, p. 3, (My italics)
315 *On Beauty and Being Just*, pp. 22-29.

I understand her discussion of beauty's qualities above to point to some action of seeking resemblance, or mirroring, and to move into attunement or in accord with the beautiful. Here she taps one of the wellsprings of mimesis: the desire or impulse or energy that gathers around an aesthetic experience that nudges one to discover, create, or to invent in order to draw one deeper into the beautiful. Beauty, as I understand her insights, would seem to prompt in me a quiet energy, a fortitude, even courage; it also incites a *poiesis*, a making or an actively imagined shaping, to create an analogy of the object or a simulacrum of the relationship of my experience with the beautiful. Perhaps we need moments of aesthetic presence to align or re-align our courage to be and to do, rather than to have. Aesthetics does not provoke desire for possession but is instead an impulse to promulgation. Aesthetics is a call in the soul for abundance.

Scarry further observes that beauty 's elastic capacity to hurl us forward and back, "requiring us to break new ground, but obliging us also to bridge back...to still earlier, ancient ground—is a model for the pliancy and lability of consciousness in education."[316] Now these elastic qualities of pliancy and mutability are the necessary ground, it seems to me, for transforming something of ourselves into another level of resiliency, of malleability and elasticity. Beauty aids us in avoiding an arthritic sensibility where our movements can become too narrow and restricted. I believe this is the stuff and stature of compassion: a willingness and openness to be softened, reshaped, re-formed and remade within the architecture of unfamiliar ground, as Ishmael experienced in the presence of Queequeg earlier and that I felt deeply in front of the woman who related the loss of her pet.

I say this because of a further development in Scarry's argument: [that] "beauty and truth are allied is not a claim that the two are identical. It is not that a poem or a painting or a palm tree or a person is 'true,' but rather that it ignites the desire for truth...."[317] But beauty is, she claims dozens of pages later, an awakening of perception[318] so that one sees more, not less of beauty's impact on a sense of justice and "fair" play. Beauty can do so because it "affirms the aliveness of the other"[319] in a cooperative of mutual respect. "Fairness," she claims, implicates "loveliness of countenance" as well as an ethical requirement of playing fair, being fair and acting fairly.[320] Justice,

---

316 *On Beauty and Being Just*, p. 46.
317 *On Beauty and Being Just*, p. 52.
318 *On Beauty and Being Just*, p. 81.
319 *On Beauty and Being Just*, p. 89.
320 *On Beauty and Being Just*, p. 91.

therefore, captures both the beauty of fairness and the ethical quality of being fair. In this sense, Justice is closer to Aristotle's idea of a right ordering of the soul, a "'just right' is poetic knowledge."[321] To love what is beautiful is at the same time to love what is good, which is an impulse to what is just.

I end this discussion of beauty and mimesis by citing a large influence on Scarry in her deliberations on beauty and ethics as a call to being more just: Iris Murdoch. In a talk she gave in 1967 on the nature of goodness and ethics, Murdock argued that, "anything which alters consciousness in the direction of unselfishness, objectivity and realism is to be connected with virtue."[322] She aligns herself with Scarry's interest by affirming what in our surroundings is an occasion for "unselfing," and that is what is popularly called beauty."[323] Beauty, rightly congealed in the imagination of the heart, places us "in the service of something else."[324] We step off the center stage of importance and allow the other—be it an image, an idea, a person, an impulse—to assume greater prominence. This may be the moment in which we have engaged the most equality, by attending to the role, as Scarry calls it, "of the lateral figure."[325]

Poetics and Beauty

Earlier I used two poems of mine to engage dual realities: the lived experience of the woman grieving over the loss of her pet, and the poem that such engagement prompted in me to give it a form and shape that, to my mind, went beyond the event and into the invisible workings of an imaginal experience. I also gave a new form to Resentment. I end with a poem that arose out of the act of reading, another complex and rich rite that engages the imagination on several levels at once and often prompts the memory to engage the present.

After many years of my first reading of the Book of Job and then Jung's now classic *Answer to Job* (1952/1956), I returned to both works and read them in succession. As with all archetypal figures in fiction, legend and myth, Job had altered profoundly in

---

321 Halliwell, *Aristotle's Poetics*, p. 23.
322 Scarry, E., *On Beauty and Being Just*, p. 112.
323 *On Beauty and Being Just*, p. 113.
324 *On Beauty and Being Just*, p. 113.
325 *On Beauty and Being Just*, p. 113.

my imagination. After rereading both works, I found myself reflecting on this mysterious mythic figure and decided to allow Job's complex character to present itself in a new form, to witness in an image or through a glass starkly how this great poetic figure had begun to live in my memory. The creation that emerged below is both my own representation of Job as well as the archetypal figure in the two texts that birthed him.

Job's Cycle

In dirt the texture of his
own sadness Job covers
his scabs with the day dust of
the desert and speaks words
to wet the inside of the Earth.

Suffering suffers its own wounds.
Eliphaz believes no accidents
happen without some beast aroused
in night waters; it stirs into life
the smallest coin of joy
because sadness carpets its way.

Throwing jewels before Leviathan
brings from the deep afflictions that
pass him by—scales from scabs
turn to beetles, crawl
across his face seeking forgiveness
searching for solace
in the red glow of an exhausted sun.

Eager to dissolve along earth lines,

mockery's effort is futile.

Job reaches for his cane, enters

his tent haunted by sweet confusion.

His love of the dust emerges from hiding

offers him manna (the bandage has not

yet been invented).

Inside his tent a small fire

cooks to cinders each whirlwind

that spirals through the flaps of

hide.

Far in the corner against the

animal skin

the moon rises in red splendor.[326]

Certainly it is not possible to give any exact correspondence of the original with what affected me about this grand, even epic figure, in history and poetry. But what is visible in the poem is a mimetic representation, or a correspondence with the original figure, as well as actions that depict him for me in a lived, embodied way. The Job in my poem is a sliver of the original but no less real as an imaginal presence. I agree with the philosopher and literary theorest Jacques Maritain, who writes that "in poetic knowledge emotion carries the reality which the soul suffers—a world in a grain of sand—into the depth of subjectivity, and of the spiritual unconscious of the intellect, because in the poet...the soul remains, as it were, more available to itself....[327] His idea of a spiritual unconscious suggests that poetry's force lies partly in its ability to descend into the spiritual depth of the soul and to extract from it an apt analogy of the original's being that is both personal and universal in design. My Job was birthed out of the original as I experienced it and thus may carry some of the original's shards with it; the created poem extends and deepens my engagement with this figure of the

---

326 Slattery, *A Hudson View*, pp. 32-33.
327 Maritain, J., *Creative Intuition in Art and Poetry*, p. 122.

imagination. He becomes more, not less real and relevant to my psychic landscape for having been forged anew.

It also carries with it an aesthetic felt sense of the original and, if I can phrase it this way, justifies, for me, Job's extended life span in the world. Job is present to be made anew in the way myths remain vibrant when they are allowed to develop, transform, and accrue new life in history's unfolding.

Finally, what my rereading the Book of Job and Jung's commentary that brought the desire to recreate this loveable figure in my own mirrored neurological way, was an active wondering about him in revisiting his world. Aristotle writes in the *Metaphysics* with passion on this capacity in the soul to become enchanted with what is and then to know it anew through what can be: the quality of wonder:

> It is owing to their wonder that men both now begin and at first began to philosophize; they wondered originally at the obvious difficulties....A man who is puzzled and wonders thinks himself ignorant (whence even the lover of myth [poetry] is in a sense a lover of Wisdom, for the myth is composed of wonders....For all men begin, as we said, by wondering that things are as they are.[328]

Wonder continues, I believe, by taking in things as they are and then crafting them as they might be, as I attempted to do in my own poems presented in this essay. Poetry allows for such a thrust into the future based on the past's intrusion into the present. The Egyptian wise man who read the story of Ra to the snake-bitten man both acknowledged his pain in the present and imagined his cure through narrative in the future. Poetry lives in the tension between past-present-future and takes in the entirety of the person: imaginal, embodied, spiritual and psychic. The fullness of poetic utterance offers such a pleroma of being by which we may measure the miracle of our days.

As to what I risked saying about my own work, I am compelled to relay the advice Jung offered in one of his best portrayals of the creative process (1966):

> Poets are human too and what they say about their work is often far from being the best word on the subject. It seems as if we have to defend the seriousness of the visionary experience against the personal resistance of the poet himself.[329]

Such a cautionary note modulates any and all explications I have made about the process of my own creative temper.

328 Halliwell, *Aristotle's Poetics*, p. 24.
329 Jung, CW, ¶ 147.

References

Aristotle, (336 B.C.E./1968). *Aristotle's Poetics.* (Leon Golden, Trans.). Commentary O.B. Hardison, Jr. Englewood Cliffs, New Jersey: Prentice-Hall.

_____. (336 B.C.E./1961). *Aristotle's poetics* (S.H. Butcher, Trans.) Introduction by Francis Fergusson. New York: Hill and Wang.

Armstrong, R. P., (1981). *The Powers of Presence: Consciousness, Myth and Affecting Presence.* Philadelphia: University of Pennsylvania Press.

Butcher, S.H., (1920). *Aristotle's Theory of Poetry and Fine Art. With a Critical Text and Translation of the Poetics.* Third edition. London; MacMillan and Co., Limited.

Campbell, J., (2004). *Pathways to Bliss: Mythology and Personal Transformation.* Novato, California: New World Library.

_____. (1993/2003). *Mythic Worlds, Modern Words: Joseph Campbell on the Art of James Joyce.* Novato, California: New World Library.

_____. (2001). *Thou Art That: Transforming Religious Metaphor.* Novato, California: New World Library.

Cowan, L., (2007). "Poetic Knowledge." Lecture at the University Dallas, Irving, Texas.

Gebauer, G & C. Wulf, (1995). *Mimesis: Culture, Art and Society.* Berkeley: University of California Press.

Halliwell, S., (1987). *The Poetics of Aristotle: Translation and Commentary.* Chapel Hill: The University of North Carolina Press.

_____. (2002) *The Aesthetics of Mimesis: Ancient Texts and Modern Problems.* Princeton, NJ: Princeton University Press.

_____. (1998). *Aristotle's Poetics.* Chicago: University of Chicago Press.

Hillman, J., (2006). *City and Soul.* Vol. 2 of *The Uniform Edition of the Writings of James Hillman.* (R. J. Leaver Ed.). Putnam, CT: Spring Publications.

Joyce, J., (1982) *Ulysses.* Foreword by Anthony Burgess. New York: Modern Library: Book-of-the-Month Club, 1982.

Jung, C.G., (1938/1984*) Dream Analysis: Notes of the Seminar Given in 1928-1930.* (William McGuire, Ed.). Princeton, NJ: Princeton University Press.

_____. *The Collected Works of C.G. Jung.* (H. Read, M. Fordham, G. Adler & W. McGuire, Eds. R.F. C. Hull, Trans.) London: Routledge & Kegan Paul.Vol. 9,ii. *Aion (*1959).

_____. Vol.15. *The Spirit in Man, Art and Literature* (1966).

Maritain, J., (1954). *Creative Intuition in Art and Poetry. The A.W. Mellon Lectures in the Fine Arts.* Bollingen Series XXXV.1. New York: Pantheon.

Mellon, N., (2008*). Body Eloquence.* Santa Rosa, CA. Energy Psychology Press.

Melville, H., (1851/1977). *Moby-Dick, or, The Whale.* Norwalk, Connecticut. The Easton Press.

Scarry, E., (1999). *On Beauty and Being Just.* Princeton, NJ: Princeton University Press.

Siegel, D., (2008). *The Mindful Brain: Reflections and Attunement in the Cultivation of Well-Being.* New York: Norton.

Slattery, D., (2004). *Grace in the Desert: Awakening to the Gifts of Monastic Life.* San Francisco, CA: Jossey-Bass, Inc.

_____. (2004). *Just Below the Water Line: Selected Poems.* Goleta, CA: Winchester Canyon Press.

_____. (2010). Job's Cycle. *A Hudson View: Poetry Digest.* Winter 2010. Vol. 5, #3. Stormville, New York: Waterforest Press. pp. 32-33.

_____. (2010). Psychic Energy's Portal to Presence in Myth, Poetry and Culture. *Eranos yearbook: 2006/2007/2008,* pp.435-474. (J. van Praag and Riccardo Bernardini, Eds.), Einsieldeln: Daimon-Verlag.

_____. (2011). Zone of Resentment. *Hudson View Poetry.* 62-63. Spring 2011. International Collection, vol. 6, #2. Stormville, New York: Waterforest Press.

Taylor, J., (1998*). Poetic Knowledge: The Recovery of Education.* Albany, NY: SUNY Press.

II

Cultural Essays

6

Motorcycling as Myth and as Metaphor

I do not claim any inside skid marks on riding motorcycles, repairing them, sleeping with them or treating them as a god or goddess. But I do believe that owning and riding a motorcycle, whether alone or in clubs, groups, or even gangs, offers more than simple travel. I state boldly at the beginning that there exists in the motorcycle and in its operation some mythic underpinning, something invisible working on us, changing our behavior, shifting our gears from one attitude to another. Some imaginal quality surrounds the motorcycle in our culture: it carries a passenger load of promises, some of which I will try to elucidate.

Riding evokes in us—perhaps I should shift the pronoun and say ME—for I cannot speak for you—a hunger, a desire, some deeply satisfying emotion in motion, not only in riding a motorcycle, but equally critical, in cleaning, waxing, maintaining, and repairing it. Something in the imagination is fired up in owning, operating and maintaining a motorcycle. While individuals may indeed "bond" with their cars or trucks, that intimacy does not begin to touch the attachment that grows up between a person and his/her motorcycle.

Now the unreflective may claim quickly: "Hell, I just ride for fun and to drink beer and hang out. What's the deal here?" Well, if that is where you are, God bless. What I have to say probably won't make much difference to you and I don't want to upset your equilibrium with any reflections that would tarnish the above attitude or throw a pothole in your road to send you skidding off balance. But others of you may have thought, while riding or cleaning your bike, changing the oil and filter, replacing

129

spark plugs, adding air to the tires, or in feeling the growing excitement stir in you over buying a new bike and fantasizing a road trip: What is the appeal here? What is the source of the surge I sense in riding, or even in anticipating riding?

I believe we are talking about a shifted attitude, a style of seeing, through motorcycles. To call it mythic is not an overstatement as I think more about it. Some fundamental questions, then, might be worth posing: What history do you bring to the ride? When did you begin riding? What kind of motorcycle has appealed to you? Has that appeal changed over the years? What satisfaction do you feel in riding? Has it diminished? Intensified? These and like questions might move us closer to the myth of motorcycling, which can be both intimately personal and yet touch some universal quality or feeling in the soul.

A short story—and don't we ride in part, to have stories to tell one another? Get two or more motorcyclists together at a restaurant or in a parking lot, even along side of the road, then count how many seconds before one starts telling the others a story about a ride or about their own history of riding, or what bikes they have owned over time. The stories are as much a part of ownership and riding as the rubber is to the tires that support you. My wife and I, for instance, have on many Saturday mornings ridden either the Honda Goldwing or Harley Davidson Electra Glide Classic to Luckenback, Texas some 70 miles northwest of our home. There we hear and tell our motorcycle stories to a growing crowd. Riders come to tell their tales and display their chromed out cycles while being entertained by other storytellers.

I grew up in Cleveland, Ohio, in a home that was pretty much traumatized every weekend by a seriously committed alcoholic father. During the week his demeanor was very mild, his reticence palpable. He bussed to work, spoke little to us during the week and kept pretty much to himself. On the weekend the transformation was rather abrupt and intense. He grew increasingly cantankerous, mean even, and slowly transformed the house into an unlivable chaos. He was, in short, one of the main reasons I took to motorcycles early—as an adventurous and exotic escape from the bedlam, from emotional assaults and demeaning attacks.

When I was 15 a close friend, a "double winner" with two alcoholic parents, saved enough money to buy a used 650 BSA, a great British bike with straight pipes, lots of chrome, black paint, high bars and a seductive guttural-sounding engine. No windshield. That was cheating. He rounded off his ensemble by buying leathers and having a tattoo of a large and menacing panther scratched into his right bicep, complete with claws that eternally made my friend Rick's arm bleed. In the summer he wore white t-shirts without sleeves so no one would miss his tattoo hanging there aloft on the high bars, toasted by the sun, so that the once luminous blue cat lost some of its luster and vitality after several years, and the original red blood lines from the claws turned a harmless domestic pink. All the charm and numinosity bled slowly from it. Nonetheless, Rick wore it proudly as part of his biker ensemble and an emblem to his windy spirit.

Rick was the one who taught me to ride, to balance myself on the bike at a stop, to coordinate clutch and throttle so that it did not stall or lurch forward and hurl me into a pit of embarrassment. What sent me off in all this was the amount of raw power I suddenly had in my right hand with the simple torque of a gritty rubber handle grip. I can still remember the dizzy thrill of accelerating from a dead stop, without a license, helmet or much sense or skill, in the early 1960s. Cranking up from a dead stop without stalling, which is the worst offense, shifting the gears, learning to coordinate hands and feet, comprised my introductory curriculum.

But most of all, I remember the sound of the engine just inches away from my crotch, and the feel of all that metal beneath me suddenly roar into life, its fierce heat toasting my Levis and tennis shoes. What did I feel at this time? I felt the first deep stirrings of something I think I still grasp for as I approach 70 (that's years, not miles per hour)—a deep sense of freedom, of boundlessness, of a life, even temporary, without boundaries, restrictions or conventions—just a clean and unobstructed view of what was coming up at me so fast I could hardly process the road looming into my vision. I now know that part of the thrill of riding solo for the first time was my inability to think through where I was heading because it was unimportant. I just headed at it, shifting gears, watching the tack and speed with just a fraction of a glance, so frightened and pumped was I to look good and to ride the bike with competence that the squeal inside me that wanted out had to be muted. My identity as a person was absolutely welded to how well I rode. And I knew it. In learning to ride and to feeling independent, I gained some of the lost self-esteem and confidence that living in an alcoholic household tends to vacuum out of its members.

My perception was being shaped toward reality in a way that I could never have imagined. I looked down at the clean, newly painted tank of Rick's BSA and there I saw a distorted image of my fat face reflected—happy, smiling, and joyful, in the moment, with no other thoughts, desires, and ambitions clouding the chrome. Home worries, past cares, future anxieties, all washed-out underneath the plush sound of the motorcycle's perfectly-tuned engine. Past and future dissolved in that instant. I was riding a motorcycle, staying successfully upright, goosing it to hear the pipes respond; it was not an engine groaning under me, tappets clicking beneath the sound of the baffled pipes; it was something alive, organic, tame, kind-of, but always able and willing to destroy me if I lost control or attention to what I was doing, even for an instant. The motorcycle was indeed shaping and customizing my personal myth as well as setting my balance in life in a new way.

This old, but healthy and horsy BSA was a living thing—not like a car or a truck; it was smaller, more organic, and more muscular, more exposed than covered with a hood, and thus more connected to me. I did not ride in it: I rode ON IT, a very different perch from which to view the world going by so quickly that my eyes streamed tears, bugs bounced off my forehead and stung so badly I cried out when their egg-yoked innards splotched against my tender visage. I grimaced and sucked in the pain in an attitude that said I do not give a shish kabob. My feet danced on the pegs, slipped under the shifting arm and hammered down on the back brake lever; my hands squeezed an overly aggressive clutch handle, and my right arm ached from holding open an ornery resistant throttle. Nothing mattered, however, but the fact that within minutes I was now miles from my friend, thinking of whose house I could cruise by and, depending on the current status of our relationship, wave or greet them with one finger extended in salutation. I was completely and totally and irresponsibly—FREE. I still today feel the shades of such freedom when I push my current Honda Goldwing or Harley Davidson Electra-Glide Classic out of the garage, full tank, cell phone, bottles of water all checked in, some cash hidden in the recesses, a plastic Triple A card, all of my contemporary and necessary security nets. But none of these goodies really block, impede or interrupt that old, lively and palpable sense of freedom that I first felt almost 55 years ago. My sense of feeling and solidarity is now enhanced when I ride with one or both sons through the ranch roads to breakfast in Wimberley or Blanco, Texas.

So one part of the myth of motorcycling has just spun its rubber on the road: Freedom. Escape from the mundane; a feeling that shifts like a gear from being or feeling like nobody to being SOMEBODY, somebody who attracted attention and could now be identified. My stock value rose among friends and strangers at my high school; I was now connected with something I loved, rather than shamed by something that pained me, that was a secret I prayed would never be known. I was now recognized, marked out, had a name and a context. I had a viable identity and that identity was inseparable from this machine. When I finally returned his motorcycle to Rick after a joyous and threshold-crossing scoot around the city, dropped its kickstand and walked into his house, I left something of myself back there with it, stuck to the saddle, sticking to the pegs and to the soft heated rubber of the throttle grip. Later I was to learn in reading the works of mythologist Joseph Campbell, that I had activated the archetypal figure of the hero and that my own hero's journey had begun in earnest. I had the heat for the steed; now I needed a grail to pursue, one I could snap up from this two-wheeled perch.

When I completed that first ride, I felt something of the uncanny, of the mysterious, of the unutterable—I felt, in short, the bike's mythic resonance. It had within the molecules of steel and ports a numinosity that was more spiritual and real than anything my religion had ever promised or produced. From my current perspective I have the sense that motorcycle riding may be one of the most powerful mythic encounters one can have. I believe that a motorcycle's power resides in part its ability to spawn or evoke the mythic imagination, where one feels in touch with something out of the ordinary, numinous, and dare I use the word, even Sacred. The god hidden in the recesses of this travel is the figure of Hermes, for the ancient Greeks, the patron saint of the journey. Why no company has yet to call one of their motorcycle models Hermes is surprising.

Now I have used the word "myth" several times already. The Greeks called stories *mythoi;* they were narratives that in their telling and in their content revealed something true and common in human experience; they revealed through symbols, metaphors, figures, and action something of the truth of life that was not measured, quantified or otherwise explainable on a quantitative or rational level. Myths speak of what we value, fear, desire, strive for, and dream deeply about. Joseph Campbell, the foremost cultural voice of myth in the modern world, believed that "Myths are clues to the spiritual potentialities of the human life."[330] They put us into contact with the symbolic order in proportion to the level of energy that the symbol is capable of carrying. Now, is a motorcycle a symbol? Yes and no. Not intrinsically, but in my own life, in the myth I am living out, for we are all engaged in unfolding our own myth. So, yes, a motorcycle can be a symbol—but of what? I think I already mentioned

---

330 Campbell, J., *The Power of Myth*, p. 5.

one: freedom. Others would include self-determined, autonomous, powerful and self-reliant. Another is the dissolution of conventional boundaries. Wear a business suit or high heels during the week, leather and engineer boots on the weekend. Move between two myths. Motorcycles are psychological, symbolic and mythic in addition to being seductive physical transports. They fulfill the definition of a metaphor: as carriers from one world or domain to another. A motorcycle allows boundaries to be suspended for a time, for travel to take on additional piquancy, for the open road and the outdoors to be experienced with an in-your-face sense of reality that enclosed vehicles cannot compete with.

Now I don't want to get too top heavy here, load the saddle bags with too much unnecessary baggage; but think of the word *metaphor*: it comes from two words, as Joseph Campbell maintained: *Meta*=to pass over, going from one place to another, and *phorein*, to move to or carry.[331] So we can fantasize that a motorcycle is a metaphor, for it truly transports us from one reality to another, from one mythos to another, from one narrative to another. Joseph Campbell again: "metaphors let us cross boundaries that are otherwise impossible."[332]

The first time riding a motorcycle was matched by another powerful experience happened not long after my initiation on the same bike with Rick. When we were just 17, I rode as a passenger with him from Cleveland, Ohio to his boyhood home on Long Island, New York and then on to Montauk Point at its tip. We might as well have ridden to the moon and back. Something was promised in the journey, some nugget of value, some treasure hard to attain, some identity still unformed, and landscapes deliciously unknown. Journeying too is a mythic activity, perhaps *the* oldest mythic action humans have initiated, the longer, the more mythically promising. Perhaps it is because the journey occasions events that may then turn into experiences that are then transformed into stories. The journey offers each of us experiences that can potentially transform us.

We left one hot Ohio evening in July around 7, with a tiny suitcase between us, no helmets or leather, just jackets and sweat shirts. We rode south in the lingering dusk light to the Ohio Turnpike, climbed aboard and sailed east at 65 mph towards Pennsylvania. I can still see the brown mole on the lower right side of Rick's neck, just down from his jet-black hairline. I knew it well, for I saw it anytime I looked forward,

---

331 Campbell, J., *Thou Art That* p. 8.
332 *Thou Art That* p. xvi.

which was most of the time. I settled into the ride as a passenger, content to enjoy the feeling of escaping a chaotic couple of weekends at home. I think this is why I associate motorcycles so intimately with freedom, to escaping pain, conflict and to feel instead the evenness and the forgiving nature of the journey.

With every mile my tensions eased; my blood boiled with excitement as we hummed into thinner and thinner traffic until only huge Peterbilt and Kenworth semis were our companions on the road late into the dark night. They and the soothing guttural sounds of the chrome pipes heating up the bottom of my tennis shoes. We had shifted gears into another dimension. We were, to tap the guru of the road the poet, Jack Kerouac, ON THE ROAD. Drowsy and exhausted, I fell asleep leaning against Rick's back and would lurch awake every time I began to fall sideways. How I did not fall on to swift-moving pavement beneath us is one of those mysteries of motorcycle riding I have never grasped. Hermes, I suspect, kept my balance for me as I slipped periodically into his terrain—the landscape of dream.

Around 1a.m. somewhere in Pennsylvania, we pulled into a truck stop. The first thing we heard when our ears ceased ringing from the exhaust pipes, was rolling thunder to our west, bearing down on us through lightning flashes that lit up our tired and road- besmirched faces. We ate, filled the tank and rode out on to the Pennsylvania Turnpike into the mountains just ahead of a storm that within an hour had caught up with us and deluged our unprotected hides on the dark and deserted highway with buckets of rain. We pulled under a bridge, shivering and now completely aware of how inadequately we had prepared for this trip, and suffered the whipping hiss of vapor as semis cruised past us leaving wakes of dirty mist to coat our less-than-white t-shirts.. We were able to fall asleep up under the highway and eventually woke hours later to a dry road and warmer air. We pushed on, shivering in our wet clothes that soon dried in the dawn breeze.

By morning, after 11 hours of riding, we pulled into downtown Manhattan. We had changed our clothes and left some of the wet things hanging from the rear view mirrors to dry. I can see in my memory as if yesterday: driving beneath the Empire State Building, watching New Yorkers heading to work but pausing with curiosity at two red-eyed fugitives on a dirty motorcycle cruising past in frazzled disarray. We loved it and felt very important in the moment. We were eventually to ride some 1300 miles round trip. Years later I could look back on this endurance run and grasp how we had unknowingly entered ritual space, the geography of transition, of a threshold, a liminal zone of living we each did not want to end. Home was never the same after this voyage, as it was never the same when, 3 years later, at age 20, I shipped out from the Cleveland harbor on a German freighter bound for Bremerhaven Germany, but that is another narrative, a sea journey pilgrimage.

Think for a moment, if it applies, of your first motorcycle purchase. How different from one's first car. Everything is different. Space is experienced in a unique way, as is time. Does it seem strange to suggest that motorcycles have their own temporality? The space of a motorcycle is less interior and separate, from outside external world space. On a motorcycle, one traverses space, not quite in it, but in the space of two wheels. "Not the goal but the journey is important" became the motto of Harley Davidson, and it is so. How much motorcycling shifts our perspective from destination to the journey itself. Most of our lives are geared to a goal, a completion of an aim or a purpose, a final result, an ending, a telos; our cultural lives are guided, even possessed by this order of being, of a results-oriented action that is part of our cultural myth to achieve something. The journey is an excuse or a necessary reason for the end, even serving at times as an impediment to the completion of a task.

Part of the myth and mystique of motorcycling shatters this mode of functioning; it dismantles and reverses it. On a motorcycle ride, yes, you may have an end in mind and sight, a rally, for instance, or a weekend ride with a friend within a group or alone. But now, instead of the journey being a necessary condition to the end, which is the central focus, the end is the excuse for the journey. Over time, and with some reflection, we may sense that the destination is indeed the journey itself. In our world of results-orientation, this is a radical departure, a breakthrough. And something else: the austerity, the economy, the smallness and self-contained quality to motorcycle riding that seems to make the journey more intimate, more compact.

Now, fast-forward 16 years from the New York trip. For years, as a graduate student in Dallas, when the academic year ended, I would load up my BMW in mid-May and ride for days to Gethsemane Monastery in Trappist, Kentucky, then on to Cleveland to visit family. At night I pitched my small tent at a public or private campground. Round trip was a little over 3000 miles. This journey became an important annual ritual for me, one wherein my freedom from studies and working two jobs was complete and as desired as it was deserved. It was my reward for completing another school year while working a job at night as a Pinkerton rent-a-cop at a Dallas steel company.

136

I remember how much I enjoyed the ritual of preparing for the trip, packing everything in due measure, careful of the limited space of saddlebags and passenger's seat. Packing would bring out in me a certain care, an economy of mind and heart, along with an economy of goods and an austerity of purpose. Part of the trip's rationale was to escape responsibilities for a couple of weeks; part of it was to forge into the unknown alone, to step across a threshold, to see the world and be seen by it. Journeying is perhaps, as I've said, the oldest action we humans have engaged. So many of the great epics of world literature are comprised of intricate stories of the one journeying. I believe the motorcycle is a mechanical and organic remnant of this ancient tradition. A good friend of mine in Santa Barbara, who had done two tours of duty in Vietnam and was wounded twice, makes the Rolling Thunder ride to the Vietnam Memorial in Washington DC each year on his Harley Davidson. He is one of the main voices in a documentary on this journey for Vietnam vets who need the ritual to reconcile themselves with the experiences that traumatized so many in that conflict. While I did not serve in Vietnam, I can relate to their relationship with trauma, having known many who did.

My gear as I prepared for my own pilgrimage, would consist of a K-Mart pup tent, a sleeping bag, some changes of clothes, a rain suit, an extra pair of shoes, a jacket, an extra tire tube, an air pump, some canned goods of beans and soup, crackers, a leather jacket, a few books and some writing material, and an old anthology of poetry. This last item, along with a roll of duct tape, was central to my travels. I formed the habit, after the boredom of reading license plates had grown intolerable, of tearing out of a used volume of poetry, a new or a favorite poem, taping it to the black BMW tank or cloth travel bag strapped to it and reading it aloud, even memorizing it over time while cruising the interstate, which is actually a pretty safe place in which to read. When I stopped for gas or at a rest stop, I would tear off the poem and replace it with another. I memorized many poems over the years with this habit. I found, for example that the poetry of John Donne and Emily Dickinson, Mary Oliver and W.B. Yeats traveled well on the tank; Rainer Maria Rilke, Wallace Stevens and Ezra Pound are tough tank poets to memorize. They require way too much attention that traveling at 70 miles per hour neither invites nor inspires.

My myth was in the machine. My changing life cycle was mirrored in the motorcycle. In some ways, the motorcycle reflected the myth I was living, as this personal myth shifted gears, changed, matured, enriched, found a new focus as well as a new balance and sloughed off what was no longer operative. As I changed, the motorcycle accommodated the fluctuations within me.

In 1974, as I prepared for my annual junket to the Cistercian Monastery in Kentucky, a graduate student friend gave me a copy of a recently published book with an intriguing title: *Zen and the Art of Motorcycle Maintenance* by Robert Pirsig. This book had a profound effect on me then and again years later when I finished reading the 25th Anniversary edition while hiking the Cinqueterra in Italy with my wife. It is still a profound philosophic reflection on the history of philosophy and the nature of life's qualities. I initially read it at every rest stop, every meal break and at night by candlelight in my pup tent. So powerful was his discussion of technology and the imagination, of the nature of Quality and right attitude which is couched within a story of a journey he and his son Chris took from Minnesota to California on an old motorcycle, that one morning, while the mist was still hanging heavy over the still, private campground in Tennessee, I woke to gray-blue light, blessed the deep silence, fixed some atrocious instant coffee and ate a sweet roll for breakfast. I then turned the BMW to the East, in full ritual compliance, where an orange sun was just rising, carefully unfurled a small canvas bag filled with tools from under the seat where they were stored in a fiberglass container, undid the valve covers one at a time, removed the spark plugs and adjusted the valves in priestly, meditative silence. I might as well have been saying Mass. Mythic? You bet? Ritual? Of course! Transformative? Certainly. Spiritual? Profound. It became one of the most spiritual moments of the entire trip. I felt through Pirsig's book and my own ritual "setting-of-the-valves" something of the numinous quality of motorcycle maintenance.

I want to get heavy-handed here for a moment, while in the pages of Pirsig's book, and suggest to you that motorcycles are both mechanical *and* ontological. By that I mean that when fully engaged, when I am fully in gear and in synch with my ride, I enter a state of mind that gives me a feeling of being at one with everything. I am being consciously vague here. It affects my imagination. Some fullness of NOW takes over me as I settle into the ride. Some power of living NOW moves in to cancel out the workweek, the responsibilities that keep me living much of the time either in the past or in the future. I believe motorcycling allows me to live most fully in the NOW, neither fore nor aft. Joseph Campbell's observation, as he studied mythologies from around the world, found a common nugget in all of them. Myths, he believed, are guides to move us to where we can be transparent to transcendence."[333] If myths do not achieve this status, then one may be outside a viable myth.

In 45 years of riding, in stepping into the garage to don the treated leathery skin of an animal and gloves made from an animal's hide, to back the bike out, check the machine over, examine tire pressures, look for fluid leaks on the garage floor, start it up, put on a helmet, and head out, that sense of a quickening never diminishes. When it does I will sell both the Goldwing and the Harley Electra Glide Classic.

Some shift in being takes place that is wondrous, adventurous, open and singular in its effect. And let me not gloss over too quickly this leather we don if we are smart; it is to encase ourselves in the skin of an animal—some material from the natural order, some primordial throwback to a time when the human and animal imaginations were intimate, when animal hides were the preferred fashion statement, and then to spread our legs astride an engine with only some leather and padding separating us from its violent hot internal explosions that divides the two tires below. Up there, just above the heat, sitting on leather, wrapped in leather, we are propelled down the highway just inches from the soles of our boots and the asphalt or concrete surface. I think there is a little madness in exposing ourselves to such a condition. What revs up is the blood that rises in temperature with the ride.

Now if we truly imagine this uncanny posture, we see that we are living in two worlds at once; something of our own animal nature is allowed to express itself. Does the motorcycle allow this depth penetration into the animal powers within us? Style and substance combine in a two-wheeled harmony.

I have been hit three times: once I skidded around a corner and went under a car when I was 24; if I had not been wearing a helmet I would never have been alive to compose this essay. On another occasion I was hit once from behind so hard it tore a saddlebag off the motorcycle and threw its contents all over an access road in Dallas. On another occasion, I was hit from behind by a driver who did not see me in broad daylight in San Antonio. Each time, I swore that I would sell the bike; each time I kept it, so deep in my own psyche is the importance of the ride. That is what I mean about ontological; the motorcycle is a state of mind, a state of being. Choose your Harley, your Kawasaki, your BMW, your crotch rocket; each is a state of mind and heart, and that reality you can never explain sufficiently to anyone. Like Hermes, the god of thresholds and new beginnings himself, it remains elusive, defies being fixed,

---

333 Campbell, *Inner Reaches of Outer Space,* p. 18.

pinned down or quantified in any comfortable way. Is one "Better" than another? On an absolute scale, no. On a relative scale, well, it depends on what cult you want to belong to, what tribal identity you want to assume, along with your leathers. So I suppose there is.

When I first arrived at the Trappist monastery in Kentucky, about 12 miles south of Bardstown, the monks at first would be a little skittish about a biker staying with them. I in turn did not like having the bike out in the parking lot, so I asked them if there was a sheltered place for it. After much discussion, they agreed to let me park it inside the cloister, in the post office building. This I did regularly for years. And it never failed: each time I would come down from my room to fetch something from one of the Craven saddle bags, there would be one or two monks hovering around it, discussing it. I knew they wanted to go for a ride, but it was discouraged; they were content to point out to one some features that interested them.

I want to shift gears here to bring in another perspective as I ride rhetorically to the end of this journey. In my teaching duties, I work with students who are designing, outlining and writing dissertations for a Ph.D. in Mythology and/or Depth Psychology. Many of my students are already therapists returning to school for advanced degrees. Several are my age, some older, some younger. One of these students, an analyst in Los Angeles by the name of Lisa Garber, who has given me permission to use her work, discovered that I rode a motorcycle and asked me to be her advisor on a dissertation that was eventually titled: *Women Who Ride: The Psyche of the Female Motorcyclist.*

Lisa discovered in her research that little to no exploration of the female motorcyclist had been done, even with the exploding number of women who ride their own motorcycles rather than perch behind a man on his. She anchored her study in two arenas: her own as well as the interviews of 5 other women who ride; and the two mythic figures: the god Hermes and the goddess Brunnhilde as "progenitors" of the psyche of the female motorcyclist.

What she found, in summary, was that female motorcyclists all shared some fear of becoming completely who they were in their own skin. All shared the experience of purchasing and riding their own bikes, and all in her study were Harley riders, which became part of their own cycle of independence, a more conscious and articulated self- emerging as they gained confidence and autonomy as motorcycle riders.

All of the women in her study were very successful professionals who nonetheless carried some emotional hindrance in themselves that arrested their development. With the purchase of their motorcycles, each woman, as Lisa writes, "moved toward a union with nature—which included the image of mother, a fuller attention to powerful father dynamics, finally to emerge from the family with a desire to be seen. This process culminated in an enhanced sense of self, supported by an impassioned relationship to the motorcycle."[334]

Lisa herself rides a sportster, which she has named "Panther." In her own evolving desire to be seen, not to be hidden, silenced, or pushed to the back of the social stage, she learned in her research and interviews that the motorcycle is a vehicle used by women to reveal themselves more fully and with some splendor. She wanted to imagine the female motorcyclist mythically and to understand if through the interviews there was credibility for choosing Hermes and Brunnhilde as the couple that spawns, imaginally, the female motorcyclist. I want to close by quoting a segment of the last part of her groundbreaking work:

> Like many contemporary women who are moving into areas previously the aegis of men, their experience and psychology has meaning and consequence for all women. The psyche of the female motorcyclist is part of every woman who finds her passion and is willing to express and expose her Self. The riders do not disparage what has come before; rather, they borrow from the patriarchy, integrating what was taken and make it their own. These are rebellious but not angry women. They are women who are at the leading edge of change. Multi-talented and empowered by desire, they ask only for a mirror and a motorcycle to further their task. This dissertation provides a partial mirror on this leg of the journey. These women share a desire to be successful, coupled with an acceptance and embrace of the unknown.[335]

Lisa ends her work with a "Recommendations" section that I want to cite partially as a way to pull the bike up, set it on its kickstand, and end the ride. The questions she poses opens up to further exploration:

> The psychological and psychic relationship between human and machine is an important line of inquiry. These women have passionate attachments to their motorcycles. What is the nature of this attachment and what are its components? Is the nature of the attachment different from one type of machine to another? The motorcycle car-

---

334 Garber, Lisa, *Women Who Ride*, p. 110.
335 *Women Who Ride*, p. 112.

ries the rider; how does this impact the relationship? How are these attachments the same or different from the relationships men develop with machines? The findings for this line of research could have a broad range of implications and applications. For instance: research into human computer interfaces, automobile-driver coupling or the change in human psychology and body perception which may be the result of spending long periods of time interacting with machines."[336]

All of us are on a road that is both physical and symbolic, temporal and spatial, external and interior. Motorcycling is one way that road can be spoken about, reflected on, imagined more deeply and fully, even allowed to reveal to us who and what we have been, are, and are becoming. Go easy on the throttle and use both brakes; when you come up to a fork in the road, take it; keep the rubber on the road and the tank to the sky. Otherwise you will never know what is just around that next curve, there, where your own personal myth must enter the landscape alone. Then you are truly on your own path.

References

Campbell, Joseph, *The Power of Myth*. With Bill Moyers. Ed. Betty Sue Flowers. New York: Doubleday, 1988.

_____. *The Inner Reaches of Outer Space: Metaphor as Myth and as Religion*. Novato, California: New World Library, 2002.

_____. *Thou Art That: Transforming Religious Metaphor*. Ed. Eugene Kennedy. Novato, California: New World Library, 2002.

Garber, Lisa, "Woman Who Ride: The Psychology of the Female Motorcyclist." Unpublished dissertation. Pacifica Graduate Institute, 2000.

Pirsig, Robert, *Zen and the Art of Motorcycle Maintenance: An Inquiry into Values*. Anniversary Edition. New York: William Morrow, 1999.

336 *Women Who Ride*, p. 202.

7

The Power and Poetry of Love

The story of Valentine's Day is not well-known today, so on the occasion of this memorable day next week, I offer this shortened version of Love. St. Valentine was a Catholic priest in Rome at the time that Claudius II was emperor from 268-270 AD.

That time in Western History was a period of transition from one mythology to another: the older pagan gods of Rome were being challenged by the new religion of Christianity. The challenge was great between a polytheistic worldview and a more monotheistic one with the advent of Christ's historical presence and the force of his teachings, most specifically, in my mind, on the nature and practice of love. Through it we might see best, the embodiment of charity, one of the Church's cardinal virtues, along with Faith and Hope.

St. Valentine was arrested and interrogated regarding his refusal to worship the older deities. He was, the story has it, turned over to one of the judges of Rome, Asterius, and during his house arrest the two men spoke about the two forms of worship. Asterius challenged Valentine by asking him to heal his daughter's blindness, and if he did, he and his entire household would convert to Christianity. The young girl was brought to the priest, who restored her sight in a miraculous transformation. Perhaps we are being asked to consider that Love is not as blind as we have been led to believe. In gratitude to the Saint and to his God, Asterius and his family converted to Christianity by being baptized and in the process of their conversion they destroyed all images of the pagan deities in their household. Asterius' household consisted of 40 members: servants, various assistants and his family members. They were all subsequently assassinated for their new faith. Valentine himself was thrown into prison and beaten until dead. He is buried, the story has it, on the Via Flaminia in Rome.

In ways that can be debated, his name became associated with romantic love in part because of what some have called a chance coincidence between the dates of his death and a pagan spring festival dedicated to the goddess Juno. The festival was in honor of the young boys and girls of the city and some suggest passed the romantic association on to St. Valentine. In a conflation of two religious belief systems, the early church leaders adopted the pagan Roman lover's festival and assigned Valentine's name to it.[337]

I use this history of Valentine's Day to introduce one of the great theological love poems in Western Literature, Dante's *Divine Comedy*, what he himself called his *Commedia*. It would not have been born, however, without two events that preceded it: 1. the chance meeting in approximately 1274 when Dante was nine, of Beatrice Portinari, a young Florentine who, when Dante came upon her in the streets of their city, was immediately transformed by what James Joyce centuries later would call a moment of "aesthetic arrest." My hunch is that none of us has escaped such a paralyzing and galvanizing moment in one's life. In an instant when on seeing or experiencing the presence of the Other through the quickening power of Love, one realizes that one's life has just been altered in some permanent and profound way, so powerful is the presence of this all-encompassing pressure on the heart, with its capacity to transform one in an instant. We are not surprised then, to see Love itself elevated to the level of divinity in world religions.

The other event is Dante's creation of what he called *La Vita Nuova,* the new life, as a consequence of his meeting with Beatrice, whose presence renovated the world for him. Often less read than his *Commedia,* it nonetheless serves as prologue of sorts to the longer work, for in it, and through the emotional upheaval of meeting Beatrice, Dante found one of life's most mysterious and complex themes, that of Love itself in so many of its spiritual, physical and psychological permutations. C.G. Jung himself, influenced mightily by Dante's poem as he crafted *The Red Book*, wrote in *Liber Secundus*: "Therefore you should have reverence for what has become, so that the law of love may become redemption through the restoration of the lower and of the past, not perdition through the boundless mastery of the dead."[338] For Dante himself, and

---

337 Castledon, Rodney, *The Book of Saints*, p. 28.
338 Shamdasani, Sonu, (Ed.), *The Red Book*. p. 297.

as many of us have experienced, love can destroy and it can redeem, depending on our orientation to this fierce force of nature.

Here is what Dante writes of Beatrice: "She appeared in the most patrician of colors, a subdued and decorous crimson, her robe bound round and adorned in a style suitable to her years." Dante goes on to use language that perhaps we can all connect to:

> At that very moment, and I speak the truth, the vital spirit, the one that dwells in the most secret chamber of the heart, began to tremble so violently that even the most minute veins of my body were strangely affected; and trembling, it spoke the words: 'Ecce deus fortior me, qui veniens dominabitur michi.' (Here is a god stronger than I who comes to rule over me).[339]

Dante is fully conscious that something has entered him with an energy capable of deflecting his life's trajectory: "Let me say that from that time on, Love governed my soul, which became immediately devoted to him and he reigned over me with such assurance and lordship, given him by the power of my imagination"[340] that he had no longer any choice but to follow Love's guidance. One can be smitten with such a potency of love that it disorients, disturbs and distributes one differently in the world.

Love then ramps up his presence in the form of a vision that he delivers to Dante while he sleeps. A handsome man, both terrible and joyful, appears to the poet holding two figures. In one hand Love holds "a sleeping figure, naked but lightly wrapped in a crimson cloth." In the other appears an image we might find intimately connected to the experience of love: "he seemed to be holding something that was all in flames," as he spoke these words: "Vide cor tuum" (behold thy heart).[341]

Then, in a dramatic gesture that is at once compelling and unforgettable, "he seemed to awaken the one who slept and he forced her cunningly to eat of that burning object in his hand; she ate of it timidly," after which he "folded his arms around this lady, and together they seemed to ascend toward the heavens."[342] This dramatic event is the heart beat of Dante's first sonnet as well as the subsequent theme of its execution. The figure of Beatrice eats a portion of the poet's heated heart in an im-

---

339 Alighieri, D., *Dante's Vita Nuova*, p. 4.

340 *Dante's Vita Nuova*, p. 4.

341 *Dante's Vita Nuova*, p. 5.

342 *Dante's Vita Nuova*, p. 6.

age both sexual and spiritual, and certainly an embodied emblem of his emotional turmoil.

At this first erotic devouring of his flaming heart by his beloved, Dante not only discovers, as his *Vita Nuova* progresses through 41 more chapters in the service of Love's exploration, that his work is inadequate to convey the richness and even the epic grandeur of his theme—it needs in fact a larger vessel as well as a more substantial verse. That container will be 14,000+ line poem in terza rima rhyme scheme that embraces his *Commedia,* and in it, perhaps the most memorable couple, Paolo da Malatesta and Francesca da Rimini, who appear in *Inferno* 5 in the realm of the Lustful shades. To that couple and their lasting effect on Dante the pilgrim and poet's psyche, I wish to turn now for a disposition of Love that achieves no further lift-off than lust.

In the second circle of Hell is the realm of the Lustful swirling like birds in a windstorm. We recall that almost the entire poem occurs in the domain of the afterlife—*animarum statem post mortem*—the state of souls after death. Here in Inferno, souls suffer what was called a *contrapasso*, namely, that what one did in life is carried into the afterlife, intensified and suffered eternally. The condition of souls after death is essentially the "just counter-penalty in Hell," as translator and commentator, Allen Mandelbaum describes it,[343] and consists of no more than an extension of what one loved in life.

The weather in the terrain of the Lustful consists of an eternal violent storm; all who inhabit this region are buffeted about, "now here, now there, now down, now up, it drives them."[344] Like the Lust that drove them wandering and out of control in life, they now and forever suffer that same condition in the afterlife.

Virgil, guiding Dante, first offers as examples throughout history individuals who were caught in the violent circuitry of Love diminished now to Lust. Furthermore, each "sin," or we might say the soul's afflictions and deformations, is a manifestation of love in at least one of the following categories: Love excessive, Love diminished and Love distorted; they are the remedies for the forms of love that have refused to accommodate due measure.

Dante is dizzy with all the stormy necessities of this region when Virgil recounts over a thousand historical and mythic examples of Lust. Far less ambitious than his mentor, the pilgrim limits his vision to only two doves flying through the air overhead

---

343 Alighieri, *The Divine Comedy*, p. 555.
344 *Inferno*, 5, p. 43.

and notices that they seem to be stuck together; he asks Virgil if he might speak to them. His guide responds:" "'You'll see when they draw closer/to us, and then you may appeal to them/ by that love which impels them. They will come.'"[345] On hearing Dante's call, the two doves, at a moment when the winds abate enough for them to control their own flight, approach Virgil and Dante "through the malignant air; / so powerful had been my loving cry."[346]

The subsequent scene of Paolo and Francesca may be the most popular of all the hundreds of vignettes in the *Commedia*. What accounts for such attraction? What is it about illicit love and clandestine lovers who, while married, begin an affair with another that violates the boundaries of both of them? Hardly ever does it end well, but that seems to be a weak impediment to its persistent survival throughout history and its attraction within so many cultures.

Dante is no less excited to hear their story, for his response signals both intense curiosity as well as disarming pity. Perhaps we have birthed in this passage the infancy of the Romance Novel, and by extension the more contemporary "Soap Opera" in the excitement of illicit behavior outside the conventions of social norms as well as the challenge of pulling it off.

The intact couple alights next to Dante. Francesca steps boldly forward while Paolo forever attached beside her, only weeps during the entire exchange between the pilgrim and her. She immediately launches into their story of how she and Paolo, the brother of the man to whom she was married, and the latter as murderer of both Paolo and Francesca when he discovers their affair, were reading a romance one day when they were both quietly seized or indeed wounded by the arrow of Eros and, well, stopped reading in order to enjoy in the flesh what they had been imagining on the page. The human tendency to literalize is indeed thorny and risky.

But not before Francesca, in a moment of seduction of Dante himself, quotes from the latter's sonnets from *La Vita Nuova*: "Love that can quickly seize the gentle heart, / took hold of him because of the fair body taken from me—how that was done still wounds me."[347] Dante becomes so engaged in her verbal seduction that Virgil looks at him in puzzlement and asks: "What are you thinking?"[348] The seduced pilgrim seems

---

345 *Inferno*, 5. II. 76-78.
346 *Inferno*, 5. II. 87-88.
347 *Inferno*, 5. II. 100-03.
348 *Inferno*, I. 111.

to come out of a reverie and, ignoring Virgil and Paolo, speaks directly to Francesca: "Francesca, your afflictions / move me to tears of sorrow and of pity,"[349] followed quickly by a request to hear the details of their story, to which she without hesitation, obliges. She recounts their reading of a medieval romance, that of Lancelot"—how love had overcome him. / We were alone, and we suspected nothing. / And time and time again, that reading led our eyes to meet, and made our faces pale, / and yet one point alone, defeated us."[350]

Through the power of story to ignite their own physical love, Paolo leans over to kiss Francesca in an impassioned imitation of the passage they just read when Lancelot kisses Guinevere. Francesca, however, is quick to blame the book for their transgression: "that day we read no more."[351] So powerful was the fiction to move in both lovers the desire to create it in reality. Most all of us know, however, that from the blueprint to the bedroom is never an exact match.

Dante, listening in complete rapture, feels the glow of Eros ignite in him at her story, in which is embedded his own anticipation of meeting his former love, Beatrice, whom he recalls with great ardor; that emotion, coupled with the pity he feels for the speaking and weeping couple he addresses, overwhelms him: "I fainted as if I had met my death / and then I fell as a dead body falls."[352] He is betwixt past and future, which is where love often situates us, sometimes in paralysis and in others at an instant of a critical breakthrough that can sweep in after breakdown.

In *Civilization in Transition* C.G. Jung offers that "love is always a problem, whatever our age may be. Love is a force of destiny whose power reaches from heaven to hell."[353] He goes on to suggest that fewer instinctual and emotional impulses in the human being can surpass those that love adumbrates and witnesses. Love, believes Jung, is,

> not confined to any particular province but covering every aspect of human life. It may be an ethical, a social, a psychological, a philosophical, an aesthetic, a religious, a medical, a legal or a physiological problem, to name only a few aspects of this many-sided phenomenon.[354]

---

349 *Inferno*, 5. II. 117-18.
350 *Inferno*, 5. II. 128-31.
351 *Inferno*, I. 138.
352 *Inferno*, 5. II. 141-42.
353 Jung, CW 10 ¶ 198.
354 CW 10, ¶ 200.

Yet Love in its fullest expression is an umbrella huge enough to cover all the landscapes from heaven to hell, as he observes.

He then migrates to the German poet, Goethe, certainly one of the most influential writers in Jung's life, to allow another voice in verse to convey Love's complexity and ubiquity:

> Let now the savage instincts sleep
> And all the violence they do;
> When human love stirs in the deep
> The love of God is stirring too.[355]

The power of this meeting with the two lovers cemented for eternity, cannot be overestimated. It reveals to Dante the paralysis love can engender where instead of love leading, within the poem, to the transcendent mystery of the Primal Love of God, it becomes, itself, a god that enwombs or enshrouds the lover. My sense is that Dante wishes us to feel viscerally the power of love to paralyze and to polarize—to paralyze the lovers in their own appetites as well as to polarize the individual from the deeper love which the early Christian faith called Agape, love of God, accomplished or realized in and through the love of another. Jung observes in Vol. 7 of his *Collected Works*, in discussing a patient who has a strong urge in her parceled out to a close friend and to her mother: Jung believes she suffers " a violent sentimental demand for love, so impassioned that she feels herself overwhelmed." The demand, he continues, has the character of an overpowering infantile craving, which, as we know, is blind.[356]

When love is not balanced, moderated or held in due measure, but gains instead access to extreme excess, the soul becomes disoriented, often slips into delusions and dissolutions and may even defect from its path. In due measure, love allows us to serve something beyond ourselves in the form of compassion for others and a desire to serve them. Dante's pilgrimage from Paolo and Francesca through the remaining descent through Hell and then the arduous journey up the spiraling path of Mount Purgatory brings him to a measured place in his soul that allows him to face the harsh love—we might call it today "tough love"—of Beatrice. Her stern presence in Dante's awakening brings him to a balanced love that honors his feelings for her but goes beyond to the source of all love discovered in *Paradiso*.

355 CW 10, ¶ 199.
356 CW 7, ¶ 133.

References

Alighieri, Dante, *Dante's* Vita Nuova. Trans. and Introd. Mark Musa. Bloomington: Indiana UP, 1973.

____. *The Divine Comedy*. Trans. Allen Mandelbaum. Introd. Eugene Montale. New York: Alfred A. Knopf, 1995.

Castleden, Rodney, *The Book of Saints*. London: Quercus, nd.

Jung, C.G., *Civilization in Transition*. Trans. R.F.C. Hull. Vol. 10 of *The Collected Works of C.G.* Jung. Princeton: Princeton UP, 1964.

____. *Two Essays on Analytical Psychology*. Second Edition. Vol. 7 of *The Collected Works of C.G.* Jung. Princeton: Princeton UP, 1966.

Shamdasani, Sonu, (Ed). *The Red Book: Liber Novus*. Trans. Mark Kyburz, John Peck and Sonu Shamdasani. New York: Norton, 2009.

8

The Soul's Claim: Choose it or Lose It

I was guided to a general interest in psychology and then (by divine grace) to C.G. Jung's work through my father's disease: alcoholism. When I was 16, I could not understand how my father, drunk on a Saturday night and in a full-blown rage, could begin shouting as I came home after a twelve-hour shift at the supermarket: "You are useless, no good, a waste!" How could I be useless? I had paid for my own tuition at a private high school, bought my own cars as soon as I could drive, and provided my father with weekly bus fare with my earnings. What else could I possibly do to win his approval? I did not know at the time what projection was or what demons roiled just below the surface of respectability, ready to uncoil each weekend in a drunken rage. So I began to search for answers. Beginning at a community college in downtown Cleveland, Ohio, I enrolled in as many psychology courses as I could fit into my full schedule. This was my tentative initiation into the study of soul and the unconscious as well as my own initial departure from the house of the illness.

In these classes I sought answers to my deeply-embedded wound: in the face of all of my successes and achievements, I was still dubbed by my father "Sir Worthless." However, the psychology classes I enrolled in were too embedded in the world of "knee-jerks, myna birds, and rats," as the best of my professors, Blake Crider, a practicing analyst in Cleveland, called the clinical perspective of the day. He taught "Abnormal Psychology of Everyday Life," and from him I began to learn of the imagination behind the words of my alcoholic father. I was drawn to the word "abnormal" like a moth to the flame. "This has relevance to my life," I remember admitting one day after class. I began at the same time to discern that there were *schools* of psychology, although the degree program I entered as a psychology major at Kent State University in the mid-1960s relied heavily on experimental psychology. But I also began pursuing a double major and enrolled in upper-division literature and poetry courses. I soon realized that there was more psychology on any page of Fyodor Dostoevsky's *Crime and Punishment* or Malcolm Lowry's *Under the Volcano* or Graham Greene's *The Power and the Glory* than in a chapter (or even an entire textbook) of experimental psychology theory and practice. For me, knee-jerks and rats were displaced by the mind of a murderer and the lost faith of a whiskey priest. These images I could live with; they were nutrients for the life of imagination and closer to the home I had recently fled from.

Although I was delighted with literary studies and the nuanced expressions of poetry, I was still disappointed with what psychology delivered as the voice of the soul. Disappointment gave way quickly to delight, however, when a graduate student in comparative literature at Kent State befriended me and encouraged me to read a book he had recently discovered: C.G. Jung's *Modern Man in Search of a Soul.* This was in 1967. I still have that reprint of the original black paperback copy, published by Harcourt, Brace & World, with what looks like a galaxy or an atom spinning about its cover; it sits by my side as I type these words. If a work other than scripture can be called a spiritual guide, then Jung's book was my new lodestar for both spiritual and psychological awakening. A life can turn in a new direction as quickly as a chapter of a book emphatically grips one's interest and pivots the compass reading of one's life.

I turn its pages now and see the red underlining I added so neatly with a ruler and the marginal notes in my scrawling, choppy 23-year-old handwriting. I can still feel the excitement in those scrawls, which I made hastily, wanting to move on to the next page, the next discovery, the impending idea, the further insight that would make my stomach grumble, roll, and rejoice in new insights.

What did I feel was important enough to mark in bright red? In the chapter "The Aims of Psychotherapy," Jung wrote:

> About a third of my patients are suffering from no clinically definable neurosis, but from the senselessness and emptiness of their lives.[357]

In a later chapter, "The Stages of Life," he discusses the place of the intellect in daily matters, and then observes:

---

357 Jung, C.G., *Modern Man in Search of a Soul,* p. 61.

> But beyond that there is a thinking in primordial images—in symbols which are older than historical man; what have been ingrained in him from earliest times, and, eternally living, outlasting all generations, still make up the groundwork of the human psyche.[358]

Finally, a third revelation moved me so much that I wrote in red at the top of the page "Reread" and next to the passage a star and the command: "Know:"

> Sensation establishes what is actually given, thinking enables us to recognize its meaning, feeling tells us its value, and finally intuition points to the possibilities of the whence and whether that lie within the immediate facts.[359]

I was spellbound by these four functions that orient us in the world; they help us discover and create meaning. I was also staggered by a style of psychological writing that represented and reflected something tangible in my interior life that I no longer had to ponder as mine alone. Instead, I was part of a universal psychological order that was ancient, accessible, and worthy of further deployment. Psychology and poetry began to meld into one vision of human life in these passages, which I absorbed like a starving animal seeking sustenance.

I immediately ceased my pursuit of experimental psychology courses at Kent State and began to devote much of my spare time to reading Jung's work, rereading his descriptions of the personal and collective unconscious, anima energy, shadow qualities of the soul, and the hunger for purpose in life. I felt all of humanity begin to wrap around me. I was in a chrysalis of my own self-discovery. Here was a psychologist, I realized, who was more in touch with the labyrinth of my life than with laboratory experiments with rhesus monkeys and experimentally-naive albino rats. But the biggest surprise was still waiting in the wings. It arrived in the form of another essay in the book that yoked depth psychology and poetry in new and exciting ways.

The Poetic Psyche

In this small paperback that was changing my interests, my perspective, and my life's study in major swaths was an essay that intrigued me with its title: "Psychology and

358 *Modern Man in Search of a Soul*, pp. 112–113.
359 *Modern Man in Search of a Soul*, p. 93.

Literature." Its coupling of the two disciplines that attracted me the most infused hope into my grand design, hope that the poetic imagination might indeed have collegial, even intimate conversations with the psyche as Jung had defined it. The timing was extraordinary, for at this juncture in my undergraduate career I had joined the staff of the literary journal, *The Kent Quarterly,* and was just beginning, with the encouragement of a creative writing teacher, Barbara Child, to write and submit poetry. I felt a certain shame about her pushing me, for to go public with such private utterances was to step boldly outside what I had never allowed myself. I did not know what I was doing, but the call to express myself in a medium that I loved to read would neither dissipate nor decline. Jung's thinking, in fact, provided further energy to this new phase of expression. I tracked the essay that was so seminal for my own thinking back to its original publication in *The Spirit in Man, Art, and Literature,* volume 15 of the *Collected Works of C.G. Jung.*[360]

What excited me about the essays in this volume? I think it was that Jung offered a kind of language that was at once intuitive, personal, poetic and universal. His prose carried both individual import and timeless significance, in part because he so often addressed and amplified the meaning inherent in the myth of a person's life. I found myself elated by his observation: "it is obvious enough that psychology, being a study of psychic processes, can be brought to bear on the study of literature, for the human psyche is the womb of all the arts and sciences."[361] Two issues sprang at me from his observation: the idea that the psyche has ancient processes and patterns within its being that continue to recur, and the idea that the psyche is a womb, a metaphor that gave it a power as the genesis of all the creative work one engages. His language itself was poetic! He thought, at least here, like a poet and an explorer. No other psychologist or theorist in my experience thought like that at the time, except for Rollo May, who also used literature to great effect in his study of human behavior. But May's work was not to influence me until several years later with his publication of *Love and Will.*[362]

Jung's attitude toward creativity and the soul encouraged me to submit two poems to *The Kent Quarterly* in my junior year. Both were accepted. I share my first

---

360 Jung, *The Spirit in Man, Art, and Literature.* This thinnest volume of the *Collected Works* was to assume enormous formative power in helping me bridge the poetic landscape and the psyche.

361 *The Spirit in Man, Art, and Literature,* para. 133.

362 May, Rollo, *Love and Will* (New York: Norton, 1969).

publication here. It tells the story of something I witnessed in a restaurant close to the boarding house off campus where I rented a room. Harry, another boarder in the same house, was blind. In spite of this formidable obstacle, he was pursuing a master's degree in sociology. He and I had become good friends and at times I would read his textbooks to him as part of a government program to assist blind college students.

What I witnessed through the window of the coffee shop was Harry at the counter having a cup of soup while three coeds sitting at a table watched him and mocked his gestures. The sight infuriated me. I entered the shop, approached Harry, and began a conversation with him, which dampened the spirits of the three young women, who soon left. That night I composed this poem:

Darkness

Is the third day
When leaves are waterlogged,
Crushed without a sound,
And a blind boy in a noisy
Smoke and grease-filled
Restaurant sits and eats alone;
Opening his mouth wide so as
Not to miss the soup-filled
Spoon as
Drops of rain drip off his
Forehead and arrogant
Bastardly coeds look
On and laugh.[363]

This poem was important to write because it both eased the anger I felt and made a *public statement* of it for others. But more than that: something happened to me in the experience of transforming an event into clumsy verse. Through the poem, I began

---

363 Slattery, Dennis P., *Casting the Shadows: Selected Poems*, p. ix.

to see the world differently, in a way that was simultaneously intimate and detached. Writing the poem deepened my consciousness of an event that lasted only minutes. The event, I recalled later, was analogous to what happens to the bitter and lost young man Ishmael in Melville's *Moby-Dick* when he befriends a tattooed islander at Peter Coffin's inn early in the novel.[364] Queequeg is holding a book that he cannot read, although he is perfectly content to count the pages. In the presence of this otherly savage, Ishmael becomes aware of a strange sensation, as if something is melting in him, some feeling of his bitterness and anger dissolving in the process. I felt a similar dissolution of the anger I first experienced when I watched the college girls mocking Harry in the restaurant. Through crafting the poem, I had entered another realm, one that was larger and yet very particular in its structure—the landscape of the poetic image within the larger landscape of the imagination as a way of knowing. I had, however imperfectly, given a form to what would have, over time, faded into the forgotten past. Writing had retrieved it for future contemplation.

Images were the keys to the experience to be conveyed. The poetic images of the rainy day, the waterlogged leaves, the greasy air of the restaurant, Harry's blindness, and the soup he was enjoying, were avenues for me to organize experience along a different pathway in the embodied psyche, where emotion and intellect as well as the sensate world could commingle to create a new shape to that experience. The images are mindful ways of gathering an emotion into a bundle and then allowing that emotion to inform the image, even *be* the image. The images I used in the poem were equivalences, even emotional analogues, of my soul's response to what I witnessed; they served to fix the experience, even to ritualize it into a meaningful whole. All of this I found exhilarating and immensely satisfying.

This experience was a form of poetic expression that derived from my conscious experience, what Jung would call a psychological rather than a visionary experience. The former, he observes, is drawn "from man's conscious life," yet it is transformed by the poet, "raised from the commonplace to the level of poetic experience and expressed with a power of making us vividly aware of those everyday happenings which we tend to evade or to overlook because we perceive them only dully or with a feeling of discomfort."[365] I remember considering that poetry can be a rendering in verse of a human experience that perhaps, through the use of figures of speech and action,

---

364 Melville, Herman , *Moby-Dick* (1951; repr., New York: Norton, 1967)
365 Jung, *The Spirit in Man, Art, and Literature,* para, 139.

can raise the poet as well as the reader to a higher level of consciousness by giving emotional shape and form to what one has perceived. Suddenly the mystery of poetry, although it was by no means negated or diminished, was placed into a category of awareness that I could comprehend. Poetry's ability to charm was enhanced by Jung's perception.

But what was so provocative was how Jung took the process deeper—down, in, and through the mystery of the psyche in its poetic mode of utterance and understanding. From him I learned that many of the images, fantasies, and dreams I thought were mine were more accurately part of a larger psychic enterprise, that I was not necessarily personally "responsible" for them, and that they had a life force of their own. He revealed this powerful insight to me in these words:

> It is strange that a deep darkness surrounds the sources of the visionary material. This is the exact opposite of what we find in the psychological mode of creation, and we are led to suspect that this obscurity is not unintentional."[366]

I felt a fierce freedom attend this observation. Images that rose up in me from my reading or as a result of an experience from the day or a fantasy that suddenly abrupted itself into my consciousness or a film that I dreamt about on subsequent nights after seeing it—all these were not self-manufactured but arose from a deeper layer of being, one that was more collective and impersonal. Jung asked:

> What if there were a living agency beyond our everyday human world—something even more purposeful than electrons? Do we delude ourselves in thinking that we possess and control our own psyches, and is what science calls the "psyche" not just a question-mark arbitrarily confined within the skull, but rather a door that that opens upon the human world from a world beyond? [367]

These questions incited further speculation in me. Some mysterious otherness attended my waking and dreaming consciousness that I could neither be blamed nor praised for. The feeling of this mystery, far from frightening me, made me want to invite it in. I began to rise at 4 a.m. seven days a week so I could attend to this new project.

I began to practice a ritual in my study: Each morning, I lit a candle and burned a stick of incense. When writing, I often played classical music or Gregorian chant in the background. The space of my work improved dramatically, as if I had just made

---

366 *The Spirit in Man, Art, and Literature*, para. 144.
367 *The Spirit in Man, Art, and Literature*, para. 148.

room for something that in the past I had not even recognized existed. Moreover, just as dreams can evoke companion dreams, I learned that poetry can provoke poetic responses. I began to write more poetry on a regular basis, now with the conviction that parts of my personal myth and the larger cultural myth I was embedded in, as well as an even larger ancestral history that I was a direct descendant of, were at play in creation. My emotional response was a feeling of liberation. I recognized for the first time two images working in me: midwife and conduit. Jung's thought opened me to the reality that I was as much a disciple of history as an inhabitant and at times a creator of it that what formed in me was not my possession but something that was using me to reveal itself. Let me offer another poem to illustrate.

One morning in the early darkness, I was in my study musing in my journal, which I write in each day for twenty minutes. In this meditation I paused to recollect the day before in order to invite yesterday to shake hands with the not-yet-today. I was reading poetry and thinking about what kind of knowledge poetic utterance provides the soul even as it emanates from that same source. The following was offered in a voice that I trusted. It was not my voice but emanated from somewhere else.

Morning Muse in the Kitchen

Making poetry of pots and spoons
a dactyl of dishes
and sonnets—sunny side up
or a new scrambled rhyme scheme
that leaves no stains on the glasses
no water spots of distraction
that can enter as burnt toast
or jelly under the finger nail
that irritates a couplet into
an entire chaos of rhyme.

She patters bare feet here and there

across the red rug looking for
a spatula to turn the eggs
easy over into the light of an inspired
instant
where everything can be seen without
the mist of coffee steam or
the hard cloud of prose.

Musing over the morning paper
the kitchen goddess remembers
every item cooking; in the fridge
the ice cream hardening into stiff
quatrains that will not melt
in prosaic patterns of heat
in late afternoon.

She dries the dishes in pure
sunlight, orders their stacks
and steps out and back
and down to the Guadalupe
River for a morning memory
of her mother gliding past in
a tube atop a shallow current
amended by silent promises laid out
in neat Petrarchan echoes.

From the shore's rushes
birds of a certain genre
find comic relief in
labor pangs of free verse.[368]

---

368 Slattery, D.P., and Chris Paris, *The Beauty Between Words: Selected Poems*, pp. 94–95.

Producing this poem was provocative for me because of its intention to find analogies of itself in metaphors that provided bridges to other, deeper realms like vertical stepping-stones. I remember Jung's sense of the creative process that yokes levels of our realities to create something new, a delightful knowing in many cases: "Through our senses we experience the known, but our intuitions point to things that are unknown and hidden, that by their very nature are secret."[369] Each of us, he seems to suggest, carries within ourselves a secret life that art is often the best conduit for uncovering. Aspects of this secret life are ancient, inherited, re-membered and re-visioned anew, as with a living, organic mythos.

Poetic responses are for me a large aperture into this realm. I trust this kingdom to reveal itself in the day's early hours, much like the angel Gabriel visiting the Virgin Mary during a time of quiet meditation when, as most paintings depict her, she is reading a book, engaged by the imagination and in a meditative open and pregnant position, fertile for revelation, open to intuitive intrusions. This image of The Annunciation, which has been depicted over hundreds of years of renderings, is the perfect psychic condition of repose for receiving a revelation. I attempted one morning to give voice to this experience:

Every Word Recalls Its Silence

Every word recalls its own silence.
Poetic words glaze
a keener memory. When uttered they
coax the strongest memories
of all. Each speech an act of remembrance;
each poetic musing marries a mythic past.
If I were to utter "Beatitude," say, would
the power shift in the East for an instant

---

369 Jung, *The Spirit in Man, Art, and Literature,* para. 148.

160

so the meek might feel what it would be like
to inherit the earth?
And if I were to say "Beatrice"
would she suddenly emerge to place
a token into the subway turnstile and
ride along the window into
underworld darkness?
A token gesture? A strength in even
an awkward motion to slake thirst?
I find the word "Beatific" memorable
on a grand scale for what in the heart
flutters when I utter it.
Darkness descends on every word—a divine
darkness that carries the dust of words
at Dusk—
Solitude seems indifferent, like a desert's
right to ignore any footprint that breaks
the silence of sand and stone and
gray-green sage—ocotillo and saguaro,
wonderful sounds beneath desert
silence.
Memories play off darkness
hedging against the light. Silence glows
with a natural blush against the word
"Incarnate."
Silence surrounds Him like a shroud
cloaking the silent skin of the Incarnate
Word with a linen as white as it is breathless.
No soul might ever again clash with
such a splintered reflection. The eye

of Beatrice is a glass of silent memory

in a splash of subdued inflection.[370]

The images are given like consoling offerings to me for consideration. Not my imagination alone but another source, one that is psychic, ancient and benevolent, presents these images to be arranged in some conscious crafted way to charm the felt sense of whatever marriage exists between words and silence. Because the process is a mystery, I make no attempts to explain it. But Jung continues to help me comprehend what the source or origin of such utterances might be. In part, what "appears in the vision is the imagery of the collective unconscious. This is the matrix of consciousness and has its own inborn structure. . . . Mythological motifs frequently appear, but clothed in modern dress; for instance, instead of the eagle of Zeus, or the great roc, there is an airplane; the fight with the dragon is a railway smash."[371]

What I hope I have elucidated here is the power of analogy that Jung's examples of mythic motifs gather to themselves. One level of reality or image or narrative seems to have a propensity toward likeness, correspondence, and affectionate accord with another. I venture to say that this is at the heart of the myth-making faculty of the psyche, and it takes on its most colorful garments in the form of stories, be they poetry or prose. My own creative process begins with trust, moves to porosity, and concludes with the making of something into a coherent, formed sense that can be shared. The end result is a knowledge-in-joy.

This last emotion is why I write, for the process itself is a therapy of the word. A haiku might make this observation more palpable:

Wounding

Harsh words attack him;

　A friend grows angry with me.

　　I cannot unspeak.[372]

---

370 Slattery, D., *Just below the Water Line: Selected Poems*, pp. 64–65.
371 Jung, *The Spirit in Man, Art, and Literature*, para.152.
372 Slattery, D., *Twisted Sky: Selected Poems*, p. 28.

The haiku remembers something essential about the wound in the words we use. It offers it a new shape, a new reflection, one that may confer a moment of meditation and perhaps a scent of grace to the moment. It forms an experience into a recollection that is new. It also carries the duality that I will end this essay with by quoting from the rich lode of Jung's writings. For readers new to his work, I will offer this: a little Jung goes a long way. By this I mean that he constantly invites us to meditate on what he observes. Often his observations in prose are as tightly packed as a metaphor in a poem, and when we read these words, a nuclear core of understanding deepens within us.

Close to the end of a chapter titled "Psychology and Literature" in *The Spirit in Man, Art, and Literature,* Jung observes that, "every creative person is a duality or a synthesis of contradictory qualities. On the one side he is a human being with a personal life, while on the other he is an impersonal creative process. . . . But he can be understood as an artist only in terms of his creative achievement."[373] Anchoring the creative side of my life in fertile ground so it can bear fruit is what Jung's writing has encouraged me to do. I would never have thought that a psychologist could become one of the most poignant and often mythopoetic writers on the human imagination, but this is exactly what Jung is and does; for some forty years I have turned to his writing for inspiration and guidance.

My hope is that readers who come to this collection of essays will not turn Jung into a deity but will rather see him as someone with whom they can engage in conversation. The time that an individual invests in his writings will expand the circle of that person's awareness and put one in closer intimacy with his/her own personal myth.

---

373 Jung, *The Spirit in Man, Art, and Literature,* para. 157.

References

Jung, C.G., *Modern Man in Search of a Soul*. New York: Harcourt, Brace, 1933.

____. *The Spirit in Man, Art and Literature. The Collected Works of C.G. Jung.* Volume 15. Translated by R.F.C. Hull. New York: Pantheon Books, 1966.

Slattery, Dennis Patrick, *Casting the Shadows: Selected Poems*. Kearney, New Hampshire: Morris Publishing Co, 2001.

____. *Just Below the Water Line: Selected Poems*. Goleta, California: Winchester Canyon Press, 2004.

____. *Twisted Sky: Selected Poems*. Goleta, California: Winchester Canyon Press, 2007.

____. *The Beauty Between Words: Selected Poems* by Dennis Patrick Slattery and Chris Paris. Stormville, New York: Water Forest Press, 2010.

9

Humanities Education:
Necessities for Cultivating the Whole Person

Why, if man can by patience select variations most useful to himself,
should nature fail in selecting variations useful, under changing condi-
tions of life, to her living products?

—Charles Darwin[374]

Not so long ago I was with my granddaughter McKenzie, aged ten at the time. We were returning from seeing the film, *Despicable Me,* and were talking about the parts we each liked best. As we discussed the film driving home, and as the mystery of conversing with an astute ten year old can turn, we began to speak of mythology, especially the Greek stories of gods, goddesses and heroic models. I remarked that I liked the myths very much, especially the story of Demeter and Persephone. At that, McKenzie began to relate the story to me and was excited about the pomegranate that Demeter, now held by Hades in the underworld, ate, thus insuring that part of every year would be spent in this nether region. She found the fruit wonderful and felt it was the most delicious part of the story.

---

374 Darwin, *Origin of Species*, 1859

I was surprised by this narrative as well as others that she began to relate: of the three brothers, Zeus, Poseidon and Hades, and of what made the middle brother so perpetually angry and discontented, or the uneasy marriage between Zeus and Hera, and the powerful beauty and wisdom of Athena. As she relayed one set of figures after another, I finally interrupted and told her: how great that you attend a public school in San Antonio and they teach mythology. Of that idea I was quickly corrected. "No papa," she responded, "they don't teach mythology to us. I go to the library and check out books on Greek myths because I love the stories." "You taught yourself these stories?" I asked. "Yup," was her succinct reply. At that moment I resolved to buy her as many books on Greek myth as she could handle and have done so ever since.

This young lady is also an Honors Student in math and science studies; she fully enjoys a special privilege three times a week of having class upstairs in a seminar arrangement where she and seven other students from multiple grade levels converse broadly across several disciplines. I cannot applaud her public school enough for accelerating the learning in their program through conversation that spans both arts and sciences. McKenzie is a student of the humanities; her seminars reveal to her and others the interconnections between disciplines of study and help them discern relationships between the sciences and the humanities. She loves it and waits for those three times per week to play with ideas among like-talented students.

In our trip home I marveled at her natural desire to know and to know broadly. She checked out the books on mythology because her appetite to know about these mysterious and wondrous characters could be satisfied in no other way. I suspect as well that, given her gift to express herself so well at such a young age, that she also loves words, language, and their power in conversation to shape ideas, opinions and worlds of meaning.

Under the growing mechanistic model of learning, however, the humanities are being assaulted as unnecessary and often superfluous arenas of study for they do not necessarily, the thinking goes, lead to job procurement and financial security. Underneath this thinking roils the myth of capitalism, which fundamentally reduces everything it brushes against into a commodity to be purchased or a price tag to reflect value. Direct cause-to-effect formatting places all learning on the procrustean bed of efficiency and job acquisition while dismembering the rest as irrelevant. The danger here is that the myth that guides such thinking, both capitalistic and corporate, is strong enough to dissolve an entire culture, and by extension, civilization. Such is the power of the myth that extolls learning as a way into job procurement. If all learning has such a goal, then yes, humanities education has no part in the process and as a consequence both the individual and culture at large are de-humanized. The totality of our humanness is sacrificed when the humanities are subverted. Recently on a local news segment the newsreader revealed a list of subject areas to avoid if you are seeking a job; among them was philosophy and religious studies—hardly job currency, in the cultural imagination, for job training.

Former Assistant Secretary of Education and Counselor to Secretary of Education Lamar Alexander in the George Bush Administration, Diane Ravitch, laments how she felt betrayed in the transformation of the "No Child Left Behind" movement because while it promoted testing and accountability for students, it dismissed the quality of the curriculum content. She writes in her 2010 publication that her hopes for real improvement in public education were dismantled when she saw that such a vision had turned into " a measurement strategy that had no underlying educational vision at all."[375] Accountability without a corresponding devotion to improving the substance of what a student learns offers a sterile method of improving learning. What dismayed her was, administrators ignoring "such important studies as history, civics, literature, science, the arts, and geography."[376] She then poses the right question: "How did testing and accountability become the main levers of school reform?"[377] For her, the bottom had dropped out of the push to leave no child left behind. Behind what?

In his Introduction to a fine collection of essays, *What's Happened to the Humanities?* Editor Alvin Kernan notes that "Historically, the humanities are the old subjects, which in many forms and under a variety of names—the nine muses; the liberal arts; quadrivium and trivium; rhetoric, dialectic, and logic; humane letters—were the major part of Western education for over two millennia.[378] Today, funding is being carved from the National Endowment for the Humanities study programs, which are dismissed by the corporate model as just another entitlement that we must downgrade or eliminate in the service of "fiscal responsibility." Recently, in the state where I reside, a legislator in the Austin capital in Texas went so far as to call public education itself "another entitlement program that needs to be trimmed back." To do

---

375 Ravitch, Diane, *Death and Life*, p. 16.
376 *Death and Life*, p. 16.
377 *Death and Life*, p. 16.
378 Kernan, Alvin, (Ed), *What's Happened to the Humanities?* p. 3.

so is to assassinate history itself and with it, the tradition that we have grown out of as well as others that have helped to shape our own. Such is one of humanities' tasks: to keep history itself alive and relevant. The ahistorical imagination, however, reduces all learning to the bankrupt bedrock of economics. To exacerbate the quagmire, many of those in power to pass judgment on public curricula are themselves poorly educated because woefully limited in their own learning history.

Not surprisingly, Texas ranks at the bottom of the national education ladder as a state in which the highest number of adults without a high school degree reside; furthermore, it holds the title as a state with one of the lowest expenditures per student in public education. In the years 2011-2012 Texas will spend $800.00 less per student for public learning. These figures are symptomatic of the disdain that some feel towards learning generally as a useless activity if it does not point directly to job-acquisition. So a work force that is incapable of discerning, of seeing problems from many points of view, which is satisfied with knee-jerk bromides for our many crises seems to be most favorable. No one is surprised that, of this writing, over 600 of the school districts in the state—which equals over 2/3 of the total number, have filed suit against the governor because teachers and administrators cannot do their job of educating students effectively.

Texas, of course, is not the only state eviscerating its public education budget. What has dropped out of the civic discussion in large measure is the intrinsic value of the humanities for the health and vitality of a culture. It seems imperative to keep alive what value such learning can have on the texture of a people's imagination, and, by extension, the degree and quality of a people's liberty as self-determined rather than reduced solely to the limited band width of economic ends.

Brave New World is Now

In a recent interview in *The Progressive,* journalist and senior fellow at the Nation Institute, Chris Hedges, offers a sobering assessment of the news media, the two party system and the corporate take-over of United States governance. In the course of the interview he admits: "I used to wonder: Is Huxley right or is Orwell right? It turns out they're both right."[379] Both *Brave New World* and *1984* might with great reward be retrieved as essential reading for anyone interested in challenging the assaults on the humanities and, more generally, on the quality of learning itself. Both novels can be found today even in airport bookstores, so ubiquitous are these texts decades after their initial publication. Their easy availability is no accident. My interest here, however, is to address only Huxley's dystopic vision.

In his Foreword to a relatively new edition of *Brave New World*, cultural critic Christopher Hitchens notes that "Huxley was composing *Brave New World* at a time when modernism as we know it was just coming into full view" [1931].[380] The question Hitchens suggests Huxley proposed in his modern allegory was a simple one: "Can the human being be designed and controlled from uterus to grave 'for its own good'? And would this version of super-utilitarianism bring real happiness?"[381]

Within the Central London Hatchery and Conditioning Centre which holds aloft its motto: COMMUNITY, IDENTITY, STABILITY,[382] the Director of this central office points proudly to the persuasive techniques in which infants are conditioned at an early age to recoil from books and flowers. These two images are metonymies for cultural learning and for the order of nature. Connections with learning and with the natural order are enemies to the state's desire to control all its citizens. Inside the INFANT NURSERIES, NEO-PAVLOVIAN CONDITIONING ROOMS[383] the director is delighted to demonstrate to the uninitiated the successful conditioning of 8 month olds: "all exactly alike (a Bokanovsky Group, it was evident."[384]

Initially, all of the infants are placed together on the floor. Shortly thereafter, flowers and books are placed in their vicinity. Immediately attracted by the bright colors and shapes, the infants begin eagerly to crawl towards them. They begin to play with the flowers and crumple the pages of the books. The director waits for a few moments, and then signals the conditioning process to begin while the infants continue to delight in their play. He nods to a nurse, who throws a switch that unleashes a violent explosion of horrifying sounds. "Shriller and ever shriller, a siren shrieked. Alarm bells maddeningly sounded. The children started, screamed, their faces were distorted with

---

379 Hedges, Chris, *The Progressive*, p. 35.
380 Hitchens, Christopher, *Brave New World*, Foreword xiv.
381 *Brave New World*, p. xiv.
382 *Brave New World*, p. 15.
383 *Brave New World*, p. 28.
384 *Brave New World*, p. 29.

terror."[385] Then phase two: an electric shock is sent through the floor the infants are playing on: "Their little bodies twitched and stiffened; their limbs moved jerkily as if to the tug of unseen wires."[386]

After the power is turned off and the infants cease their terrified crying, the Director tells his nurse to "Offer them the flowers and the books again."[387] When she approaches the infants with these objects a second time, they recoil in horror; the Director proudly yawls that "what man has joined, nature is powerless to put asunder."[388] This treatment will be repeated some 200 times, which will seal what the Director has blueprinted: "They'll grow up with what the psychologists used to call an 'instinctive' hatred of books and flowers....They'll be safe from books and flowers all their lives."[389] The conditioning here is based on two tropes: the book, symbol of learning through reading, contemplation, discussion and thought; the flower as symbol of the natural order, aesthetics, wildness, the untamed part of nature which promotes pleasure through escape from the city, and into the openness of the world's body. Replacing these are constant conditionings while one sleeps, including clichés that repeat their pseudo-truths ten thousand times as one is growing up in the *Brave New World*, so that all conditioning has one end: to increase consumption.[390] Thought disappears and programmed responses fill in the gaps where the imagination once held a more prominent, persuasive and civilizing presence. The spirit languishes and cries out for nourishment but receives now only literal enjoyments to consume; such a hunger can never be satisfied with such cheap substitutes.

The leading deity adopted by this new world is Henry Ford, whose proclamation, "History is bunk," assumes the mantra of the new society. Replacing history, human memory, and the standards bequeathed future generations by tradition through, among other sources, the wisdom of the ancestors, are drugs that offer instant nirvana, sexual experimentation with others in casual relationships and diversions in abundance to keep the mind and body occupied and thought-less. The individual commits to nothing but distracted self-gratification. The head Controller of Western Europe as well as the program to eliminate cultural memory from the

385 *Brave New World*, p. 29.
386 *Brave New World*, p. 30.
387 *Brave New World*, p. 30.
388 *Brave New World*, p. 30.
389 *Brave New World*, p. 30.
390 *Brave New World*, p. 38.

population—his ford-ship, Mustafa Mond—repeats slowly for all: *History is bunk.* As he repeats this mantra to the students he addresses, "he waved his hand, and it seemed that "with an invisible feather whisk, he had brushed away the dust of history, covered with spider webs, and the webs consisted of Thebes and Babylon and Cnossos and Mycenae:"

> Whisk, Whisk—and where was Odysseus, where was Job, where were
>
> Jupiter and Gotama and Jesus? Whisk—and those specks of antique dirt called
>
> Athens and Rome, Jerusalem and the Middle Kingdom—all were gone.
>
> Whisk—the place where Italy had been was empty. Whisk, the cathedrals; whisk,
>
> whisk, King Lear and the Thoughts of Pascal. Whisk, Passion; whisk, Requiem;
>
> whisk, Symphony; whisk.....[391]

To erase the past, tradition, cultural and world histories, is effectively to assassinate the Humanities in the Brave New World, ironically a line stolen from Shakespeare's last play, *The Tempest.* Abolished in this new world is the presence of individual meaning that resides outside what the state mandates as the purpose of life. Repetition of thought content heard in one's sleep over 62 thousand times erases all individual thought with "hypnopaedic proverbs" like: "Everyone belongs to everyone else"[392] and "Ending is better than mending"[393] or "you can't consume much if you sit still and read books."[394] Passivity, indifference, manipulation, diversion, distraction, seeking bodily pleasures and passions—all comprise the formidable terms of the new society. Huxley's allegory of a disposition of passive indifference through the voice of the corporate state is the final consequence of a populace that has lost the virtues of learning, inquisitiveness, wonder, philosophizing and a broad-based humanities education that promotes reflection, discernment, taste and freshly-languaged articulations of the ailments attendant on human destiny and choice. The price tag is one's complete abdication of liberty on all levels, replaced efficiently by its more trivialized version:

---

391 *Brave New World*, p. 41.
392 *Brave New World*, p. 46.
393 *Brave New World*, p. 55.
394 *Brave New World*, p. 55.

choice of commodities and entertainments to further enforce a life of distraction and digestion.

Before turning to an alternative to such an infernal world view, one which could be argued we are fast approaching in Western culture today, I want to mention a chapter from the Canadian cultural historian, Jane Jacobs, whose classic, *The Death and Life of Great American Cities* is as relevant now as when she wrote it decades ago. Her last book, *Dark Age Ahead*, published in 2004 before her death, and one which opens with the line, "this is both a gloomy and a hopeful book,"[395] contains a chapter entitled "Credentialing Versus Educating."[396]

Arguing that a degree and an education are not necessarily synonymous,"[397] Jacobs asserts and then argues effectively for her thesis that "Credentialing, not educating, has become the primary business of North American universities."[398] She tracks this move to the turbulent 1960s when students, sensing a change in the quality of education they were receiving, began to complain that they had expected "more personal rapport with teachers who had become only remote figures in large, impersonal lecture halls." They also felt short-changed by professors who attempted to transmit culture "that omitted acquaintance with personal examples and failed to place them on speaking terms with wisdom."[399] These students sensed a sea change in the delivery system of learning; administrators, on the other hand were concentrating on "applying lessons from profit-making enterprises that turn expanded markets to advantage by cutting costs" because their interests resided in "increased output of product [which] can be measured more easily as numbers...."[400] Much of education had been seduced and consumed by the corporate model, itself a tumorous outgrowth of the scientific mechanistic model. Students were now numerically interchangeable while learning as an act of imaginative inquiry was on all fronts now to be measured along the well-grooved route of standardized tests. Mechanization had indeed taken command.

Jacobs goes on to delineate how in the 1960s the purpose of education began to be recalculated for credentialing that would lead to job security and financial safety. Job acquisition became the purpose of all learning; what did not promote a salaried

---

395 Jacobs, Jane, *Dark Age Ahead*, p. 3.
396 *Dark Age Ahead*, pp. 44-63.
397 *Dark Age Ahead*, p. 44.
398 *Dark Age Ahead*, p. 44.
399 *Dark Age Ahead*, p. 47.
400 *Dark Age Ahead*, p. 49.

position was deemed irrelevant. Damage to the environment, mass consumption of natural resources, even war itself, were seen as job-creating enterprises and thus must heel under the banner of more people working: "To this day, no alternative disaster, including possible global warming, is deemed as dire a threat as job loss."[401] This icon of industry—the impulse in education to promote its most important purpose, credentialing as the only relevant element in cultural continuity—appears to be more prevalent today than when she minted this observation seven years ago.

In the process of making credentialing the most important work of institutions of higher learning in the 60s, Jacobs observes, the good students lamented being treated as raw material to be moved through the system to graduation as quickly as possible, which often meant dropping electives that included humanities courses that one wished to study for the sheer joy of learning. The other attitude of students, to the chagrin of passionate teachers, was indifference to anything said or studied that did not directly feed the appetite for credentials, hence, their work in the classroom and outside in assignments was minimal and lethargic.[402] It is not difficult to discern the short line between Huxley's 1931 observations and Jacobs' some 75 years later. The pattern is clear in history, as is the imagination that develops such an austere education whose one purpose is job preparation through training. What is sacrificed in such a narrow corridor is cultural memory, a flexible imagination as well as discussions of the deepest problems that affect us as human beings. Along with such a paring to the bones is the squelching of a sense of wonder about how things were and are and just might be.

Humanities and the Revival of Learning

The disciplines that comprise the humanities might be viewed on one level as multiple ways of remembering the traditions of thought revealed by history. To recall the wisdom of the past, to rework these mythologies that gave rise to earlier civilizations and cultures, to see ourselves in light of what has been discovered—all these can be beneficial to an intelligent and vigorous work force. To lose the points of view as ways of imagining and knowing that the humanities continue to offer the thoughtful

---

401 *Dark Age Ahead*, p. 60.
402 *Dark Age Ahead*, p. 62.

person is to lose our collective cultural identity. Without it, we free-float and free-fall as a people because our common heritage is sabotaged right out from under us. We become victims of any propaganda that assaults us, as with the repeated clichés that invaded the sleep of people in Huxley's programmed world. The result is the loss of a critical and thoughtful moral imagination that can discern the difference between knowledge and kitsch.

But if we stopped at simply assessing the loss of content that the humanities gift us with, we would have failed to tap into the deeper levels of its intrinsic value, for the humanities offers us a particular way of being present to knowing. As early as 1980, a report formulated by "The Commission on the Humanities," expressed concern about this cluster of studies' future and offered a succinct statement of its value: "Through the humanities we reflect on the fundamental question: what does it mean to be human? The humanities offer clues but never a complete answer."[403] The report goes on to suggest that "They reveal how people have tried to make moral, spiritual and intellectual sense of a world in which irrationality, despair, loneliness, and death are as conspicuous as birth, friendship, hope and reason."[404]

The humanities explore, each in its varied language and method, the place of paradox, mystery, contradiction through the particular and unique turn of mind, which is always "toward history, the record of what has moved men and women before us to act, believe, and build as they did."[405] These ideas outlined by the Commission are what I wish to cultivate in my last observation.

In his now classic text, *Leisure: The Basis of Culture*, Josef Pieper, a German philosopher and theologian, argued in 1948 Germany for a way of knowing that allows time, reflection, and musing which can promote a deeper knowing. Part of his book's intention, retranslated in 1998, is to retrieve some of the ancient ideas about knowing that bear directly on the intrinsic value of humanities learning.

Early in his discussion, Pieper retrieves a dual way of knowing practiced by both ancient and medieval philosophy. He observes that the medievals "distinguished between the intellect as *ratio* and the intellect as *intellectus*."[406] The former is "the power of discursive thought, or searching and researching, abstracting, refining and

---

403 Lyman, Richard W., (chairman). *Report of the Commission on the Humanities*, p. 1.
404 *Report of the Commission on the Humanities*, p. 1.
405 *Report of the Commission on the Humanities*, p. 3.
406 Pieper, Josef, *The Basis of Culture*, p. 11.

concluding."[407] By contrast, *intellectus* "refers to the ability of 'simply looking' (*simplex intuitus*), to which the truth presents itself as a landscape presents itself to the eye." Both forms of cognition are necessary to satisfy what the ancients believed constituted "the spiritual knowing power of the human mind....All knowing involves both."[408] *Intellectus* is more conducive to receiving, to waiting in openness, "a receptively operating power of the intellect."[409] This latter way of conceiving knowledge is closer to contemplation, a disposition that is non-aggressive, non-manipulating, non-egocentric and less bent on explanation; instead it is more porous and patient, willing to see what wishes to be revealed. I believe it is a form of being present that the humanities cultivate most effectively, as a disciplined way of being receptive and open, not in charge and not always guiding the reins of the intellect. Nor are the humanities seeking a definitive answer to complex questions; its instinct is not to simplify and so control.

In fact, as Pieper develops the distinction between the low "canopy" of the work world and the more transcendent canopy-breaking of liberal learning, he suggests that "the Philosopher is akin to the Poet; both are concerned with the *mirandum*—'the wondrous', the astonishing or whatever calls for astonishing, or wonder."[410] In the work world such activity is useless and irrelevant; in the world of total work "all the various forms and methods of transcendence must themselves become sterile...."[411] It is my belief that the humanities promote the philosophic and poetic act of wondering, which is the beginning impulse to philosophizing.

Poetic Knowledge and the Recovery of Education

In his far-reaching and deeply historical work, *Poetic Knowledge: The Recovery of Education*, teacher and literary historian James S. Taylor crafts a persuasive case for retrieving and replenishing this form of knowing. He is quick, however, to point out that poetic knowledge is not concerned with the wisdom that poetry affords us, but rather with a certain attitude towards learning that I have been developing up to this

407 *The Basis of Culture*, p. 11.
408 *The Basis of Culture*, p. 11.
409 *The Basis of Culture*, p. 12.
410 *The Basis of Culture*, p. 69.
411 *The Basis of Culture*, p. 69.

point. For this mode of knowledge is what the humanities foster, each in its own way, of perceiving and interpreting the world. Taylor reveals early on what qualities comprise poetic knowing: it is intuitive; it is comfortable with obscurity and not with the fast and fixed; it allows the seen and the unseen to emerge in a unity; it cultivates the imagination, intuition, emotions and silences; it is based on a philosophical intuition; it is "a poetic (a sensory-emotional) experience of reality"; it is non-analytical.[412] Thus, poetic knowing "makes present a sensate knowing"[413] wherein the embodied person contemplating such a form of knowledge is not dis-incarnated but fully present "connaturally."

This last term, *connatural,* Taylor retrieves from the writings of St. Thomas Aquinas and, more currently from its further development by the philosopher Jacques Maritain, to designate a stance or an attitude towards knowing that I am arguing is at the heart of humanities learning: "To be connatural with a thing is to participate in some way with its nature, as distinct from its intentional form, to share a likeness of nature."[414] It is one of the central modes that leads to right judgment. Discernment, taste, right order, a sense of the relation of parts to parts and to a greater whole are all assembled in connatural knowing, which stems from, according to Taylor, "all unpremeditated intellectual acts of knowing."[415] In the process, within humanities learning or knowing, one grasps that facts are insufficient; rather, the humanities is more a gathering of a world view that opens the mind to historicity itself in its profound and often perplexing continuity.

Maritain designates this attitude or stance a *habitus,* a term he pulls from the history of the ancients to express what he calls "the qualities of a class apart, qualities which are essentially stable dispositions, perfecting in the line of its own nature the subject in which they exist." So for example, he suggests that "Health, beauty are *habitus* of the body; sanctifying grace is a *habitus* (supernatural) of the soul."[416] My sense is that humanities study can have as one of its ends the development of an "operative habitus"[417] wherein the contemplation of the disciplines that comprise its terrain can

---

412 Taylor, James S., *Poetic Knowledge*, pp. 5-6.
413 *Poetic Knowledge*, p. 5.
414 *Poetic Knowledge*, p. 64.
415 *Poetic Knowledge*, p. 65.
416 Maritain, Jacques, *Art and Scholasticism and The Frontiers of Poetry*, p. 10.
417 *Art and Scholasticism and The Frontiers of Poetry*, p. 11.

lead to action, to the promotion of social justice, to a sense of authentic liberty, and to a desire to promote balance and fairness in the world.

To lose humanities education is to forfeit our collective moorings, our anchors and our sense of being placed in a world with a history and a future. Humanities education is one of imagination and vision, a means of seeing both panoramically and scenically; it develops "not simply an alert mind but an overall alertness of keen senses....It is the habit of noticing what is happening here and now and reflecting with the natural powers upon that experience that cultivates the connatural degree of knowledge."[418] For my purposes, I believe, *humanities knowing* begins in both trust and wonder and ends in love and respect for all that was, is and will be.

A mythic sensibility, a way of thinking along mythic corridors, is immensely facilitated through humanities-leaning learning. Notice the work of Marie-Louise von Franz, C.G. Jung, Joseph Campbell, Marion Woodman, James Hillman, Sigmund Freud, Gaston Bachelard, Fyodor Dostoevsky, and earlier, Homer, Plotinus, Plato, Aristotle, Sophocles, Aeschylus, Virgil, Sappho and one sees how many disciplines they exploit to deploy new ideas, not old ones repackaged but finally insubstantial in their construction.

The qualities as well as actions of invocation and evocation grow organically from the analogical bent of the imagination to see the pattern, to discern the underlying principles governing a thing, to remember the connection from earlier sources, to retain the qualities of *then* to pull them into *now,* as well as the energic reality of form beneath the structure of things, to spiral back into history and across disciplines and return to where one was in contemplation so to discern its pattern anew. The power of knowing the tradition in several disciplines gives one's hip a range of motion that an arthritic grinding bone on bone prohibits; it is one of the strongest attributes in allowing a mythic sensibility to gestate and grow in the soul. Humanities cartilage gives to culture a flexible form of knowledgeable rotation.

I have thought for some time that any presidential cabinet should include not only a humanities learner but also a mythologist in the room when any big decisions are being contemplated in order to give a cultural and multifaceted depiction of a country and its people under discussion. In each discipline of learning lurks a nuclear reactor, a unique energy field that is activated when we step into it. It is revved up even

---

418 *Poetic Knowledge*, pp. 64-65.

more when we enter sporting the suit of another discipline so that some nuclear, core reverberation may be set in motion because of just such a confrontation/conversation.

In his essay that introduces Sigmund Freud's *Civilization and its Discontents*, the biographer Peter Gay opens with the opinion that "it was Freud's fate, as he observed not without pride, to 'agitate the sleep of mankind.'"[419] I like this idea of agitating the sleepers, those needing a bit of prodding towards wakeful consciousness. The humanities behave like a constellation of consciousness-altering disciplines; when taken together, they can evoke and provoke one into a fuller awareness to see below the phenomenal world into those principles and patterns that give them their structure and form. Without the humanities, this slumber will continue and deepen in the modern mind and so darken the possibility of an informed and thoughtful collective that up to now has been evaporating on the horizon of culture for decades.

Finally, I offer the following reflections on humanities education:

- It is interdisciplinary in nature
- It is complex, subtle and consonant with the disciplines that comprise its rich field as well as the created order in all its imperfections
- It cultivates integrity
- It grounds the person and the collective in place by making one feel at home in the world
- It promotes a sense of authentic freedom
- It places us in contact directly or analogically with the world's large universal and sustaining symbols
- It guides one towards the inner truth of things
- It serves as a compass for suffering humanity
- It aids one in recognizing the larger essential patterns and energies that direct human and natural existence
- It promotes care and compassion for self and others as well as the planet in its complex interplay
- It points one to the large realm of the invisibles
- It serves as a critique or caution to excess and to appetites out of control
- It is less a method for explanation and more a willingness to be in the face of mystery and at ease, for there is always more to realize

---

419 Freud, Sigmund, *Civilization and Its Discontents*, p. ix.

- It promotes a sense of wonder
- It develops a habit of mind that can be transferred to any study in life and to a life lived in its fullest comprehension and satisfaction
- It fosters or makes present a sense of caution in the present by redeeming and recollecting the past so as not to duplicate its malfunctions in the present or future
- It allows space to forgive ourselves and others by outlining the imperfect nature of being and becoming
- It reveals the paradox of unity within diversity
- It opens us to the mythic and psychic substructure of the seen world so we may contemplate the invisible presences in their rich multiplicity and diversity
- It brings joy and a sense of spaciousness to the one studying because one is now in touch with forces and energies far transcending the self

References

Freud, Sigmund, *Civilization and Its Discontents*. The Standard Edition. Introduction Peter Gay. Trans. James Strachey. New York: Norton, 1961.

Hedges, Chris, "The Progressive Interview." *The Progressive*, volume 75, Number 8, August 2011. 33-37.

Hitchens, Christopher, "Foreword." *Brave New World and Brave New World Revisited*. New York: Harper Perennial, 2004. vii-xxi.

Huxley, Aldous, *Brave New World* and *Brave New World Revisited*. New York: Harper Perennial, 2004.

Jacobs, Jane, *Dark Age Ahead*, Vintage, May 17, 2005

Kernan, Alvin, (Editor) *What's Happened to the Humanities?* Princeton: Princeton UP, 1997.

Lyman, Richard W., (chairman). *Report of the Commission on the Humanities: The Humanities in American Life*. Berkeley: U California P, 1980.

Maritain, Jacques, *Art and Scholasticism and The Frontiers of Poetry*. Trans. Joseph W. Evans. New York: Charles Scribner's Sons, 1962.

Pieper, Joseph, *Leisure: The Basis of Culture*. Trans. Gerald Malsbary. South Bend: St. Augustine's Press, 1998.

Ravitch, Diane, *The Death and Life of the Great American School System: How Testing and Choice are Undermining Education*. New York: Basic Books, 2010.

Taylor, James S., *Poetic Knowledge: The Recovery of Education*. Albany: State University of New York Press, 1998.

10

Poetics of Soul:
Revisioning Psychology As Mythical Method

Every text reveals the weaver's predilections
—James Hillman[420]

The beauty and complexity of James Hillman's *Revisioning Psychology* rests substantially in how it creates a new metal as an amalgam of poetics, mythos and archetypal psychology; its consequence is iconoclastic, insightful and innovative for any of us interested in the cross currents of poetry and psyche. Where the two meet and converse is quite possibly one matrix where myths have their genesis.

I can remember so many evenings in the early years of the Dallas Institute of Humanities and Culture when James stood at this podium and dazzled us with his reading of a fairytale or reworked a passage by Jung or entered into a reverie on some cultural phenomenon, like the importance of culture for the health of the city or the presence of Aphrodite in the revelation of beauty, that he invited us to see with new eyes. Only the literary critic Louise Cowan, to my mind, carried the same intense cache of dazzle at this podium; both were in some sense mirrors of one another as visionary innovators and instigators of a deepening imagination, which is where their

---

420 Hillman, James, *Revisioning Psychology*, p. ix.

individual works united most forcefully and most fruitfully. I know I am not alone on this point.

I imagine *Revisioning Psychology* as James' *Moby-Dick,* with all the complexity, episodic turns of plot, and meditations on the soul of matter and the mothering of soul that Melville's whaling voyage invited on board the Pequod. The white whale, for James, is the psyche itself—seductive, slippery, sagacious, serious, serene, twisted like the crooked lower jaw of the elusive whale, fierce in its seduction, oblique as well as ubiquitous and occupying multiple latitudes at once. Moreover, like the white whale, soul itself in James' lexicon is the *anima mundi,* the world soul, which only the deepest philosophic and poetic meditations are capable of approaching, much less grasping.

In addition, we each comprise qualities of the figures of Ahab in his quest to disarm what cannot be affected, really; Ishmael in moments of quiet reflection when something subterranean reveals itself in a breach of imagining; a bit of Stubb who wants to seize the whale as a commodity and pin it to the main mast of nature or cut a slice and have it served raw on a dinner plate; and even a sliver of Pip, who, upon jumping from the whale boats not once but twice, sees the immensity of soul in the waters of the mind and matter and speaks a foreign language from that day forward, influenced by the grammar of divinities that stir mysteriously in the deep.

Sometimes I think that James is most like Pip, however; it is as if he jumped from the boat chasing whales and entered the immemorial immensity of the ocean to see with altered optics the mythic creatures swarming there. Yet unlike Pip and more akin to Ishmael, he survived the vision to give us the story of that deep diving in *Revisioning Psychology,* which his legacy and history may affirm, is the most original sea voyage from which all other soul explorations emanate.

Its waters are vast and deep, its themes enormous and universal. Ishmael observes at one point in the voyage: "To produce a mighty book you must choose a mighty theme. No great and enduring volume can ever be written on the flea, though many there be that have tried it."[421] Choosing mosquitoes or flies to further spiritual development will not carry the load. *Revisioning Psychology* shows clearly in its wake the leviathanic theme of the soul itself—not only the individual soul we are personally guided by, but the *anima mundi* herself. His vision, however, is that large, that epic because it engages one of the grand qualities of this inclusive genre: re-founding old verities into a new order of nuanced and complex understanding. Only a few souls

---

421 Melville, Herman, *Moby-Dick,* p. 487.

will and have been called to muster the courage to explore such a region that stretches both horizontally across the landscape of history and downward mythically to the depths of pathology and afflictions. Grand courage must be part of one's cargo in order to witness fully, without flinching, the soul's enormous motions. In one of his memorable insights, James affirms that, "the soul can exist without its therapists but not without its afflictions."[422] Few have understood both the voice as well as the value of our infections and wounds as has he.

Lyn Cowan, a Jungian analyst and no lightweight in her own books on the soul, once told me in an email that it was she who, working closely with James in Zurich, typed the manuscript of *Revisioning* and created the index from the galleys. When one evening over dinner, after the manuscript had been shipped out to Harper's Publishing, she told James: "You know, it's your masterwork. You'll never write anything that reaches this level again." He looked startled and then reflective: "Yes....you're probably right."[423] Privileged to be so close to every word of the work as she typed them, I imagine her musing on what was unfolding before her eyes with each click of the keys and then as she constructed the index for it, another form, perhaps, of the "Extracts" of *Moby-Dick* and the *prima materia* of the entire opus. Getting to know Lyn recently, and agreeing with her assessment of James' opus, I realize what can and does happen to readers of a writer's work: they can in moments of clarity, see into it as readers more deeply than can the writer and thus have the advantageous capacity of fathoming depths of its waters of which the writer may be unaware. Such is the power of the work's mythic enormity.

Revisioning is a work that taught me it must be read slowly and meditatively. In the fall of 2010 when I entered ¾ time employment at Pacifica Graduate Institute and so would not be flying out for two week stretches between August and January, I was drawn, after 30 years had passed, to re-read and take slow notes in my own hand, not computer-generated, of so many passages that had so puzzled me when I was a graduate student at the University of Dallas. I recall at that time how little money my wife Sandy and I had. I could not afford to buy the book, so I checked out a copy from the library and took it to my night job as a Pinkerton Security guard at Delta Steel Company in Dallas.

---

422 *Revisioning Psychology*, p. 71.
423 (email: 11/14/2011, 9:03 A.M.).

There, after much sleuthing at 1 or 2 in the morning, I succeeded in locating the key to the Xerox machine, a fairly new invention at the time in the mid'70s. Under cover of guarding the offices and rolls of sheet metal created for buildings to be constructed across the United States, that night I copied the entire book, accompanied by great glee and a little fear. I still possess the Xeroxed copy as a keepsake of those leaner but nonetheless abundant years of study. I can still recall the strongly-worded memo from the company's president that went out to all employees the following day; in it he demanded to know who it was that made so many copies on the machine, an expense he could do without along perhaps with the employee as well. I kept my head down, beyond suspicion; what in heaven's name would a security guard be doing copying something at night? I hid neatly under the stereotype, safe behind my shiny Pinkerton badge. That is how I procured my first copy of *Revisioning:* by theft. I never told James that story; now I wish I had. I think he would have been delighted to learn that Hermes was alive and active in duplicating his creative work, as James himself carried that Hermes energy through every page of *Revisioning.*

At the time, accompanied by literary theorist Louise Cowan's rich insights into the nature of poetics and genre theory on one side of my studies, and James' astonishing breakthroughs, often following on C.G. Jung's own excavations into psyche on the other, I wondered for a considerable period of time what I had done correctly in my life to deserve such largesse.

Revisioning is so large that one could spend a lifetime studying it, as one might the narrative of the white whale, for its own context and for what it leads us to consider. I am going now to take just a small parcel from James' work, one of my favorite sections that I recently typed from the hand-written notes that number some 150 pages and blends his insights with my own thoughts and analogies gathered in my rereading; in this way I feel a joint stock company of mutual participation as a revisoner of his *Revisioning.* I believe it was one of his main intentions, if not hopes, that we each would take up the challenge of his take on the soul's mythical method and extend it along our own corridors of understanding. No wonder he dedicated the book to "The Reader, without whom all is Vanity." A stronger invitation to take up the author's words and rework them has not been issued.

Recovering the Soul

James' work, you may remember, is divided into four sections: 1. Personifying or Imagining Things; 2. Pathologizing or Falling Apart; 3. Psychologizing or Seeing Through; 4. Dehumanizing or Soul-Making. The structure comprises his own genre wheel of the soul and perhaps they could with beneficial effect be seen as analogies of the four genres worked out so elegantly in Louise Cowan's genre wheel: Lyric, Tragedy, Comedy, and Epic. Something of these respective quaternities, as C.G. Jung noticed repeatedly, offer images of wholeness and completeness.

In each of these sections James wrestles with, so to realign the work of psychology—the logos of the soul—with the imagination, something lost, he affirms, with the development of psychology along the sluices of fantasies heavily naturalistic and scientific. A too literal reliance on one's history flattens the power of the imaginal life into insignificance. Moving between a phenomenology that returns us to the lived experience of an event and an imaginal mythology that seeks primarily through afflictions the movement of the soul to a fuller awareness of itself, *Revisioning* recalibrates the nature and purpose of psychologizing as a form of mythologizing. Its overarching aim regarding psychology James is very clear about when he affirms in his Preface to the 1992 edition: "to revert its vision to poetic principles and polymorphic Gods... of ensouling the nonhuman."[424] Each section of his quaternal structure can stand alone, but each assumes a deeper richness when placed in relation to the others.

My interest warms up considerably over the last part of section Two: Pathologizing or Falling Apart. It is most interesting right now for a couple of reasons: 1. It most intensely expresses some of the major terms for one to discover through uncovering layers of one's personal myth; 2. It rests heavily on the seminal movement of reversion essential to archetypal psychology's mythical method, namely, a return to the origins, through memory, of one's life story. It also clarifies further the nature of fantasy not as make-believe but as the presence of analogy, metaphor and what Jung earlier, borrowing from the work of philosopher Hans Vaihinger, called the "als ob" or "as-if" nature of our psychological turns. It further highlights the central act of pathologizing, what James calls an "iconoclasm; as such it becomes a primary way of soul-making. Its method is to break the soul free from its identification with egocentric seeing through the upperworld heroes of light and high Gods who provide the ego with its models...

---

424 *Revisioning Psychology*, p. ix.

and have cast our consciousness in a one-sided, suppressive narrowness regarding life, health and nature."[425] Finally for my purposes, it asserts as well what James calls the "polytheistic perspective," which writer of theology and mythology David Miller was to successfully amplify later in his own book, *The New Polytheism* (1974).

One of many innovative ways of seeing anew that *Revisioning* introduces as part of its mythic method is polytheism; it allows for an escape hatch to rescue the soul from the belief that a single, uniform perspective has the heft or the validity to voice with sufficient nuance a full spectrum of psychological life. In fact, such reliance on a systematic way of univocal seeing arrests and silences the poetic subtleties of psyche's insistence. Needed, he writes, "is a deeper perspective that takes full account of the ceaseless interconnections and fantasies going on among the persons of the psyche. I mean here the polytheistic perspective described in myths where norms are the myths themselves in their structuring and governing of experience."[426]

Revisioning Psychology's Mythical Method

Almost ten years after the publication of *Revisioning*, James was to return to mythos and plot in one of his most popular books, *Healing Fiction*, my second favorite of all of his writings, after *Revisioning*. There, early on, he proposes a startlingly new way for us to understand the plot of a story when he outlines Freud's seminal contribution to psychology, both positive and negative. First the negative: Freud's theory of the Oedipus story became the foundation for his theory of human development or its absence, in the form of libido. James observes: His [Freud's] double style of writing required that what was plot and myth on one level was theory and science on another."[427] James' quarrel with Freud's theory is not that it fails as an empirical hypothesis of human nature, but that it fails poetically; it is in essence neither deep nor embracing enough nor an "aesthetic enough plot for providing dynamic coherence and meaning to the dispersed narratives of our lives."[428] In the last qualifier, note in passing the polytheistic method appearing in the phrase, "dispersed narratives."

---

425 *Revisioning Psychology*, p. 89.
426 *Revisioning Psychology*, p. 88.
427 Hillman, *Healing Fiction*, p. 11.
428 *Healing Fiction*, p. 11.

Now to the positive regard James holds for Freud's theory, its own form of myth, for our theories, he reveals, are forms that our myth assumes. Always a myth peers out from under theory's clothing. Freud carried his own mythic genius, as James asserts: "Freud developed his one plot after a myth, Oedipus. With this move Freud too placed mind on a poetic basis. He understood that the entire narrative of a human life, the characters that we are and the dreams we enter, are structured by the selective logic of a profound *mythos* in the psyche."[429] In this move of his, Freud had hearkened back to Aristotle's *Poetics,* which was the first literary theoretical work to earmark plots as myths: "wherever 'plot' appears the original Greek word is *mythos.* Plots are myths. The basic answers to *why* in a story are to be discovered in myths."[430]

Two items gain undeniable importance here. First, James' development of these ideas relating psyche to poiesis to mythos has its genesis in *Revisioning*, where he intuited this connection and built an edifice (even an Oedipus to it!) in the form of a mythical method. His breakthrough was in recognizing the enormous achievement of both Freud and Jung when in their respective works, and in spite of their disagreements about the range and nature of psychic energy and the layers of the unconscious, they "took the step into understanding human nature in terms of myth;"[431] in doing so "they moved from human nature to the nature of religious powers. Here James implements a term he will use throughout his writing: "the poetic basis of mind [which] suggests that the selective logic operating in the plots of our lives is the logic of mythos, mythology."[432]

The second reason for pausing at the way station of *Healing Fiction* as a supplement to *Revisioning Psychology* is that this principle resides behind the 80 or so riting meditations in my book, *Riting Myth, Mythic Writing: Plotting Your Personal Story.* For not only the stories that we have been and are becoming but also the stories we remember, are seminal inroads to contacting the deeper strata of our personal mythos. I want to suggest that the act of remembering is itself a mythic act, a mythic meditation: not their historical accuracy in fact but rather their imaginal veracity as remembered are the *prima materia* for writing. They are, in the language of *Moby-Dick,* the "Extracts" from which we develop and see unfolding the larger map of our voyage, the rigging and mastheads of our mythology, and the shrouds of our secret life. In

---

429 *Healing Fiction*, p. 11.
430 *Healing Fiction*, p. 11.
431 *Healing Fiction*, p. 12.
432 *Healing Fiction*, p. 12.

fact, the act of writing is itself a ritual way of reenacting our narrative in mytho-poetic ways by memorializing them from within, then writing out our remembrances and mythologizing them in the creative process of recollection.

No wonder then that the Greek imagination discovered and gave shape to Memory as a goddess, Mnemosyne, who first aligned and subsequently mated with Zeus, a divine presence of mind itself, gave birth to the nine muses. Moreover, while we do not know a great deal about Mnemosyne, we are made aware that she it is who makes possible narratives themselves, for the plots of the stories we encounter, including the unfolding complexity of our own, assumes the ability to remember and to imaginally retrieve what has been, to help each part find a place, bit by bit, in the fabrication of our own fiction. Such is the power of this goddess to offer us coherence that events themselves are incapable of delivering.

The four modes of consciousness that comprise the large sweep of James' mytho-poetic method mentioned earlier might be taken up individually in a series of lecture-discussions and meditated on slowly so to see the whole through each of these rich and episodic parts. I want, however, for the remainder of this presentation to return to my intention to explore a section from "Two: Pathologizing Or Falling Apart" and most specifically, the section entitled "Myths,"[433] In these five pages he returns to one of his most pervasive influences in his own writing, the neo-Platonist Plotinus, who believed that "all knowing comes by likeness."[434] "Reversion," another and most essential mode of psychological movement in James' mythical method mentioned above, is one main artery back to recognizing or discovering "likeness." One versed in the ways of Louise Cowan's imaginative construct of poetry might readily recognize the quality of mimesis outlined in the *Poetics,* which now hovers around both *likeness* and *reversion.*

Pathology is less crafted around literal events, sicknesses, excesses, natural events and more deeply around "mythical figures" which James calls "eternal metaphors of imagination," and "archetypal resemblances" present in literal events and persons but, more conducive to our concerns, in mythical figures in action that allow one to ask imaginally: which figure am I like "and the patterns I am enacting [that] have their authentic home ground?"[435] The impulse at work here is James' belief that "soul

---

433 *Revisioning Psychology*, pp. 99-104.
434 *Revisioning Psychology*, p. 99.
435 *Revisioning Psychology*, p. 99.

events are not parts of any system"; rather, they reveal an independent primacy of the imaginal. It creates its fantasies autonomously, ceaselessly, spontaneously,"[436] not as compensation but as illumination. Reversion is such a formative principle at work in this action of soul because it seeks a return, a retrieval, and, indeed, a revisioning. *Revisioning* is at the same instant a Psychology of Reversion, of a return, of seeing once more, not in the spirit of a repetition compulsion but more through the disposition of a renewed constellation, a terza rima of the soul's eternal return and renewal, a return in order to renew or a reversal into the unfamiliar. Reversion comprises the new spiral of archetypal psychology. Spiraling down, far from being a motion of degeneration, is here a movement of meditation and remediation.

In this spirit, another tenet of his mythical method is to be wary of taking the myths literally. Rather, and closer to the workings of the imagination, one might enter the spirit of "as if" mentioned above, what Jung called in his writings the "als ob" of the soul, and at about the same time the German Kantian philosopher Hans Vaihinger called his massive study *The Philosophy of 'As If'*. Less so "what if" but rather "as if."

Originally published in 1924, *The Philosophy of 'As If'* brilliantly traces and makes connections between a host of disciplines that gather around the nature of metaphor and analogy. Vaihinger understands our ways of comprehension as being founded largely on "analogical fictions."[437] He goes on develop the idea that "all knowledge, if it goes beyond simple actual succession and co-existence, can only be *analogical*," followed by an observation he develops from the philosopher Grun. "Grun is therefore quite right when he says that metaphysics is metabolic, *metaphoric*. What Grun calls metaphors are in the main indispensable fictions."[438] Metaphors work along circuitous lines, around and about, obliquely making connections that are not causal but imaginal, allowing the psyche its poetic toe hold into comprehending by analogy, rooted in the structure of likeness.

Vaihinger's thought, which influenced C.G. Jung as well, here offers another angle into James' work through metaphor as an example of an "as if" mode of revisioning, an imaginal correspondence unconcerned about the fact of the event, and more curious about its imaginal circuitry, its energy transfer and translation, through reversion.

---

436 *Revisioning Psychology*, p. 100.
437 Vaihinger, Hans, *The Philosophy of 'As If'*, p. 29.
438 *The Philosophy of 'As If'*, p. 29.

Earlier, James offered the intention of his entire project: to see the soul anew "I began by examining various psychological syndromes *as if* they were mythical enactments, *as if* they were ways in which the soul is mimetic of an archetypal pattern."[439] On the other hand, if reversion becomes too literal, too close to a univocal matching A to B, then we have fallen, he warns, into the same kind of reduction from which his opus is seeking to extricate the thought of the soul from. His caution bears repeating:

> Mythical metaphors are not etiologies, causal explanations, or name tags. They are perspectives toward events, which shift the experience of events, but they are not themselves events. They are likenesses to happenings, making them intelligible, but they do not themselves happen. They give an account of the archetypal story in the case history, the myth in the mess.[440]

The afflictions we live within and that live through us are to be seen as crucial markings of our fiction. Mythic stories, including the ones we embody through our own woundings, must include a reading of all the figures present, not this or that one that we believe most represents us.

I can remember Louise Cowan instructing us in her course, "The Russian Novel" several decades ago: "Do not settle on one character in the story; be open to every one of them, for each character embodies part of the mosaic of the total form of the work; not to include all of them is to read in a woefully incomplete way."[441] Not her exact language but certainly her insistent sentiment. Spoken like a true archetypalist. For another dictum of James' sense of mythic awareness of the soul's yearnings and actions is to pay attention to all segments of the myth. "By means of the myth is the experiencing of their working intrapsychically within our fantasies, and then through them into our ideas,

To separate one or another out and to marginalize the rest usually results in calling the marginalized parts of the myth psychopathological. Not always are we to be blamed for such an exclusion, because, when the myth is experienced along the contours of the above terms, then it is least apparent "for each one characterizes the notion of consciousness itself according to archetypal perspectives; it is virtually impossible to see the instrument by which we are seeing."[442] Yet we may be conscious in

---

439 *Revisioning Psychology*, p. 100. (My italics)
440 *Revisioning Psychology*, p. 101.
441 University of Dallas Lecture, Fall, 1972
442 *Revisioning Psychology*, p. 103.

the way of Apollo, full of light, or willful like Hercules, or the smooth flow of Dionysus.[443] Each divinity is then a style of consciousness, a disposition towards what is present, and an attitude towards a particular interpretation.

Pathology offers pathways to the soul's deepest nature and temper. Recognizing our own form of pathologizing is an essential dimension of gaining a fuller self-consciousness, for "pathologizing is itself a way of seeing; the eye of the complex gives the peculiar twist called 'psychological insight.'"[444] Eyeing pathos is another vision of gazing at the soul through the analogy of affliction, which I wish to extend to include the analogy of affection. I suggest that in our afflictions prowl the deepest plots of our unfolding fiction. The archetypal dominants of these fictions are the stories embodied in myths. *Revisioning* involves rereading mythic stories as analogies of the soul in its suffering. Remembering mythic plots is an imaginal and archetypal method of recollecting ourselves: "we could look at the high-flying young champions—Bellerophon falling from his white winged horse, Icarus plunging into the sea, Phaethon hurtling in flames, unable to manage his father's chariot of the sun—to understand the self-destructive behavior of the spirit...."[445] Herein the mimetic marriage between mythopoiesis and soul-making assumes active presence; both share a love for the imagination's power to make present what would perhaps lie under the floorboards of consciousness, lessening our ability to live more fully, more poetically, more psychologically.

To write as a way of remembering often puts us in touch with our own personal myth. To recollect, to remember, to retrieve and to renew some of these patterns of awareness that craft, contour, and codify the fictions that we are as well as the afflictions that seed and celebrate the deeper mystery of our continual unfolding, can then amplify and even befriend our self-knowledge.

---

443 *Revisioning Psychology*, p. 103.
444 *Revisioning Psychology*, p. 107.
445 *Revisioning Psychology*, p. 103.

References

Hillman, James, *Revisioning Psychology*. New York: Harper Perennial, 1975.

_____. *Healing Fiction*. Woodstock, Connecticut: Spring Publications, 1983.

Melville, Herman, *Moby-Dick, or The Whale*. Introduction by Clifton Fadiman. Illustrations by Boardman Robinson. Collector's Edition. Norwalk, Connecticut: The Easton Press.

Vaihinger, Hans, *The Philosophy of 'As If': A System of the Theoretical, Practical and Religious Fictions of Mankind*. Trans. C.K. Ogden. London: Routledge & Kegan Paul, 1968.

11

The Memorable Teacher: Father Zosima's Active Love and Learning in Dostoevsky's *The Brothers Karamazov*

People talk to you a great deal about your education but some good,
sacred memory, preserved from childhood, is perhaps the best education.

—Alexey Karamazov, *The Brothers Karamazov*[446]

Introduction

As a teacher of 44 years, I have discovered that I move between two poles: faith and doubt. Faith that I will be led by the texts I teach to some insight that warrants remembering, and yet doubt that I know what I am doing and what is being done to me. That is how I understand myself as a teacher: as a pilgrim on a continuous but unclear path between faith and doubt. Because of these two poles, I continue to love teaching because it is the most satisfying and challenging way to learn.

I watch for books both fictional and non-fictional that can shed more light on the art and practice of teaching. One of the great works of literature that has long

---

446 Dostoevsky, *The Brothers Karamazov*, p.734. (All page references throughout this chapter refer to *The Brothers Karamazov*.)

instructed its readers in the areas of teaching and learning by a master teacher is the Russian writer, Fyodor Dostoevksy's last and perhaps most profound work, *The Brothers Karamazov*, completed in 1881, just months before its author died at the age of 60. It represents the last of a series of five novels written over decades after Dostoevsky was released from a Siberian prison camp where he spent several years following being convicted of participating at a reading of a radical pamphlet the Russian authorities found seditious.

Emerging from the frozen tundra and a life of extreme suffering that revived violent epileptic seizures originating when he was only 20 years old, Dostoevsky suffered them for the rest of his life. Nonetheless, one of Russia's greatest writers in its history, though having published and gained a mixed notoriety with earlier works, was poised to create his greatest poetic expressions. He began with *Crime and Punishment* (1866), followed by *The Idiot* (1868), *The Possessed* (1873), *A Raw Youth* (1875) and finally *The Brothers* (1880), agreed by most as encompassing his greatest psychological and poetic insights. In January 1881 Dostoevsky died in St. Petersburg.

As he was called to write, some of us are called to teach. Two questions present themselves at the outset of exploring the teacher in this novel: *What* is a good teacher and *who* is a good teacher? The first question concentrates on attributes, the second on person and persona. A third question asks what this magnificently complex and beautifully-structured novel can impart about the soul of the good teacher and the disposition that allows for learning on a deep and communal level. Instead of the more current terms *facilitator* or *classroom manager*, we might think of the teacher as a midwife, or as one who inspires the teacher in the student, who offers a way of being present to whatever the subject matter is in order to bring the learner to a place of self-instruction through insights gained after being led to the right landscape of inquiry. Can one, moreover, teach well and effectively if one has ceased learning, who is no longer thinking about how that mysterious imaginative encounter with a work's subject matter could be conveyed to another? I don't believe it is possible if nothing more than data-processing or alternating hunting/gathering of information is the purpose of such activity. Clearly something greater and more lasting is at stake in the dedicated and insightful teacher. Towards the end of his life, Dostoevsky chose to make the image of the teacher the principle presence of his last novel as a witness to the sacred acts of teaching and learning.

If poetry offers us by analogy, or by imaginative correspondence, something that resides deep in the soul of our collective humanity and that the narrative of a novel like *The Brothers* is informed by such insights that we can excavate as readers, then what might it reveal about the nature of the good teacher as well as authentic and memorable teaching? Such is the intention of this essay: to see by means of indirection what and who the good teacher is as embodied in one of the novel's major figures, an old and sickly monk, Father Zosima, as he offers instruction and compassion in the last days of his life before his illness consumes him. We might consider, then, what he is guided by, what informs his meetings with a host of varied characters throughout the novel and what qualities constellate around teaching to make it both meaningful and memorable. Zosima inhabits as its central figure a complex plot. Here are the broad outlines of the story.

The narrative focuses primarily on one family, the Karamazovs, comprised of the old patriarch, Feodor Pavlovich Karamazov and his four sons: Dmitri, Ivan, Alyosha and a bastard son, Smerdyakov. Dmitri and his lecherous father compete for the affections of a young woman, Grushenka, which ends with the murder of the father. Dmitri is charged with the killing, but as the novel unfolds it becomes clear that he is innocent and that the bastard son, Smerdyakov, influenced by the intellectual half-brother Ivan, interprets his half brother's teachings as confirmation that old Feodor should be killed. The young son, Alyosha, drawn to the monastery and the monastic life, introduces his teacher, Father Zosima in the novel and records much of what he learned from him. In the course of the action, just before the middle of the story, Ivan recites to his younger brother a prose poem, "The Legend of the Grand Inquisitor," which surveys the terrible burden of freedom of mankind, especially when guided only by the image of Christ rather than by the authority of the Church, with its dogmas and rules, which blueprint the old Inquisitor in Ivan's poem both redesigns and executes.

The now universally known poem tells of Christ's return during one of the most intense periods of the Inquisitions in Seville, Spain in the 16th century. The old Inquisitor has him arrested and subsequently visits him his first night in prison. He admits to Christ that his return will throw into chaos centuries of developing miracles, mystery and authority to ease the burden of freedom for mankind. He tells Christ that his image as the central guide for human action, grounded in active love and responsibility for all, asks too much of human beings in their exercise of freedom.

Ivan eventually disintegrates under the burden of his tormented imagination. His half-brother, Smerdyakov, is eventually arrested and tried for murdering his father, and Dmitri is set free. The action also includes the sudden death of old Zosima and his rapidly corrupting and putrid-smelling corpse, which inspires a scandal amid accusations that such corruption of his body is proof that the old monk was really not as holy as he wished to appear. At Zosima's funeral Alyosha experiences in a dream state a transformative moment of death and rebirth and through them discerns that he must follow his mentor's instructions to leave the church and enter the world, marry, and teach. The novel concludes with Alyosha, carrying within his soul the image of his mentor's active human love, teaches a group of young boys, the future of Russia, who in turn praise their teacher with passionate accolades and declarations of love for him and for one another.

Father Zosima as Paradigm of Inspired Teaching

By turning to several scenes in the novel where Father Zosima engages members of the larger community, often in his monastic cell as his classroom, we can become more fully aware of the spirit of an inspired and effective teacher. That we first encounter the old priest greeting guests in his cell, with its worn but comfortable furniture, suggests a quality of his teaching throughout the novel as both a social as well as spiritual practice. Engaging others through active love weds social interaction with spiritual largesse that represents a pillar of his pedagogy: that each person is responsible for all others. In the human act of teaching and learning, no barriers should exist, though that does not exile disagreements. Zosima's guiding vision, the most important text that inspires his own life and teaching, is the New Testament and its great teacher, Jesus Christ, an image that Ivan's Grand Inquisitor, mentioned above, claims is impossible for human beings to aspire to because it demands more than the human spirit can tolerate. Zosima patterns his disposition towards others and his teaching on unconditional love as a way of both knowing and being. Without a deep and nonrestrictive love for the student, he believes he is incapable of being both effective and persuasive.

In appearance Father Zosima is unimpressive: he "was a short, bent, little man, with very weak legs" (*Brothers*, p.32.) and appeared older than his 65 years because of his illness. "His face was very thin and covered with a network of fine wrinkles, particularly numerous about his eyes....His pointed beard was small and scanty, and his lips, which smiled frequently, were as thin as two threads." (p.32.) Likewise was the furniture in his cell old and wrinkled, well-worn and faded to match its occupant. We can understand his cell as a *temenos,* a sacred space, like the classroom itself; it indicates that setting has a responsible and critical place in the act of learning. The conditions of place and space in which teaching and learning occur can humanize and promote these actions or it can alienate and retard them by muting their sacred nature.

Moreover, what Zosima reveals in this initial appearance with the visitors who have found seats in his cell, is his hospitality. He treats all who enter his living space with reverence and respect, much as one would engage honored guests. As a teacher, Zosima's disposition is one of a welcoming presence wherein a host/guest relationship is established to create an atmosphere and energy favorable to learning. The compassionate teacher consciously creates an atmosphere so that those listening to be instructed and to participate in the conversation that grows from it will be porous, open and receptive to entertaining both the matter and the manner of instruction.

When he addresses old Fyodor Pavlovitch Karamazov, who often portrays himself as a buffoon so that it is difficult to discern when he is to be taken seriously, Zosima responds to his question: "'what must I do to gain eternal life?'" (p.36.) by reminding old Karamazov of what he already recognizes: "'You have known for a long time what you must do. You have sense enough: don't give way to drunkenness and incontinence of speech; don't give way to sensual lust; and above all to the love of money.'" (p.36.) Zosima discerns what infections reside in the soul of the lecherous man; his teaching then is more prescriptive and invites Fyodor to remember what he already knows. Memory itself, the act of remembering, resides at the heart of learning in the novel. Perhaps learning itself is a perpetual imaginative act of recollection that the effective teacher inspires in one's students. Zosima himself, as I mentioned, teaches through the memorial conduit of Christ's guiding words in the gospels; they are his teaching lodestars and direct him in all he says and does in both attitude and in his angle of understanding. In this respect, the effective teacher, among other strategies, engages the students in acts of remembering, which includes here the imaginative act of recollection rather than the mechanical act of memorization of material, so that not data-retrieval but purpose and meaning may slowly emerge in the material meditated on in new ways. Teaching as recollection can lead often to learning as renewal of what one had known but forgotten. It must be remembered anew.

Soon thereafter, Zosima leaves his cell, accompanied by Alexey (also called Alyosha), and addresses a group of peasant women who have gathered, like a chorus of students, each seeking some insight and wisdom from the old monk. He engages several of them directly, but not before listening to them with complete attention. Now this gift and trait of being able to listen closely and with full attention to the other is a signal quality of good teaching: absorbed listening. For how else can the teacher interested in the welfare and learning capacity of one's students further those aptitudes if one is not able to be attentive to their limits and, in the case of these women, their afflictions? Zosima understands that effective teaching spreads out to include one's ability to listen with full attention, which I understand as an act of generosity and respect for the other, in order to better calibrate what and how one responds to where the learner is. Listening with unconditional attention to the other allows the student to become fully present to what he/she understands and expresses. Listening is a form of teaching because of what it allows the other to be present to. To listen with attention is to witness learning on the part of the student as well as to assess where further instruction may be most fruitfully deployed.

With one of the women in particular who has lost many of her children and has just buried her young son, Nikita, Zosima sees before his eyes, in an imaginal moment of recollection, an analogy to the Biblical story of Rachel. "'It is Rachel of old,' said the elder, 'weeping for her children, and will not be comforted because they are not…. Be not comforted. Consolation is not what you need. Weep and be not consoled, but weep. Only every time you weep, be sure to remember that your little son is one of the angels of God, that he looks down from there at you and sees you, and rejoices at your tears….'" (pp.41-42) Zosima reveals by way of a poetic insight in the figure of Rachel how the teacher may actually allow who is being instructed to respond not as one would think one should, but more authentically, more intimately with the actual experience one is suffering. This level of authenticity, students detect intuitively and know what teachers they can trust and which they might best be less forthcoming in their presence.

Such an amazing instance of compassionate pedagogy is revealed by analogy at this moment of instruction. Here the teacher does not attempt to fix or cure the grieving mother, nor does he leave her to suffocate in her grief. What he achieves in his act of loving her in her grief is placing her suffering into another narrative context, into an ancient story, while respecting her right and need to grieve and to shun consolation. It is a brilliant moment: Zosima sees her suffering in the remembered context of the Biblical figure, then encourages the suffering mother not to be consoled, not to be denied her grief-in-loss. He then provides that grief a new space as well as a spiritual vision that modifies or allows for another imagining of the suffering. Here his teaching is an act of love and generosity without sentimentality, without *a fix* attached to it. It now has an alternate image to be experienced by, a more sacred imagination that allows the grieving mother to find in her suffering an image that gives it another life while simultaneously placing her in a new context of a wider human narrative. He guides her to an image of faith that can indeed *console* but not *erase* her great loss as it gains an alternative imaginative form. Teaching here on several levels is based on remembrance—"be sure to remember"—as a way into integrating her suffering. Of course, the grieving mother is free to choose this alternate narrative or simply cling to the one she has been in; the theme, however, is not lost: learning involves fundamental and profound choices, a freedom to engage an alternative image than the one that has sustained and/or at times incarcerated the intellectual and emotional life of one so the individual suffers a paralysis of the will in exchange for not having a supple enough presence to what afflicts, in this case, the woman who grieves.

As a counter to this authentic and compelling moment, Zosima turns finally to Madame Hoklhakov, "a sentimental society lady of genuinely good disposition in many respects" (p.44.) and the mother of wheel chair-bound, Lise, a young woman who Alexey feels affection for and may eventually wed. Her mother has returned to Father Zosima after having recently been in his audience. She suffers, she claims, from an inability to love the people though she wishes to and believes she must; she gushes to the old monk in feigned helplessness. We might understand her as the kind of student who idealizes the teacher beyond all bounds, projecting her own inflated sense of herself on to her mentor and confessor. "'Forgive me! I am suffering!' And in a rush of fervent feeling she clasped her hands before him." (p.47.) The discerning teacher understands the idealizing student and is careful not to be caught by his/her hooks so to avoid being manipulated.

Admitting to her teacher that she suffers from lack of faith, she inquires of Zosima what he thinks of her now. As an idealizing student, she can suck enormous energy from her teacher with a vampire-like neediness. Zosima does not reprimand but rather encourages her to engage in authentic active love of others: "'If you attain to perfect self-forgetfulness in the love of your neighbor, then you will believe without doubt, and no doubt can possibly enter your soul.'" (p.48.) In the same instant he appeals to her inflated sentimental notions of suffering and offers an antibody—authentic active love lived in self-forgetfulness. He ends by encouraging her to avoid all forms of falsehood, "'especially falseness to yourself. Watch over your own deceitfulness and look into it every hour, every minute.'" (p.49.) Never ceasing to love even the most self-involved of his charges, the generous teacher does not shy away from the fundamental flaw exhibited by the student, but has the skill to turn it by suggesting that one be vigilant about one's own motives in constant acts of self-reflection. Honesty and forthrightness, coupled with a generous spirit and an attitude of reverence for the suffering of others, scripts Father Zosima's discerning generous teaching. As a mentor he sees what is noble and redeemable in his students; they do not need answers or cures so much as direction and guidance; then the responsibility rests directly with them, not with the teacher. Knowing whom one is teaching is as crucial as the subject matter being presented for exploration. Blaming the teacher for the student's failure to learn is both shortsighted and too convenient; it also deflects responsibility away from the student on to the shoulders of the teacher. Zosima reveals the value of keeping the student engaged in the process of learning and in calculating the competence of the student approximate to the demands of learning.

Now not all students will learn in spite of the best teacher's efforts. Breaking through the case-hardened crust of a calcified imagination held hostage to a concept or an attitude, with no other possibilities on the student's horizon, poses a challenge for the most seasoned mentor. Such is Zosima's experience with the tormented but brilliant Ivan Karamazov, author of "The Grand Inquisitor" prose poem mentioned earlier that he reads to his brother Alexey with scandalous delight. In Zosima's cell earlier, Ivan and Father Zosima state their respective positions on the nature of virtue and what forces sustain virtues' presence. Zosima argues that the Church of Christ, with Christ as the salvific image of love, is essential; without it, "there would be nothing to restrain the criminal from evildoing, no real chastisement for it afterwards; none, that is, but the mechanical chastisement spoken of just now…which embitters the heart'" (p.55.) but is no real deterrent because it does not soften the heart "'which lies in the recognition of sin by conscience.'" (p.55.) Taken most broadly, no teaching or learning occurs without some formative boundaries or property lines. The freedom that the teacher imparts to the student in order to encourage a variety of ways of knowing cannot happen in boundless space.

In his argument, Zosima fastens his conviction to the recognition of one who transgresses the law, that he has violated something essential to the community. By contrast, Ivan argues that "'there is no law of nature that men should love mankind" but virtue under any color exists only "because men have believed in immortality.'" (p.60.) To Zosima's questioning of his belief, Ivan rejoins: "'Yes. That is my contention. There is no virtue if there is no immortality.'" (p.60.) He will in fact admit to his brother Alexey later that "Christ-like love for men is a miracle impossible on earth." (p.218.) Zosima has no rebuttal for Ivan's argument; instead he sees through to something dark in the young man's soul and addresses it. Now the perceptive and loving teacher can address his student with the truth of the other's nature in such a way that the student becomes aware of himself with a depth and penetration previously unavailable to his awareness. Conceptual thinking has alienated Ivan from himself and Zosima detects just such a cleavage in his soul. He tells him, without rancor or malice: "'in your despair, you, too, divert yourself with magazine articles, and discussions in society, though you don't believe your own arguments, and with an aching heart mock at them inwardly....That question you have not answered and it is your great grief, for it clamors for an answer.'" (p.61.)

We witness a different moment of learning in their exchange. Mentoring includes at times not teaching the material of a discipline when the student recoils from it or remains indifferent to it. These are student choices, not the teacher's. But such a situation of resistance can be transformed by the discerning teacher who can grasp the internal workings of the imagination of the student to such a degree that s/he is in a position to assist making the student known to himself, a knowledge or awareness that one may not possess. In the moment above, Zosima reveals to Ivan where his suffering is most active and, by implication, where in him the sacred may co-inhabit with it: "'But thank the Creator who had given you a lofty heart capable of such suffering; of thinking and seeking higher things, for our dwelling is in the heavens. God grant that your heart will attain the answer on earth, and may God bless your path.'" (p.61) Zosima has turned Ivan's rebellion into a moment of gracious acceptance of who and what he is and what grace may be needed to use his gifts for nobler ends. Learning has indeed occurred; however, it did not become mired in Ivan's ideas but in the condition of his suffering heart. Here, as with other illustrations above, we detect a pattern: learning's most vulnerable region may be where one is most deeply wounded, afflicted, disoriented and dismembered. At this juncture is an opening for change that, without such a soft porous space in the soul, learning might not be invited in, however revelatory it may be.

As Zosima's death draws closer, Alexey is stirred by his words to go into the world, marry and teach: "'Remember that, young man. When it is God's will to call me, leave the monastery. Go away for good.'" (p.67) Alexey is terrified of both losing his mentor and leaving the place of his instruction. Yet this too is part of the learning process: uncoupling from the mentor and carrying his wisdom in memory is to risk losing one's moorings and place of safety where the challenges demand little of one's capacities. I sense that separating from one's central sources of instruction can certainly be terrifying but absolutely necessary so that one does not live a life by following a path already conveniently laid out by another. To do so is to live once again another's life while foregoing one's own. Finding one's own path as one transitions from student to teacher, guided by the wisdom of an ancestor, in this case his monastic mentor, both completes as well as extends Alexey's process of learning. The perceptive teacher can fathom the inchoate teacher in his student and knows that giving birth to that teacher within the folds of the student requires that the mentor step aside, as Virgil, for instance, does for Dante in the last Cantos of *Purgatorio* in the *Commedia*. Out of active love, even as the good teacher instills in the student a way of learning and coming to know that is not a Xerox of the teacher's way but an illustration of how learning can be engaged and furthered according to one's own style. Zosima's wisdom and courage is contained in the words above as his instructions usher Alexey out into the world to follow his own teaching path guided by *pamiat,* the Russian word for memory, which includes the memory of ancestors, what is most important that will sustain one. Learning itself is an act of memory and teaching is an art form in service to the art of recollection.

Zosima, in a series of talks recorded by Alexey so they are available to others, confesses: "'Brothers, love is a teacher, but one must know how to acquire it, for it is hard to acquire, it is dearly bought, it is won slowly by long labor.'" (p.297) So crucial is his insight that love itself teaches; following the strain of that love is Zosima's guiding principle that stretches vastly outside himself, back to the gospels as his fundamental learning narratives that embody love in action. As he reconfigures the gospels in his own teaching, Alexey will further this tradition by engaging the sacred texts in his own developing style as a teacher. So does the word indeed become flesh and instructs among us.

Zosima's Corrupting Body as Memorable Teacher

A teacher can be a scandal in life and in death. Zosima's teaching style, as it were, is carried beyond his life to the scandal of his death. His body's rapid corruption highlights his memory in a way that a normal death and decay would disallow. Is there something here about the scandal of teaching and in its scandalous stench carry a deeper memory to all who know of the most thought-hearted soul, from the most sacred of lives and from the most beloved of teachers? Such is the effect on the young monk, Alexey, who Father Zosima took under his tutelage and transformed by both word and example.

Moving between the language of preaching and that of teaching, Zosima reveals to all who have ears to listen to him that the fundamental impulse in learning and in living a full and meaningful life resides in the capacity one develops to love. In this regard he asks us to remember the guiding principle of Dante Alighieri's fundamental premise that attends the energies of his *Commedia: intelleto d' amore*, the intelligence of love. Love has its own manner of intelligibility, its own knowledge. Zosima carries that same insight that guided his life into his own surprising and scandalous death. The corruption of his body punctuates his words in life. The poetic power of the way in which he decomposes in effect marries his words to the flesh in a fresh reenactment of Christ's own words, his painful death and his joyful resurrection. For the belief of the Russian soul of this time, not what one knows, but what one remembers (*pamiat*) holds the greater value. To be more memorable, Zosima's dead body, which decomposes at an alarming rate, releases an odor that incites some to call him an embodiment of evil itself. These voices miss the genius of his teaching and the dramatic insights his decaying flesh proposes to those open-hearted enough to learn from him. In life, Zosima's refrain is embodied in the following affirmation:

> "Love one another, Fathers," said Father Zosima, as far as Alyosha could remember afterwards. "Love God's people. Because we have come here and shut ourselves within these walls, we are no holier than those that are outside....When he realizes

that he is not only worse than others, but that he is responsible to all men for all and everything, for all human sins, general and individual, only then the aim of our seclusion is attained." (pp.148-49)

In sum, his words that live on with fierce force after his death captures the monk's essential teaching that each is responsible for all, that no one remains outside the purview or range of responsibility for anyone else. Assumed in his belief is that there is no division between people and that individual diversity harbors beneath it a mysterious unity. Conducting one's life with this guidance is the deepest teaching that Zosima shares with the world, including his death.

Post-Mortem Pedagogy

Not long before the middle of the novel, Father Zosima suddenly passes, to the grief of most of his fellow monks and the town generally. But what is most memorable about this great teacher is the rapidity of his decay and the intensity of his stench. The narrator draws attention to this fact that "Before three o'clock in the afternoon that something took place..., something so unexpected by all of us and so contrary to the general hope, that, I repeat, this trivial incident has been *minutely remembered* to this day in our town and all the surrounding neighborhood." (p.308, my italics) Such a memorable incident is to have a profound effect on his most devoted student, Alexey, "forming a crisis and a turning point in his spiritual development, giving a shock to his intellect, which finally strengthened it for the rest of his life and gave it a definite aim." (p.308) With all of the teachings that emanated from his holy mentor, nothing seemed to have a more potent pedagogical effect on the young monk than did the terms of his teacher's passing. Even in death, one can instruct; even post-mortem what one advances can assume a memorableness that informs us about the power of the teacher.

The scandal emanating from the recently deceased is "an odor of corruption [that] began to come from the coffin, growing gradually more marked, and by three o'clock, it was quite unmistakable. In all the past history of our monastery, no such scandal could be recalled." (p.309) There is brilliance on Dostoevsky's part in revealing how teaching can be scandalous, that scandal can school one into a remembrance that would not be present without such exaggeration. The scandal of Zosima's death can attend excellent teaching and underscore the rich irony that accompanies his decaying body. In his death he becomes even more memorable because of this acceleration of corruption, "in excess of nature" (p.313) that informs us of how powerful the good teacher can live, now as an ancestor, in recollection. Zosima's death italicizes a pedagogy of putrefaction. It gathers together qualities of the teacher that perturb many of one's students to both excess and access. It also contains a delicious pun on the assault of the nose and gnosis, the Greek word for "knowledge," especially as it relates to Christian mysticism and mystical enlightenment. All of these areas are an essential part of Zosima's post-mortem offensive bouquet; none of the senses is more intimate or more memorable than smell. We might reconsider the adage as applied to Zosima's corrupting corpse which begins to stink to high heaven, for he is the elder most known for winning over "many hearts, more by love than by miracles, and had gathered around him a mass of loving adherents...." (p.310) But for some, the terms of his decay will deconstruct the old monk's life of active love and expose the weakness of their own beliefs in his sacred life.

First, the surprise and confusion of the odors emanating from his coffin quickly invade the conventional wisdom and expectations of the town's people. Their hope is that miracles prayed for will soon appear fulfilled, emanating, as they must from such a holy man. The teacher, who provokes, however, can disrupt, corrupt, dissolve and dismantle common beliefs and conventions, letting all their previous assumptions fall apart. To break asunder these secure altars of knowing is to allow for other forms of insight, other angles of vision, to intervene. If the student can withstand these assaults on convention in order to claim something new and move it forward, then other options for knowing escalate. However, these new ideas brought forth by the teacher can stink, offend, and assault in such measure that it becomes the task of the student to be permeable to such possibilities, to see where they might lead. Upsetting conventions in one's thoughts and prejudices can be one of the teacher's most potent pedagogies.

The good teacher also has a nose for knowing, a way of sniffing one's way into new crevasses and cracks of what is generally assumed to be true, and to question their veracity and authority, less to dismiss than to amplify, modulate and deepen them. Following one's nose, guided by the teacher, can lead students to promising new possibilities so that what has become dead in them as information devoid of imagination will be sloughed off. But this same teacher may be considered a real stinker for upsetting what one was comfortable knowing, as Zosima is accused of being. He breaks into both expectations and assumptions and rocks them until they begin to break open. For this he unleashes a torrent of jealousy among many of the monks he lived among.

A certain iconoclastic impulse may attend the good teacher's approach in pushing one to question rather than to blindly follow what has been ordained as fixed beliefs and surmises. Not without merit, Zosima's body begins to exude its putrescence at 3 o'clock in the afternoon, the time generally believed of Christ's death on Good Friday. This time is repeated throughout the novel to draw attention to the historical analogue of the monk's offensive odors in death. One might suggest that Christ's death in sacrifice and Zosima's stinking corpse in sympathy with this historic event is also a sacrifice to the safety of religious beliefs that have lost all sense of mystery, all grasp on the imagination's power in faith and any authentic connection to the image of Christ's active human love of being responsible for all. The odor of corruption that the perceptive teacher brings to learning signals the decomposition of held-fast certitudes, prejudices and "truths" one clings to. To this antiseptic and safe manner of believing Zosima's stinking corpse enters to assault and astonish with irony: the holy man's putrefaction.

The townspeople feel betrayed as well; the holy man's death was not supposed to be so real, so embodied and so devastating compared to conventional norms of death. They seek instead the miraculous, while easily blinded to the miracle of this "excess of nature" decomposing before them. Putrefaction is a new odor and a new order of pedagogy that attacks the tendency to complacency. Things become rank around the corpse; it is an invisible presence, only "sensed," with a combination of disgust and horror; each is thrown on one's self to interpret it as one's beliefs dictate. Father Ferapont, an envious antagonist of Zosima's, for instance, claims it is indisputable proof of how hypocritical the old monk was in life and that the stench of his body is in fact the sins and the unholiness of a life lived amongst the pleasures of the world, like the cherry jam Father Zosima enjoyed in social gatherings with the women who visited him. This same act transforms Alexey and initiates him to begin his own pilgrimage quite different from what he suspected would be his safer, because more familiar, trajectory as a monk.

Grieving by his mentor's coffin, Alexey falls asleep and dreams of the miracle of Cana of Galilee. He realizes he is part of the new wine that has been changed by

Christ into the best refreshment for the guests, who are impressed that the best vintage was saved until the end. Having fallen asleep on his knees, he suddenly awakes and walks quickly to the edge of the coffin. In his dream he had heard his mentor's voice proclaim the new wine in the story of Christ's first miracle; now he carries this new expansive feeling in his heart out of the monastic cell and into the night air, transformed by the presence of his dead mentor and the vision of a new expansive city: "The vault of heaven, full of soft, shining stars, stretched vast and fathomless above him. The Milky Way ran in two pale streams from the zenith to the horizon. The fresh, motionless, still night enfolded the earth…The silence of earth seemed to melt into the silence of the heavens….Alyosha stood, gazed, and suddenly threw himself down to the earth." (p.340) A grace-ful transformation overpowers him, as if all that he had learned and contemplated contellate at one instant into a profound change of heart, perhaps the highest and deepest consequence of learning.

This moment, described as occurring soon after the old teacher has died, expresses a resurrection of the soul as a result of what he has learned, as if all his knowledge was now in the service of a *metanoia,* where a change of heart eventuates into a sustained transformed vision of himself and his communal place in the world, where nothing will be excluded from his embrace. Dostoevsky's language captures the powerful effect of a superb teacher on the soul of his student: "But with every instant he felt clearly and, as it were, tangibly, that something firm and unshakable as that vault of heaven had entered into his soul. It was as though some idea had seized the sovereignty of his mind—and it was for all his life and forever and ever. He had fallen on the earth a weak youth, but he rose up a resolute champion, and he knew and felt it suddenly at the very moment of his ecstasy." (p.341) Within his transformed understanding, prompted and nurtured by his mentor, he comes into his own authority as a teacher and as a person: resolute, certain and yielding to his life work, which will not be in the monastic setting but rather in his "sojourn in the world." (p.341) The great teachings of Zosima lead his student to be not a copy of the original but his own unique self, imprinted, however, by the original, a station he may never have reached unless he had yielded with such unconditional completeness to his mentor's active love. All of this comes to fulfillment through the corrupting corpse that Alexey gazes on after waking from his dream. Decay delivers him to a sweet new life.

In addition, the odor of corruption is an outrage, as teaching itself can be outrageous; one's sensibilities are re-ordered into a new pattern of awareness. It signals as well that the teacher does not jettison the body, its imperfections, and its mortality for a life of the mind devoid of flesh. The body, it seems here, has its own grammar, its own unique lexicon, and a new language that those willing to entertain a less anticipated reality must submit to.

Zosima's stinking corpse is hardly the iconic presence assumed to be the postmortem response his adherents and parishioners sought. Instead, it swiftly becomes an ironic image; it becomes the thing most foreign to the sensibilities attuned to it. As such it suggests that the teacher's most effective response on certain occasions in the process of learning includes an ironic twist, for irony has the power to break down conventions, invade clichéd thought, and challenge the commonplace. Teaching can be both iconoclastic and ironic; motivated by love, not cynicism, irony can change over time the heart's way of knowing and extend yet further to a transformed person in service of the sacred.

Zosima as teacher makes himself known in death through his corrupting corpse in an act of love, one of generosity rather than simply through an excess of nature. It may at times be part of good teaching to perturb, to promote discomfort, decentering, delusion, to stir the senses, not just the mind, in an act of awareness that encompasses the whole person. Zosima's corrupting odors fuel the imagination, stir it from sleep, insist it imagine differently, to smell what assails the nose as a different body of knowledge, or a more varied landscape than conventional thought has previously deployed.

As a corollary to what is stated above, Zosima's deformation, its decaying offensive odors, preserves spirit anchored in flesh and thus avoids an intellectualism severed or dismembered from the individual's own flesh as well as the world's body. Learning, the good teacher reveals, is an embodied action of the soul, not a fractured mind-centered performance. In the spirit of Holy Mother Russia, from which Zosima emanated and to whom he returns, to the soiled-ness of the sacred, the teacher that he was and continues to be knows that losing the body can breed a form of abstracted, alienated relation to the soil, as Ivan's more intellectual theology has coerced him into. Such a union of soul with flesh originates from the Great Mother herself. Zosima's corrupting corpse soils the familiar and pollutes purely intellectual knowing divorced from the earth and from history as he guides the student back to an awareness of its genesis, the earthiness of the impulse to learn. Its putrefaction reveals how teaching and learning are spiritual acts of the soul as well as intellectual achievements of mind.

The body, like the earth herself, flourishes in decay, is fertilized by what is least attractive, for the nutrients in fertilizer provide nourishment and energy for new growth. As a seed planted in the ground begins to create new life only when it begins to decay, its shell casing decomposing to free a new rhizome to push through the topsoil, so is Zosima's putrifying corpse a fertile seed that allows the creation of a new fertile field. The scandal of teaching is composed of what it decomposes, breaks down, dis-assembles, to create a new garland of odorous order. There appears to be, then, a direct line of influence from nose—nous—gnosis, a knowledge built on decay, on breakdown, with fertile consequences and even possibilities for new communions. All are what the teacher brings to the field of learning through a cultivation of the old into the soil of what is promising. Alexey is the slender but powerful shoot or sprig that emanates from the seedy decay of Zosima's body, his corruption the richest fertilizer for the new plant that is Alexey Karamazov.

Zosima's offensive-smelling flesh infects and guides Alexey to see, to revision his life in light of his teacher's death and his eventual pilgrimage back into the world's flesh, most likely to marry the young crippled Lise, and to be intimately engaged with the world's matter, modulated by an active love, a constant guiding presence in Zosima's life and now in his death. Less what one learns from one's teacher and more what one remembers of that person and subject matter affords an index of that teacher's presence long after courses and conversations have declined. The teacher is one who actively loves both subject matter, integrating and imagining it in new ways, and one's students who learn to arrange the material in their own fashion. To love within irony is a gift and an art form that the good teacher can impart with largesse.

As a budding teacher, Alexey shares this generous quality of the mentor with his new young students who gather around to celebrate him as he instills in them love for one another even as they attend to another funeral, the death of the young Ilyushechka's coffin, where "there is practically no smell from the corpse." (p.728) Then Alexey collects the youths by the stone under which they had wanted to bury the young Ilyusha; he asks them to engage two acts of remembrance: "'we will never forget first, Ilyushechka, and second, one another….Let us always remember how we buried the poor boy at whom we once threw stones, do you remember, by the bridge….still let us always remember how good it was once here, when we were all together, united by a good and kind feeling which made us, for the time we were loving that poor boy, better perhaps than we are.'" (p.733) As a teacher Alexey conveys to the young boys a sense of their own goodness, even beyond what they thought of themselves; this attitude of self-loving and acceptance, even in the face of grief and loss, carries on the legacy of Zosima by instilling in one's students a sense of their own worth, and because of it, their capacity to excel beyond themselves.

The teacher here at novel's end exhorts, acknowledges and witnesses goodness: "'let us all be generous and brave like Ilyushechka, clever, brave and generous like Kolya,…and let us all be as bashful but also as clever and sweet as Kartashov.'" (p.734) As a gifted teacher, Alexey passes on a legacy of largesse, of a generous spirit and the virtue of remembrance that is to "live forever in our hearts from this time forth!'" (p.735) Learning is in large measure adapting and integrating a legacy of what must be remembered "eternally." (p.735) Its sensibility is what the compassionate teacher promotes and instills in his students, as Alexey does here. He has changed the hearts of the young boys for the rest of their lives; their response, in gratitude, is active love exuberantly returned: "'Hurrah for Karamazov!' Kolya cried once more rapturously and once more all the boys chimed in." (p.735).

Reference

Dostoevsky, Fyodor, *The Brothers Karamazov*. Ed. Ralph Matlaw. Trans. Constance Garnett, revised by Ralph E. Matlaw. New York: Norton, 1976. 1-735.

Also by Dennis Patrick Slattery

William Faulkner and Modern Critical Theory. Ed. Dennis Patrick Slattery. *New Orleans Review*. Winter, 1987, vol. 14, No. 4.

From Your First Mile to Your First Marathon without Injuries. Co-authored with Dr. Jerry Pooler: 1984. Unpublished.

The Idiot: Dostoevsky's Fantastic Prince. A Phenomenological Approach. New York: Peter Lang, 1984.

The Wounded Body: Remembering the Markings of Flesh. State University of New York Press, 2000.

Depth Psychology: Meditations in the Field. Dennis Patrick Slattery and Lionel Corbett, eds. Daimon-Verlag, Einsiedeln, Switzerland: Daimon-Verlag, 2000.

Casting the Shadows: Selected Poems. Winchester Canyon Press, 2001.

Psychology at the Threshold: Selected Papers from the Proceedings. Dennis Patrick Slattery and Lionel Corbett, Eds. Pacifica Graduate Institute Press, 2003.

Grace in the Desert: Awakening to the Gifts of Monastic Life. Jossey-Bass Publishing, March 2004.

Just Below the Water Line: Selected Poems. Winchester Canyon Press, 2004.

Harvesting Darkness: Essays on Literature, Myth, Film and Culture. New York: iUniverse, 2006.

A Limbo of Shards: Essays on Memory, Myth and Metaphor. New York: iUniverse, 2007.

Twisted Sky: Selected Poems. Winchester Canyon Press, 2007.

Varieties of Mythic Experience: Essays on Religion, Psyche and Culture. Ed. Dennis Patrick Slattery and Glen Slater. Daimon-Verlag, Einseideln, Switzerland. March, 2008.

Reimagining Education: Essays on Reviving the Soul of Learning. Edited Dennis Patrick Slattery and Jennifer Leigh Selig. Spring Journal Books, April, 2009.

Simon's Crossing. A Novel. Co-authored with Charles Asher. Fiction. New York: iUniverse, 2010.

Day-to-Day Dante: Exploring Personal Myth through The Divine Comedy. Bloomington, Indiana: iUniverse, 2011.

The Beauty Between Words: Selected Poetry of Dennis Patrick Slattery and Chris Paris. Stormville, New York. Waterforestpress. November, 2010.

The Soul Does Not Specialize: Revaluing the Humanities and the Polyvalent Imagination. Edited by Dennis Patrick Slattery, Jennifer Selig and Stephen Aizenstat. Mandorla Publications, May, 2012.

Riting Myth, Mythic Writing: Plotting Your Personal Story. Fisher King Press, Carmel, California. May 2012.

CDs:

Casting the Shadows: Selected Poems. Recorded/ Mastered by Dan Canalos, Soundwaves Recordings, Huron, Ohio. 2002.

Just Below the Water Line: Selected Poems. Recorded/ Mastered Dan Canalos, Graphic layout Kristen Schoewe. Soundwaves Recordings, Huron, Ohio. 2006.

About the Author

Dennis Patrick Slattery, Ph.D., has been teaching for 43 years, the last 19 in the Mythological Studies and Depth Psychology and Depth Psychotherapy programs at Pacifica Graduate Institute in Carpinteria, California. He is the author, co-author, or co-editor of 20 books and dozens of articles and book reviews in magazines, newspapers and collections of essays. See his entire vitae on http://www.dennispslattery.com/ dslattery@pacifica.edu

Dr. Slattery offers writing retreats on personal myth in the United States and Europe through the work of Joseph Campbell. When not writing and teaching, Slattery and his wife ride their Harley-Davidson Electra Glide Classic on the ranch roads of Texas as well as spoil their new granddaughter.

Contact: dslattery@pacifica.edu www.dennispslattery.com

Index

Also from Fisher King Press

Marked By Fire: Stories of the Jungian Way
edited by Patricia Damery & Naomi Ruth Lowinsky,
1ˢᵗ Ed., Trade Paperback, 180pp, Index, Biblio., 2012
— ISBN 978-1-926715-68-1

The Dream and Its Amplification
edited by Erel Shalit and Nancy Swift Furlotti, 1ˢᵗ Ed., Trade Paperback, 230pp, 2013
— ISBN 978-1-926715-89-6

Lifting the Veil: Revealing the Other Side
by Fred Gustafson & Jane Kamerling, 1ˢᵗ Ed, Paperback, 170pp, Biblio., 2012
— ISBN 978-1-926715-75-9

Resurrecting the Unicorn: Masculinity in the 21ˢᵗ Century
by Bud Harris, Rev. Ed., Trade Paperback, 300pp, Index, Biblio., 2009
— ISBN 978-0-9810344-0-9

The Water of Life: Spiritual Renewal in the Fairy Tale
by David L. Hart, Rev. Ed., Trade Paperback, 158pp, Index, 2013
— ISBN 978-1-926715-98-8

Divine Madness: Archetypes of Romantic Love
by John R. Haule, Rev. Ed., Trade Paperback, 282pp, Index, Biblio., 2010
— ISBN 978-1-926715-04-9

Tantra and Erotic Trance: Volume One - Outer Work & Volume Two - Inner Work
by John R. Haule, 1ˢᵗ Ed., Trade Paperback, 215pp, Index, Biblio., 2012
— ISBN 978-0-9776076-8-6 & — ISBN 978-0-9776076-9-3

Eros and the Shattering Gaze: Transcending Narcissism
by Ken Kimmel, 1ˢᵗ Ed., Trade Paperback, 310 pp, Index, Biblio., 2011
— ISBN 978-1-926715-49-0

Jung and Ecopsychology: The Dairy Farmers Guide to the Universe Volume 1
by Dennis Merritt 1ˢᵗ Ed., Trade Paperback, 242pp, Index, Biblio., 2011
— ISBN 978-1-926715-42-1

The Cry of Merlin: Jung the Prototypical Ecopsychologist: DFG Volume 2
by Dennis Merritt 1ˢᵗ Ed., Trade Paperback, 204pp, Index, Biblio., 2012
— ISBN 978-1-926715-43-8

Hermes, Ecopsychology, and Complexity Theory: DFG Volume 3
by Dennis Merritt 1ˢᵗ Ed., Trade Paperback, 228pp, Index, Biblio., 2012
— ISBN 978-1-926715-44-5

Land, Weather, Seasons, Insects: An Archetypal View: DFG Volume 4
by Dennis Merritt 1ˢᵗ Ed., Trade Paperback, 134pp, Index, Biblio., 2012
— ISBN 978-1-926715-45-2

Becoming: An Introduction to Jung's Concept of Individuation
by Deldon Anne McNeely, 1ˢᵗ Ed., Trade Paperback, 230pp, Index, Biblio., 2010
— ISBN 978-1-926715-12-4

Animus Aeternus: Exploring the Inner Masculine
by Deldon Anne McNeely, Reprint, Trade Paperback, 196pp, Index, Biblio., 2011
— ISBN 978-1-926715-37-7

Mercury Rising: Women, Evil, and the Trickster Gods
by Deldon Anne McNeely, Rev. Ed, Trade Paperback, 200pp, Index, Biblio., 2011
— ISBN 978-1-926715-54-4

Four Eternal Women: Toni Wolff Revisited—A Study In Opposites
by Mary Dian Molton & Lucy Anne Sikes, 1ˢᵗ Ed, 320pp, Index, Biblio., 2011
— ISBN 978-1-926715-31-5

Gathering the Light: A Jungian View of Meditation
by V. Walter Odajnyk, Revised. Ed., Trade Paperback, 264pp, Index, Biblio., 2011
— ISBN 978-1-926715-55-1

Enemy, Cripple, Beggar: Shadows in the Hero's Path
by Erel Shalit, 1ˢᵗ Ed., Trade Paperback, 248pp, Index, Biblio., 2008
— ISBN 978-0-9776076-7-9

The Cycle of Life: Themes and Tales of the Journey
by Erel Shalit, 1ˢᵗ Ed., Trade Paperback, 210pp, Index, Biblio., 2011
— ISBN 978-1-926715-50-6

The Guilt Cure by Nancy Carter Pennington & Lawrence H. Staples
1ˢᵗ Ed., Trade Paperback, 200pp, Index, Biblio., 2011
— ISBN 978-1-926715-53-7

Guilt with a Twist: The Promethean Way
by Lawrence H. Staples,1ˢᵗ Ed., Trade Paperback, 256pp, Index, Biblio., 2008
— ISBN 978-0-9776076-4-8

The Creative Soul: Art and the Quest for Wholeness
by Lawrence H. Staples, 1ˢᵗ Ed., Trade Paperback, 100pp, Index, Biblio., 2009
— ISBN 978-0-9810344-4-7

Deep Blues: Human Soundscapes for the Archetypal Journey
by Mark Winborn, 1ˢᵗ Ed., Trade Paperback, 130pp, Index, Biblio., 2011
— ISBN 978-1-926715-52-0